What Othe

Dr. Frank Tunstall has completed the second volume in his trilogy on the Gospel of John. He wrote it to lay out the evidence showing twenty-first century readers Jesus of Nazareth is indeed the Son of God.

The author has devoted his life to studying, teaching, and preaching the Word of God. As one reads the book, it is evident Dr. Tunstall stands in awe of the power, authority, and glory of his Lord. His deep insight into Scripture leads the reader to a new and greater understanding of Jesus as God's Son. From feeding the five thousand to raising Lazarus from the dead, Dr. Tunstall provides powerful exposition of the text along with practical instruction and excellent illustrations. His skill as a writer creates an engaging narrative of the miracles Jesus performed as well as His teaching showing that Jesus is God's Son.

This book is a valuable resource for pastors and teachers as well as an inspiration for devotional reading.

The writer has served as pastor, church planter, editor, conference missions director, college professor and president, and as a bishop in his denomination. It is this rich experience along with Dr. Tunstall's scholarly training, which makes *Jesus Son of God* such an outstanding book.

—James D. Leggett
President, Holmes Bible College
IPHC Presiding Bishop (Retired)

I loved and was blessed immensely by reading Book Two of *Jesus Son of God*.

Book Two is even better than Book One.

Every new Christian, including college students, and especially licensed clergy, should read both of these books. They are essential for believers and non-believers.

The author makes Jesus come alive in the narrative as a real person; when you read you will meet Jesus as an individual. Never has Jesus been presented in such a unique way. The reader can readily make application for his own life because the THINK ABOUT IT sections will cause you to stop and think about yourself and your culture.

John Chapter 7, "Jesus, the Master of Time," was phenomenal to me. Dr. Tunstall shows how Jesus is Lord over time, including how He managed His own time according to a specific timeline. The author also portrays Jesus as an obedient servant of His Father. My knowledge and personal relationship with God has grown tremendously by reading this book.

Thank you, Dr. Tunstall, for using your talent and abilities. You are blessing the body of Christ.

I cannot wait to get Volume III. I already have and will continue to use these volumes in my counseling and preaching.

—Bishop Chris Thompson
IPHC Vice Chairman
Evangelism Director of EVUSA

Jesus Son of God covers the Gospel of John, chapters 6:1–12:11. In his typical style, Dr. Tunstall gives attention to almost every verse in the text of the Gospel of John. As I wrote in my review of Book One and repeat here, he has combined scholarship with devotion and study with worship. Reading this volume will not only inform but will also inspire. But then again, this reflects the personality and character of the author. He is a trained scholar in theology who is well acquainted with the literature, but at the same time, more than a scholar, he is a pastor. Many profound lessons will be learned digesting this book.

When the first volume of John (chapters 1–5) was released in 2013, World Missions Ministries had the privilege of distributing copies to missionaries and national leaders around the world. It was available in print and in digital format. I am now happy to assist in distributing volume II to the same group and more.

In the not-too-distant future, we will have volume III which will complete Dr. Tunstall's study of the Gospel of John. The set will be a treasure for many years to come.

—Harold Dalton, D. Min.
Assistant Director, World Missions
Ministries, IPHC

For Additional Copies

You may contact Tate Publishing at 888-361-9472.

Or visit the following websites:
   Amazon.com
   GreatCommandMinistries.org

You may also visit your favorite bookstores.

Jesus Son of God
Book One, Second Edition
John Chapters 1–5

Jesus Son of God
Book Two
John Chapters 6:1–12:11

A Leaders Guide is also available for teaching Jesus Son of God
Books One and Two
by Shirley Spencer
(Thirteen lessons covering Books One and Two [John 1:1–12:11])

For dialogue with the author you may contact him at FrankTunstall@Cox.Net

JESUS
SON OF GOD

FRANK TUNSTALL

JESUS
SON OF GOD

BOOK TWO
John 6:1–12:11

TATE PUBLISHING
AND ENTERPRISES, LLC

Unless otherwise noted, all Scripture quotations are from the New International Version of the Holy Bible (NIV). Copyright 1973, 1978, 1984, International Bible Society. Used by permission. Citations from versions other than the NIV are duly noted, and are identified by the following abbreviations:

- CJB—Complete Jewish Bible
- TLB—Today's Living Bible
- ESV—English Standard Version
- GW—God's Word Bible
- KJV—King James Version
- LL—Living Letters
- MSG—The Message
- NKJV—New King James Version
- VOICE—The Voice Bible
- WNT—Weymouth New Testament Translation

The opinions expressed by the author are not necessarily those of Tate Publishing, LLC.

This book is designed to provide accurate and authoritative information with regard to the subject matter covered. This information is given with the understanding that neither the author nor Tate Publishing, LLC is engaged in rendering legal, professional advice. Since the details of your situation are fact dependent, you should additionally seek the services of a competent professional.

Published by Tate Publishing & Enterprises, LLC
127 E. Trade Center Terrace | Mustang, Oklahoma 73064 USA
1.888.361.9473 | www.tatepublishing.com

Tate Publishing is committed to excellence in the publishing industry. The company reflects the philosophy established by the founders, based on Psalm 68:11,
"The Lord gave the word and great was the company of those who published it."

Book design copyright © 2015 by Tate Publishing, LLC. All rights reserved.
Cover design by Carlo Nino Suico
Interior design by Jake Muelle

Published in the United States of America
ISBN: 978-1-63418-097-9
Religion / Biblical Commentary / New Testament
15.05.12

DEDICATION

To the memory of Rev. John Swails, my English Bible and U.S. Government teacher at Emmanuel College, who so positively impacted my life.

ACKNOWLEDGMENTS

I express my appreciation to my late sister, Rosa Baker, Pastor Steve Brown, and to Shirley Spencer for their invaluable suggestions and help in editing this book.

CONTENTS

Let's Get Started
INTRODUCTION

The gospel message about Jesus Christ the Son of God is now navigating a season of ever increasing pressure. This reality calls for a fresh look at the Gospel of John, the New Testament book which establishes Jesus as God's Son.

Two millennia ago, John the son of Zebedee was an apostle in the inner circle of Jesus Christ. He wrote the Gospel of John in the second half of the first century, just a few decades removed from Jesus' death and resurrection. He did it in the very dominating and enslaving era of the Roman Empire to give the evidence for Jesus of Nazareth as the Son of God. His book became one of the four gospels in the New Testament.

John expressed his thesis in John 1:1 and 14, and at the end of his book:

> In the beginning was the Word, and the Word was with God, and the Word was God (John 1:1). The Word became flesh and made his dwelling among us (John 1:14).

> These are written that you may believe Jesus is the Christ, the Son of God, and that by believing you may have life in his name (John 20:31).

To make Jesus' case, the great apostle's book offers an introduction to show the Son of God has existed from eternity (John 1:1–18). The eternal Word proceeded from His heavenly Father in an incarnation at Nazareth, and became Mary's Baby in the silent night of Bethlehem. "The word became flesh and blood, and moved into the neighborhood" (John 1:14 MSG; Luke 2:15–19).

As John developed his narrative he drew from Jesus' ministry seven miracles, seven discourses, and seven "I AM" declarations to frame the Lord's identity. John's assumption was open-minded readers would be compelled to conclude only God could do such miracles, teach so masterfully, die so nobly, and rise from the grave so victoriously, all the while loving people—all people—so totally.

The Seven Miracles

1. Turning water into wine at the wedding in Cana of Galilee (John 2:1–12).
2. Healing the nobleman's son (John 4:46–53).
3. Healing the man at the Pool of Bethesda (John 5:1–9).
4. Feeding the 5,000 (John 6:4–13).
5. Walking on water (John 6:16–21).
6. Healing the man born blind (John 9:1–12).
7. Raising Lazarus from the dead (John 11:30–53).

The Seven Discourses

1. The New Birth and Nicodemus (John 3:1–21).
2. The New Birth Illustrated: The Woman at Jacob's well (John 4:1–42).
3. The discourse following Jesus' healing the man at the Pool of Bethesda (John 5:16–47).
4. Jesus presents Himself as the Bread of Life (John 6:22–71).
5. The teaching at the Feast of Tabernacles (John 7:14–10:42).
6. The discourse at the Feast of Dedication (John 10:22–39).

7. The story of the death and resurrection of Lazarus (John 11:1–57).

The Seven "I AM" Statements

1. I am the bread of life (John 6:35).
2. I am the light of the world (John 8:12).
3. I am the gate (John 10:9).
4. I am the Good Shepherd (John 10:11).
5. I am the Resurrection and the Life (John 11:25–26).
6. I am the Way, the Truth, and the Life (John 14:6).
7. I am the Vine (John 15:5).

John sealed his case giving the second half of his book to the last week of the Lord's ministry, including Jesus' brutal crucifixion and gloriously triumphant resurrection (chapters 12:12 through 21:25).

In the contemporary era of mass communication and marvelous medical technology, these seven miracles continue to prove only God can do such things. Modernity, with all of its genius, must stand back in awe of them.

Secondary Themes

A subtheme of John's work is the stories of people who confessed Jesus as Messiah—the anointed one (a term to be equated with such additional terms as Son of God, Son of Man, the Christ, and the God-man). Another subtheme is John's faithfulness to record accounts of people who did not take this step of faith. A third portrays how Jesus kept His focus and did some of His greatest teaching and miracles amid the greatest opposition.

The Plan

"The Word became flesh and made his dwelling among us" wrote the Apostle John. "We have seen his glory, the glory of the One and Only, who came from the Father, full of grace and truth" (John 1:14).

Jesus Christ *is* this Word of God. He came to His chosen people who "did not know the righteousness that comes from God." The result was they "sought to establish their own" and "did not submit to God's righteousness." They refused to accept that Jesus of Nazareth was their Messiah and the end of the law "so that there may be righteousness to everyone who believes" (Romans 10:3–4).

Jesus' commitment was to accomplish His Father's assignment as "the lamb of God" who would "take away the sin of the world" (John 1:29, 34). It was a job description big enough to befit the Son of God (Isaiah 49:6; Genesis 22:8). But predictably, it also stirred up resistance.

The Apostle John shows the religious system in Israel held firmly to its own substitute "righteousness" and rejected Jesus. *Religion* refused Jesus' ministry before the strong arm of Rome did. After His baptism, anger toward Jesus had started to lift its ugly head in the Lord's first visit to the temple in Jerusalem. It only intensified as His ministry progressed. By the time Jesus raised Lazarus from the dead, the fury had become a murderous hatred that despised Jesus (John 11; Isaiah 53:3). It must not be missed *religion* became the first enemy of the Messiah when He "moved into the neighborhood" (John 1:14 MSG). Then religion allied with the state to kill Him. This same alliance of religion and governmental authority will ultimately usher in the reign of Antichrist.

The Sanhedrin's Strategy; the Savior's Blueprint

The Sanhedrin, the highest religious council of the Jewish people, met almost immediately after Jesus' stunning miracle in which Lazarus walked out of the tomb which held him for four days. Led by Caiaphas the high priest, the Sanhedrin proceeded to formulate a brutal plan to kill Jesus. He also gave the order for Jesus' arrest.

Jesus' sovereign blueprint called for Him to become the perfect sacrifice as "the Lamb of God," the "Passover lamb," who would "take away the sin of the world" (John 1:29; 1 Corinthians 5:7; Genesis 22:8).

Amazingly, the two plans of action were complimentary. The strategy of the Sanhedrin to kill Jesus actually meant Jesus' blueprint would be successful (Luke 23:34; Acts 3:17).

The struggle was colossal; it was an all-out war for the eternal destiny of the souls of men. For their part, these religious leaders did not voluntarily give up an inch of territory. Jesus had to "take it" every step of the way. As the struggle went forward, not one time did Jesus use their method. He was the sovereign Lord, yet He did not coerce a single participant in the drama of Calvary. This meant these leaders and their followers acted in their own free will to arrest and crucify Jesus.

Amid all of the intrigue and drama to eliminate Jesus, the Lord retained control of the timing. Jesus was determined His crucifixion would occur on the very morning of the Passover celebration and at the same time the Passover lamb was slain in the temple.

Jesus needed no sword or spear to achieve His goal; His only instrument for the struggle was the love of God. Young David a millennium earlier could not wear Saul's armor; he needed only his sling and one of his five smooth stones to end permanently Goliath's boastings (I Samuel 17:50). Time would prove the love of God, and not the sword, was the one force King David's messianic Son needed to compel Rome to bow at Jesus' Cross.

THINK ABOUT IT: The love of God does indeed "*take away* the sin of the world" (John 1:29, 36; Genesis 22:8).

Death itself was the ultimate instrument of control in the hands of these religious rulers; their fearsome willingness to kill is what so effectively silenced the Jewish population. The solemn quietness in any cemetery is deafening.

Propelled by the love of God, Jesus had a surprise weapon His enemies did not see coming—the power of resurrection. As Jesus watched their anger turn into hatred, and then into a plot to murder Him, He continued to witness how well His Father's plan was working. Jesus actually taught His disciples: "Fear not them which kill the body, but are not able to kill the soul; but rather fear him which is able to destroy both soul and body in hell" (Matthew 10:28 KJV).

The Sanhedrin leaders thought the cross would silence Jesus forever; He would be out of their hair permanently. In their wildest imagination they did not foresee Jesus walking out of His tomb!

Jesus, on the other hand, understood fully what His resurrection would achieve. His triumph would mortally humiliate death itself, wipe out its sting forever, and give eternal life to untold millions worldwide who repent and believe the gospel.

In the battle for Japan in World War II, the atomic bomb was the Allies' top secret weapon, and it forced the Japanese warlords to surrender. With Jesus Christ, the surprise was His power of resurrection, accomplished and demonstrated in the love of the Triune Godhead.

The plan Jesus came to fulfill worked perfectly!

When the Apostle John laid down His ancient quill, he had recorded the ageless story that has convinced readers in every generation, among all ethnicities everywhere: Jesus *is* God's Son. He *is* the Redeemer of all who repent and believe the gospel.

John's book makes the same powerful case in the 21st century. People can indeed experience a rebirth that changes them from the inside out, and restores all relationships with the heavenly Father. This good news remains God's answer to establish the modern gods of this age are but idols of the mind. John does so by proving Jesus alone holds the status, the Son of God.

THINK ABOUT IT: *Son of God* indeed! Moses was right when he prophesied 3,500 years ago—we "*must listen to him*" (Deuteronomy 18:15; Matthew 17:5).

Who Killed Jesus?

We answer that Israel's ruling religious authority, the Sanhedrin, triggered the process that led to His death (Mark 15:13, 14, 20; 1 Thessalonians 2:14–15). Then the Roman occupiers of Israel consented to the sentence and carried out Jesus' brutal crucifixion.

Isaiah described the participation of Jesus' own Father: "It was the Lord's will to crush him and cause him to suffer," and to make "His life a guilt offering" (Isaiah 53:10). Jesus said He voluntarily gave His life. "I lay down my life of my own accord," He told the critical Pharisees (John 10:18). In a personal sense, dear reader, you and I too were standing at Golgotha consenting to His death.

It is morally wrong to blame only first century Jews or their descendants for Jesus' death (Matthew 27:25).

The Apostle Peter and the Apostle John gave a balanced interpretation in their prayer after their confrontation with the Sanhedrin:

> Herod [the Jewish civil leader] and Pontius Pilate [the Roman governor] met together with the Gentiles [foreigners visiting Jerusalem] and the people of this city [Jews who were in on the plot] to conspire against your holy servant Jesus, whom you anointed (Acts 4:27).

Yes, there is plenty of blame to go around.

This volume is written in a commentary style with applicational inserts added throughout, intended to provoke thought.

Book One covers John 1:1 through 5:47.

This volume, Book Two, begins at John 6:1 and continues through John 12:11. It concludes John's account of Jesus' ministry leading up to Passion Week, the week of His crucifixion.

Book Three will begin at John 12:12 and tell the story of the last week of the Lord's earthly ministry. It climaxes with Jesus' horrible crucifixion and triumphant resurrection. Book Three is yet to be written.

John Chapter 6

JESUS
THE BREAD OF LIFE

This chapter quickly mushrooms into a day of dynamic action. It includes Jesus feeding to the fill five thousand men besides the women and children by multiplying five loaves of barley bread and two small fish. The Lord continues this dynamic day of action by walking on the Sea of Galilee that very night in a storm. The Apostle John records the fourth of the seven discourses of Jesus in this chapter, and records Jesus' claim, "I am the bread of life." It is the first of the seven "I AM" statements. This chapter honors Moses' greatness in Israel's national history, even as it sets Jesus apart as Moses' Messiah and unrivaled superior. It also shows the continuing build-up of opposition toward Jesus and His teaching.

Twenty-Four Hours with Jesus

6:1 Some time after this, Jesus crossed to the far shore of the Sea of Galilee (that is, the Sea of Tiberias), 2 and a great crowd of people followed him because they saw the miraculous signs he had performed on the sick. 3 Then Jesus went up on a mountainside and sat down with his disciples.

Jesus captivated people wherever He went with His teaching and His miracles. They were His road signs pointing straight to His identity as the Son of God (John 2:11). The people were motivated by their hope for help with their infirmities that had no cure. Jesus also sparked a high level of curiosity and it brought people to Him in large numbers.

One should remember Israel had enjoyed no prophetic voice for 400 years. Then the Messiah's forerunner, John the Baptist, had appeared on the scene. John was followed by Jesus of Nazareth, who began His Spirit-anointed ministry as the supreme miracle worker (Acts 10:38). As the people initially flocked to John, they quite naturally swarmed Jesus. They were drawn largely by the wonder of His miracles which so blessed the needs of people. Their desire, however, did not equally include assimilating His teachings and living by them.

The "far shore" would have been the east side of the Sea of Galilee. It bordered on the Decapolis, a territory featuring ten Greek cities, brimming with Hellenistic culture and awash with Greek idolatry and values.

Amid Jesus' ministry to the crowds both large and small, the Lord always made opportunity to pull His disciples apart and let them physically rest. During these times, Jesus encouraged them to restore their spiritual and emotional batteries and at the same time gave them special training. The Lord surely knew what was ahead in the next 24 hours, but the disciples had no clue.

THINK ABOUT IT: If we only understood the great things the Lord has planned for us as well—in our next 24 hours!

6:4 The Jewish Passover Feast was near.

Moses led the very first Passover; at the time of our Lord, it was a 1500-year-old feast. It celebrated the last of the ten plagues in Egypt followed by Pharaoh's release of the Israelites so that the exodus could begin. Moses told the Israelites to sacrifice a lamb and sprinkle its blood on the door posts of their homes.

When the angel of death went through Egypt that historic night, He saw the blood and spared the lives of all the Israelite firstborn living in Goshen, including their animals (see Exodus 12). It was one of the greatest miracles of the Old Testament.

Jesus, in His own person, is the ultimate fulfillment of the Paschal lamb; He would soon be on the cross as Israel's Passover offering, and ours too (1 Corinthians 5:7; Hebrews 10:12, 14). But before He left Galilee and made the trip again to Jerusalem, two of His greatest miracles and another of His dynamic discourses were on the Lord's schedule.

FEEDING THE 5,000

6:5 When Jesus looked up and saw a great crowd coming toward him, he said to Philip, "Where shall we buy bread for these people to eat?" 6 He asked this only to test him, for he already had in mind what he was going to do.

Tests or Temptations

The statement, "He already had in mind what He was going to do," is instructive. It goes to the heart of the way Jesus and His Father stayed in direct communication. This is summarized with the Lord's statement:

> "I tell you the truth, the Son can do nothing by himself; he can do only what he sees his Father doing, because whatever the Father does the Son also does. For the Father loves the Son and shows him all he does" (John 5:19–20; see John 5 in Book One).

In this case the interaction between the Lord and His Father had already taken place and Jesus knew "what he was going to do" (vs. 6). The Lord's first step in His plan was to add to Philip's training by giving Him a test.

The Holy Spirit examines the faith of all of God's children. But, thank God, Jesus does not tempt us by dangling opportunity to sin in front of us. Instead, He uses situations and circumstances to show us what is in our own hearts, and then motivates us to draw closer to Him and His values (Exodus 20:2; 2 Chronicles 32:31; James 1:2). This is the huge difference between the tests of God and the temptations of the devil. Satan tempts as a challenge to God, motivating people to disobey and respond to God in unbelief. Satan wants us to reach out and take the forbidden fruit—of whatever kind. For examples, theft, false witness, immorality, and greed are all grounded in a *taking* spirit—grabbing at someone else's expense and against their will. These clearly would be temptations, not tests. Unbelief would also be temptation.

THINK ABOUT IT: The quest to gain a position or a promotion using subterfuge to unseat the person currently holding the position would be grounded in the temptation birthed by greed. In addition, motivation to abuse God's plan for the body by indulging in drugs or alcohol, or other lusts of the flesh, including over eating, would also be temptation.

When the Lord confronted Phillip by asking for a plan to feed the multitude, it was not a temptation to sin, but a test. This exam was calculated to show Philip the very limited extent of his trust in Messiah's capability. Phillip was one of the first people to confess Jesus as Messiah, according to the Apostle John, and had recommended Nathaniel to Jesus (John 1:43–48). But could Jesus feed a hungry multitude? This explored the outer edge of Phillip's grasp of Messiah's authority.

6:7 Philip answered him, "Eight months' wages would not buy enough bread for each one to have a bite!"

At this time Philip's small faith saw no possibility of a solution coming from the person he had hailed as Messiah. To Philip it was totally a money issue. The only way to get bread was to purchase it, and the funds were not in the treasury to "buy bread," at least on this scale. This explains Philip's response: "It would take a fortune to begin to do it!" (John 6:7 TLB). How many people have been stopped at this juncture! They cannot see their Lord standing on the other side of their drained savings account; or, as the case may be, beyond their credit card.

6:8 Another of his disciples, Andrew, Simon Peter's brother, spoke up, 9 "Here is a boy with five small barley loaves and two small fish, but how far will they go among so many?"

Andrew, too, had confessed Jesus as Messiah, but neither did he perceive the capability of Messiah's power. He was aware, however, of a lad in the crowd with his lunch, and used the child to make his point. Andrew was about to learn Jesus' capacity to act and how far this small amount of bread and fish would go in the Messiah's hands.

The Apostle John specifically identified the child's bread as "barley loaves" (see also vs. 13). Barley was commonly known as the poor man's bread; wheat was the bread of the wealthy. By saying the youngster's lunch included barley bread, John was setting the stage to show Jesus is the Bread of Life for ordinary people too. In fact, "the common people heard him gladly" (Mark 12:37).

Amazingly, this hungry lad gave his lunch to Jesus!

"What Can I Give Him?"

Christina Rossetti wrote a poem in 1872 that only appeared after her death. About thirty years later the poem was set to music and titled "A Christmas Carol." Today, we know it as "In the Bleak Midwinter."

Rossetti was a devoted follower of Christ who for many years volunteered at the St. Mary Magdalene "house of charity," a refuge for women coming out of a life of prostitution. In the Victorian Era of her day, economic forces often caused women to eke out a living by selling their bodies. Some of the "women" were only twelve years old. Rossetti's efforts in offering them Christ's love, and helping find better jobs for these marginalized women came through in some of her poems.

For instance, this Christmas carol pictures a Savior who entered our world of suffering and brokenness—a world much like "the bleak midwinter" of Rossetti's native England. "Heaven cannot hold" [Jesus] "nor earth sustain" [Him], and yet "a stable-place" and "a manger full of hay" cradled Him.

In light of Christ's great power and love, Rossetti's poem asks:

> *What can I give Him,*
> *Poor as I am?*

Her answer says there is one thing all of us can give Christ—no matter who we are:

> *If I were a shepherd*
> *I would bring a lamb,*
> *If I were a wise man*
> *I would do my part,*
> *Yet what I can I give Him?*
> *Give my heart.*[1]

> **THINK ABOUT IT:** Regardless of your scarred past or your present struggles, Jesus wants one gift from you above all others—your heart. A heart to believe and trust His sovereign power over all problems and circumstances. A heart which permits Him to take your life as it is, and lead you into a new future which will include eternal life.

6:10 Jesus said, "Have the people sit down." There was plenty of grass in that place, and the men sat down, about five thousand of them. 11 Jesus then took the loaves, gave thanks, and distributed to those who were seated as much as they wanted. He did the same with the fish.

This was possibly the largest crowd the people living around the Sea of Galilee had ever seen. It numbered five thousand men. We know this lad was in the crowd, which suggests more children probably were present. Since children were there, it meant women surely were in the crowd as well. A conservative estimate might reach as high as eight to ten thousand people.

What happened next continues to live as one of the Lord's greatest signs regarding His position in the Godhead as the *logos*, the creative Word of divine authority over all life forms. The New Testament writers, Matthew, Mark, and Luke join John in telling the story (Matthew 14:21; Mark 6:37; Luke 9:13). Witnessing it brought the people face to face with Jesus' true identity as the creative Word. To Jesus it was a simple order: "You give them something to eat." To the disciples it was freighted with creative power.

Yes, this fourth of the seven miracles John records reveals Jesus as "the God who gives life to the dead and calls things that are not as though they were" (Romans 4:17; Isaiah 55:8; 1 Corinthians 1:28).

Kittie Suffield, based on this command from the Lord, wrote in 1924 the enduring hymn, "Little Is Much When God Is in it."

[Chorus] Little is much when God is in it!
Labor not for wealth or fame.
There's a crown—and you can win it,
If you go in Jesus' name.

The child who gave his lunch to Jesus surely lived the remainder of his life in the glow of the miracle and no doubt never tired of telling the story: *"I gave my lunch to Jesus and He gave a command that fed thousands of hungry people with my lunch. Filled them up too and had lots of bread and fish left over!"*

A Grateful Heart

"Jesus…gave thanks." The Lord's act of showing gratitude to His Father before feeding the people should encourage the practice of saying grace before a meal as part of a lifestyle of gratitude. It is important for parents to teach this special value to their children. Followers of Jesus do not take their food supply for granted. Instead, they honor God as the source of every meal, because all food ultimately comes from His generous hand. He alone supplies the ingredients necessary to produce food—the ground, the nutrients in the soil, the sunlight for photosynthesis, the rain, the seed, the oxygen, and the carbon dioxide, without which no food can grow and no person or animal can survive.

Jesus' act of gratitude also shows the selflessness in His character. He was about to perform one of the greatest miracles of His ministry. But before doing it, He thanked His Father, and gave the honor to Him. If pride had been in His heart, or any desire to take personal credit, or any willingness to act independently of His Father and the Holy Spirit, this would have been a grand opportunity. Instead of grabbing for His Deity and acting solo, Jesus humbly began to perform the miracle by thanking His Father (Philippians 2:6).

What if Jesus had not given thanks, but had taken the credit? Such a choice would have greatly increased the possibility Jesus also would have let them make Him their king, which the people wanted to do a few hours later. If it had happened, it would have stopped dead in its tracks Jesus' mission as the Lamb of God who takes away the sin of the world.

THINK ABOUT IT: It is an amazing fact of life how a little ingratitude here, and a little more there, and soon we are caught in a deadly web of selfishness which ultimately destroys. (Romans 1:21–23). But the concept of "taking" or "grabbing" does not exist is the Trinity. Agape love never "takes" or "grabs."

Jesus apparently did not respond to Philip and Andrew with rebukes for their small thinking (John 1:43–45). He simply proceeded to feed the people. By doing so He lifted the horizon of their faith in Him. It surely was a message the disciples did not miss. This great miracle should also have been a bold sign to all Israelites showing God was on the scene, for one can be sure the word spread like wildfire across the land.

Distribution and Multiplication

Matthew shares how the meal was served. The fish and bread went from Jesus' hands to the disciples, who circulated the food among the big crowd. "Taking the five loaves and the two fish and looking up to heaven," wrote Matthew, "[Jesus] gave thanks and broke the loaves. Then He gave them to the disciples, and the disciples gave them to the people" (Matthew 14:19).

The record does not tell if others helped the disciples in the distribution. But to show the magnitude of the miracle, if the crowd included only nine thousand people, and the twelve disciples did all the distribution, they each had to serve some 750 people. If each disciple averaged feeding four people a minute, it would have required about three hours of focused effort to distribute the meal—if the disciples did all the serving.

Jesus did not multiply the bread and fish just one time into a huge barley loaf and a large fish big enough to feed the crowd. Instead, Jesus broke the bread and fish and gave pieces to each of the twelve disciples. In Jesus hands, the multiplying miracle occurred perhaps twelve times. In the disciples' hands, they kept breaking the bread and the fish, and the multiplying miracle could have continued 750 or more times, until each person was fed all he wanted to eat. Then the miracle stopped.

Only God can do what Jesus did with five loaves of barley and two fish.

The disciples seated the people in groups of 50 and 100 to organize serving the meal. Pushing and shoving are not mentioned, although everyone in the crowd was hungry (Mark 6:39–44). First, the word no doubt spread—"food is being served." Then the word went through the crowd food is being served miraculously, yet no stampede. The hungry people in the multitude, including women and children, awaited their turn patiently, for some of them perhaps as long as three hours.

The marvelous crowd control here can only be explained by the power of the Holy Spirit hovering over the entire multitude. In those moments all of the people present were under the canopy of the same cloud which had guided the Israelites by day to the Promised Land. The Spirit of Jesus is the essence of the cloud. We conclude this special anointing on Jesus, the Son of God and Israel's Messiah, kept the crowd orderly.

What an experience this must have been to the disciples distributing the bread! As they broke the bread and fish, the food kept multiplying. Surely the disciples' eyes popped repeatedly as they saw this miraculous sign unfolding time, after time, after time, after time!

Eating to the Fill

THINK ABOUT IT: Have you wondered how the disciples felt—their emotions—when they saw the bread and fish continually multiplying in their hands until the multitude of people ate to the fill? Obviously, the disciples never forgot the miracle.

Interestingly, the Apostle John does not disclose how this great miracle changed Philip's understanding of Jesus' authority and capability as the Son of God. But the impact must have been life changing.

6:12 When they had all had enough to eat, he said to his disciples, "Gather the pieces that are left over. Let nothing be wasted."

One can also wonder the logistics of how this happened. Did the disciples keep serving the people seconds and third helpings until all were satisfied, and many were left holding uneaten food in their hands? Or did the bread and fish multiply in the hands of the people as they were eating it? We are not told how it all worked out, but hundreds of people in the multitude no doubt had not had a meal to the *fill* in a long time.

Jesus did not ration the miracle, telling His disciples, for example, to give each man three pieces of fish and two pieces of bread, and each woman two pieces of fish and one piece of bread, and each child one piece of fish and a half piece of bread. He did not even instruct the disciples to be generous, and then leave it to them to decide the meaning of "generous." His instructions were "as much as they want!" (John 6:11). The result was "everyone was full" (NLT); they ate until they were *satisfied*.

When the Queen of Sheba visited King Solomon, one of the many things that amazed her was the over-abundance of food on Solomon's table (See 1 Kings 4:22–23; 10:1–5). But "one greater than Solomon is here" (Matthew 12:42; Luke 11:31). The food Jesus blessed and the disciples' distributed was bread and fish, and all ate as much as they wanted. But this food was only a symbol of what was to come, for Jesus' table serves eternal life to all who believe, making Him the very satisfying Bread of Life (John 6:35).

The Scraps of Life

What Jesus did for their stomachs, He wanted to do for their souls. People through the centuries, both commoners and the wealthy, have come to Jesus equally hungry and famished. Their empty lives have left them with splitting headaches. Jesus has always been their answer, and they have left "satisfied." In the Sermon on the Mount the Lord promised, "Blessed are those who hunger and thirst for righteousness, for they will be filled" (Matthew 5:6).

While Jesus wanted everyone satisfied, at the same time He wanted no waste.

THINK ABOUT IT: People are wasteful in many ways, other than with food, such as time, talent, callings, spiritual gifts, tithes, and assets.

"When they had all eaten their fill..." (RSV), Jesus showed the mind boggling extent of the miracle by focusing on the leftover scraps. Jesus is much more than Lord of tables with plenty of food. He also sees the importance of "the pieces." In fact, He commanded, "Gather the leftovers, so that nothing is wasted" (John 6:12–13 NLT).

Many people feel like leftovers and know they have become the broken pieces of life. Jesus is the Sovereign who rescues them, demonstrating Himself as "the Lord of the scraps." Even those who have been gobbled up by abuse or a host of other causes leave leftover pieces, and they have value to Jesus; in fact, He can turn scraps into things of beauty, and He does it without fanfare or hoopla.

The first of the four servant songs of Isaiah speaks clearly to the point:

> Here is my servant, whom I uphold,
> my chosen one in whom I delight;
> I will put my Spirit on him
> and he will bring justice to the nations.
> He will not shout or cry out,
> or raise his voice in the streets (Isaiah 42:12).

Messiah came filled with the Holy Spirit without measure, committed to quenching the hunger of the soul (John 3:34, KJV). His table is rich with what we need most—the love and mercy of God. Jesus did not come with a raised voice and a clenched fist, yelling and screaming at people to get what He wanted.

We conclude much yelling is not the key to gaining the Lord's attention, nor is it the answer to winning the loyalty of people. God seeks sincerity of heart. Yet, there is a time to cry out to God (Psalms 22:2; 34:17; Mark 10:47).

> He won't brush aside the bruised and the hurt, and he won't disregard the small and insignificant, but he'll steadily and firmly set things right. In faithfulness he will bring forth justice (Isaiah 42:3 MSG).

The Servant Messiah was so tender and considerate, He would not finish breaking off a "bruised reed," and if a wick was smoldering he would not snuff it out. His goal has always been to heal the hearts and bodies of the bruised reeds of the world. Then they can make music again. He also trims the lamps burned dim, once more bringing the sparkle back into people's eyes and the glow into their faces. "He will not falter or be discouraged till he establishes justice on earth. In his law the islands will put their hope" (Isaiah 42:3–4).

THINK ABOUT IT: "If our physician, God in Christ, having rescued us from our desires, regulates our flesh with His own wise and temperate rule, it is evident He guards it from sins because it has a hope of salvation, just as physicians do not allow people whom they hope to save to indulge in whatever pleasures they please."
Justin Martyr (ca. 100–165)

Amazing: "He will not falter or be discouraged" as He does His rescuing, regulating, and guarding work. Did the Lord never feel discouraged? We answer He did not. He came to carry out a plan developed from eternity. He "knew what was in man" and needed no one to tell Him what is in man, so nothing surprised Him (John 2:25 KJV). In the Tri-Unity of the God who is One, His Father and the Holy Spirit guided Him; hence, He was never caught off guard. In addition, Jesus was an amazingly quick thinker on His feet and had total recall of the Old Testament Scriptures.

The food on Jesus' table is the answer for broken and depressed people. "He won't tire out and quit. He won't be stopped until he's finished His work—to set things right on earth" (Isaiah 42:4). Instead, He is the Great Physician who keeps working with us until He brings us back to health. And when He does, He gives us our unique place in His Great Commission, inspiring us to enlarge our tents. He knows and helps us realize even the "far-flung ocean islands wait expectantly for His teaching" (Isaiah 42:4 MSG; 54:2–3).

THINK ABOUT IT: Jesus fills the hungry with good things. Yes, He is the Messiah of the scraps of life too.

6:13 So they gathered them and filled twelve baskets with the pieces of the five barley loaves left over by those who had eaten.

What about the people? One can easily picture their eyes bulged and jaws dropped when they realized what a huge miracle was happening right in front of them—perhaps in their own hands. Others of them no doubt looked at those little baskets of food and just knew there would be no bread left for them.

Many think to this day: "*there is no bread in God's basket for me. God gives His miracles to others but He does not care about me.*" But Jesus showed time and again His concern for people who have been written off. Messiah takes "great delight in *you.*" He will "quiet *you* with his love." He will even "rejoice over you with singing" (Zephaniah 3:17).

What excited emotions must have flowed through the crowd as the process started! The people watched the disciples serving the multitude as the loaves and the fish kept multiplying. The miracle did not stop until everyone was full.

Even the naysayers were fed. The liars, thieves, and adulterers in the crowd were fed. The worst sinners among them were fed. The meal included the very Pharisees and elders who hounded Jesus with their doubts and unbelief—they were fed too. Those who despised Him and turned their heads to keep from looking at Him were fed. What a gracious and generous host Jesus was to the multitude. Jesus' table is so blessed with abundance He even sends His rain on the just and the unjust (Matthew 5:45).

THINK ABOUT IT: Since Jesus fed everybody in the crowd, should not His church be a gathering place for all people to hear the Word of God and dine on the bread of life?

The miracle of feeding the 5,000 was a very bold sign, flooded with *Son*light. Jesus is indeed the Son of God and the bread of life. This fourth miracle John records inspires people to accept Jesus as the Son of God. A striking conclusion follows: since He can create bread and meat on the spot, could He not also be the creator of all things?

THINK ABOUT IT: "If you think you are too small to make a difference, try spending the night in a closed room with a mosquito."—**African proverb**

The boy's lunch, when turned over to the Son of God in faith, miraculously blessed the lad and his world around him. Since then, his captivating story has been told wherever the gospel has gone.

A King's Crown

6:14 After the people saw the miraculous sign that Jesus did, they began to say, "Surely this is the Prophet who is to come into the world."

"*Surely,*" is quite right; it is also a huge understatement! This is a reference to Moses' prophecy predicting Messiah would be a prophet (Acts 3:22; 7:7; Deuteronomy 18:15, 18). The people were beginning to absorb Jesus' true identity, but their faith remained inaccurate regarding His mission and destiny.

6:15 Jesus, knowing they intended to come and make him king by force, withdrew again to a mountain by himself. 16 When evening came, his disciples went down to the lake, 17 where they got into a boat and set off across the lake for Capernaum.

It was such a huge miracle the people wanted to put a crown on Jesus' head. It is indeed noteworthy that Satan inserts the temptation for Jesus to become Israel's king immediately following this great miracle. After times of outstanding success people routinely face great temptations. The result has been many have walked through their worst failures shortly after their greatest achievements. But Jesus understood the mission of His life, and knew the only crown awaiting Him was a crown of thorns. The miracle was so mind boggling the Lord also knew the people would try to make Him their monarch. A sovereign who could feed the common people would obviously get a following quickly.

The Lord dealt with the magnitude of His success with decisive action. He left town.

Quiet Time with His Father

According to Matthew's account of this miracle, Jesus urged the disciples to get into a boat and cross over to Capernaum, while He stayed behind. The Lord sent them away knowing what else would follow later in the evening.

After they left, Jesus "climbed the mountain" so He could pray in solitude. "He stayed there alone, late into the night" (Matthew 14:23 MSG). Does not the prayer life of Jesus indicate Jesus wants special time with us too? He also wants His house to *be* "a house of prayer for all nations." (Isaiah 56:7; Matthew 21:13; Mark 11:17; Luke 19:46).

Arguably people need quiet time with God after their successes more than after their disappointments and failures. This story shows, after this great miracle, even Jesus needed solitude with His Father—by Himself time; *Father-time*. Since this was true for Him, how much more is it true we need *Father-time* in the ups and downs of life, and especially so in the ups.

THINK ABOUT IT: Are you in the habit of arranging quiet time, prayer and meditation time with your heavenly Father, and all the more in your seasons of success?

It's amazing what twenty-four hours can hold when you spend it with Jesus!

JESUS WALKS ON WATER

6:17 By now it was dark, and Jesus had not yet joined them. 18 A strong wind was blowing and the waters grew rough. 19 When they had rowed three or three and a half miles, they saw Jesus approaching the boat, walking on the water; and they were terrified.
20 But he said to them, "It is I; don't be afraid."
21 Then they were willing to take him into the boat, and immediately the boat reached the shore where they were heading.

A Dark Night in a Storm

In this fifth miracle, John records they had sailed only about three miles on the Sea of Galilee; a fierce storm had greatly slowed their progress. Yes, they had seen the Lord's marvelous provision for the hungry multitude, but let it be underscored: it was night, and dark, and they were in a storm. They had yet to absorb the Lord who provided bread and fish for the multitude was the Creator of the laws of nature and could take care of them in a storm, in the dark of night, in the late hours of the night (Mark 6:52).

Each of the Lord's followers, sooner or later, is caught in a storm. Surely Jesus knew the storm was ahead, so why did He "constrain them" to get into the boat and "go to the other side" of the lake (Mark 6:45)? Jesus did not give these instructions only to see them drown. Instead, the stage was set for another huge miracle, the second in twenty-four hours.

The Psalter does not name the author of Psalm 107, but he surely was a prophet: "[Messiah] stilled the storm to a whisper; the waves of the sea were hushed. They were glad when it grew calm" (Psalm 107:29–30 TLB; see Psalm 89:9; Isaiah 51:10; Jeremiah 31:35).

It was clearly a divine act.

Before Jesus turned the storm into a soft sigh, however, He showed His disciples He was the Master *inside* the turbulence of the storm. We can only marvel: apparently Jesus walked on the water in the storm the *full three miles* to join them. Another wonder is that He found them that violent evening, a needle in a haystack. At the height of the turbulence in the dark of night there would be almost no light, except perhaps occasional flares of lightning. To see a small boat out on the Sea of Galilee by the flashes of lightning from three miles away is a miracle all its own. Jesus not only knew the location of His disciples; He knows the position of each of His children to this day, no matter how remote the locality. The Lord is radar personified.

THINK ABOUT IT: There is no such thing as a storm so perfect, a night so wild and dark in your family, the Holy Spirit cannot come to you!

In those stormy circumstances, for the disciples to see the very dim outline of a man coming toward them seemed like the figure of an approaching ghost. One can easily imagine how their stomachs were churning as their blood pressure went sky high.

As for Jesus, obviously the law of gravity should have pulled Him under the water. But gravity was powerless before the might of the Creator of gravity. Instead, Jesus kept walking on the water in the storm. Additional evidence the mammoth miracle of feeding the 5,000 had not soaked into the disciples' faith was the fact they were so frightened. Every nerve in their bodies was yelling at them; they were scared out of their wits. "They cried out, because they all saw him and were terrified" (Mark 6:52). [The Greek word for "cried out" is *anakrazo*, meaning they could have been yelling and screaming.]

Regarding this miracle of walking on water while "a strong wind was blowing"—is this what Job meant when he penned, "He alone...treads on the waves of the sea?" (Job 9:8). Did Job express a prophecy? Is it possible Jesus was actually stepping on the *waves*?

Keeping balance while walking on calm and placid water is a miracle great enough to befit the Messiah and Son of God, but to keep balance and walk on the moving waves, and do it for three miles in a fierce storm is a quantum greater miracle.

Mark Twain's Explanation
Why Jesus Walked on Water

Mark Twain (1835–1910) was accompanied by his wife on one of his visits to the Holy Land. They were staying in Tiberius on the shores of the Sea of Galilee. It was a moonlit night, and the weather was perfect. Twain had the romantic idea of taking his wife for a boat ride on the lake.

They walked down to the pier and Twain inquired of a man sitting in a rowboat how much he would charge to row them out on the water. Twain was dressed in his usual white suit, white shoes, and white Texas hat. The oarsman, presuming him to be a wealthy rancher from the USA, said, "Well, I guess about twenty-five dollars." [Twenty-five dollars in 1910, allowing for inflation, would be a charge of about six hundred dollars today!]

Mark Twain thanked him.

As he turned away with his wife on his arm, he said to her, "Now I know why Jesus walked!"[2]

Jesus: Lord of Life's Rough Seas

Many families have found themselves in a midnight of rough seas—a loved one not expected to make it 'til dawn, for just one example. It should not be forgotten the Lord "saw the disciples straining at the oars" (Mark 6:48). He knew they were doing everything they could; giving the last ounces of their energy. How many times through the centuries of the Lord's church, Jesus has walked right up to families in their crises. He has never been intimidated by their turbulent desperation. Time and again "He [has performed] wonders that cannot be fathomed, miracles that cannot be counted" (Job 9:10).

When the disciples saw a figure walking on the water toward them, they were full of fear. Jesus response to their fright was to say to them, "Take courage. It is I. Be not afraid" (Matthew 14:27).

THINK ABOUT IT: It is noteworthy the Lord miraculously calmed the paralyzing fear *inside* the disciples before He quieted the life threatening storm *outside* them.

Peter received the Lord's comforting message which enabled him to ask Jesus to permit him to walk on the water too. At the Lord's command he stepped out of the boat in the storm and started walking! (Matthew 14:28–31; see also Mark 6:49). When Peter began to focus on the wind and the waves, however, and not on Jesus, he began to sink. But Jesus heard Peter's cry for help and pulled him out of the water into an upright position so that he walked on the water again back to the boat. This alone was no small miracle. While standing on the water, Jesus could actually lift Peter. Then, Jesus and Peter "climbed into the boat together and the wind died down" (Matthew 14:32).

The storm had fought the disciples with every pound of its power, and was winning—until Jesus stepped into the boat. Then the storm gave up the fight. When faced with the superior might of the Creator of the wind and the waves, the storm relaxed its grip. *Kopazo* is the word for "died down," meaning the storm tired out and relaxed.

Maybe the storm was more tired than the disciples!

Jesus demonstrated in this miracle His mastery over nature, showing even storms are at His command. This is another marvel which inspires people to conclude Jesus is indeed the creator of all things. When a believer assimilates Jesus' Lordship over nature on this scale, he is only a step away from believing Jesus is the creator of the entire natural order. The disciples in the boat, having experienced the whole drama, responded by worshipping Jesus, saying, "This is it! You are God's Son for sure!" (Matthew 14:32–33 MSG).

THINK ABOUT IT: This miracle further establishes Jesus' supremacy in the arena of world religions. Who can match him?

Without question He is more than one among equals!

How many times men of faith have stepped into unknown territory, only to lose their focus on Jesus, and begin to sink. But when they could not help themselves and were over their heads in the water, Jesus rescued them and made their ministries successful. This miracle shows Jesus as:

1. The Lord, who is the *logos*—the Word, who is sovereign over nature, including the laws of physics governing nature. Jesus did it with another simple command, without even raising His voice: "Peace, be still" (Mark 4:39). What authority!

THINK ABOUT IT: Have you ever noticed people with authority do not need to yell to get things done?

---

2. The Lord over location. Though some three miles from His disciples, Jesus knew their distress and pinpointed their position; He is radar personified. Jesus walked on the water to them—perhaps as Job described, stepping on the waves. He also permitted Peter to join Him on the water. He found them in a small boat, late at night, with high winds and powerful waves. Jesus knew their location and walked to them.

3. The Lord of our focus. The miracle shows the absolute necessity, when walking in faith, to keep our eyes on Jesus. It also demonstrates when our faith is weaker than we thought and we are over our heads Jesus is there to pull us out of the water that would have drowned our ministry. Then He walks with us back to our boat.

4. The Lord to be worshiped. The miracle had its desired effect. The disciples gave Jesus reverent respect, and declared with certainty He was "the Son of God"

(Matthew 14:33). It is also reasonable on future trips the disciples feared the Son of Man in the boat more than the worst storms on the Sea of Galilee!

THINK ABOUT IT: When leaders publicly walk through their storms people see how their role models handle their tornadoes. The result is they are inspired to deal with their own crises.

The Lord who was capable of walking on the waves will one day come back. This time the clouds will be His sidewalk. Then our moment will have come to join Him. Linda Stalls expressed this in music:

> "Stepping on the clouds, we will see him
> Rise to meet him in the air.
> Stepping on the clouds He will greet us
> Oh! The joys together we will share,
> I'm gonna leave this world behind me
> Going where the devil cannot find me,
> I'm going higher, higher, higher
> Stepping on the clouds."
>
> *Copyright 1974, Word Music, LLC.*

Ready for the Surprise

Robby Robbins was an Air Force pilot during the first Iraq War. After his 300th mission, he was surprised to receive permission to pull his crew together immediately and fly his plane home.

They soared across the ocean to Massachusetts and then had a long drive to western Pennsylvania. They drove all night, and when his buddies dropped him off at his driveway just after sun-up, there was a big banner across the garage—"**WELCOME HOME DAD!**"

How did they know? No one had called, and the crew themselves hadn't expected to leave so quickly. Robbins relates, "When I walked into the house, the kids, about half dressed for school, screamed, "Daddy!"

Susan came running down the hall—she looked terrific—hair fixed, make-up on, and a crisp yellow dress.

"How did you know?" I asked.

"I didn't," she answered through tears of joy. "Once we knew the war was about over, we knew you'd be home one of these days. We also knew you'd try to surprise us, so we were ready every day!"[3]

6:22 The next day the crowd that had stayed on the opposite shore of the lake realized only one boat had been there, and Jesus had not entered it with his disciples, but they had gone away alone.
23 Then some boats from Tiberias landed near the place where the people had eaten the bread after the Lord had given thanks.
24 Once the crowd realized that neither Jesus nor his disciples were there, they got into the boats and went to Capernaum in search of Jesus.
25 When they found him on the other side of the lake, they asked him, "Rabbi, when did you get here?"

The people searching for Jesus did not know the whole story, but they figured out Jesus and His disciples had only one boat the evening before, and Jesus did not get in the boat when the disciples headed back across the lake. "They had gone away alone." These searchers were left to wonder how Jesus had rejoined His disciples. If it was a mystery to them, it is not to John's readers. Jesus had walked on the water in a storm for about *three miles* to join them!

The discourse which follows in John's account occurred in the synagogue at Capernaum (John 6:59). The backdrop is feeding the 5,000 with five barley loaves and two small fish, and walking on the water to the disciples on the turbulent Sea of Galilee in the darkness of that very chaotic night.

John is the only gospel writer to include the account of Jesus turning water into wine (John 2:1–11), and the miracle of healing the invalid at the Pool of Bethesda (John 5:1–15). John is also the only writer to tell the story of the woman at Jacob's well, making her the first person in John's account to drink the living water and experience the new birth (John 3). In addition, only John tells the story of the woman caught in the act of adultery (John 8) and the story of Lazarus (John 11). The teaching that follows is unique to the Book of John as well. None of the other gospel writers present Jesus as the Bread of Life.

JESUS, THE LIVING BREAD

Presenting Jesus as the Bread of Life is the theme of this fourth of the seven discourses of Jesus in John 1–11. This story also presents the first of the seven "I AM" statements in the Book of John: "I AM the bread of life" (John 6:35). A sub-theme of this discourse frames a case study of six different reactions of people to Jesus.

The discussion moves from recognizing Jesus as a Rabbi, to responding to Him in unbelief, to wanting to test Him, to grumbling, to walking away from Him, and finally, with Peter, confessing Him as the Son of God.

People have always searched for Jesus. The first reaction of the six is expressed in verse 25. "When they found him," they addressed Him as "Rabbi." In their eyes He was a respected teacher qualified to interpret Jewish law. In effect, they were expressing the same assessment Nicodemus showed in his night time meeting with Jesus in Jerusalem. But they did not view Him as their Messiah (the Christ who is the Anointed One), foretold by their prophets. A rabbi—"yes," but Son of Man, Son of God, and Lamb of God—"No!"

THINK ABOUT IT: "If Jesus is not true God, how could He help us? If He is not true man, how could He help us?"—Deitrich Bonhoeffer

---

Jesus Discerns the Motivation of the Crowd

John 6:26 Jesus answered, "I tell you the truth, you are looking for me, not because you saw miraculous signs, but because you ate the loaves and had your fill."

Jesus routinely began His teaching with the phrase, "I tell you the truth." It was His own upfront affirmation of His identity and authority.

The expression is rendered in the Authorized Version as "Verily, verily I say unto you." The Greek for this verse, literally translated, is, "Amen, amen. I say to you." *Amen, amen* carries the idea of, "So be it, so be it." This decisiveness and conviction in Jesus' teaching also comes through when expressed like this, "Firmly and correctly *I say* to you." More colloquially, the phrase could be translated, *I'm absolutely telling you how it is; I know what I'm talking about and my word to you on this subject is final!*

Please note the words "I tell," (NIV) or I say" (KJV). Jesus was contrasting His teaching with that of the scribes and teachers of the law. He was asserting He is *the* Word; the *last* Word; *the final* word. This is true because His words were coming from the lips of the Messiah and Son of God (John 1:1; 2 Corinthians 1:20).

The anointing of the Holy Spirit on Jesus saturated Jesus' words with a striking sense of weight and authority. Jesus taught in true humility and without any arrogance or condescension. Yet, the authority in His voice and manner of speaking exceeded that of any Old Testament king, prophet, or priest, or all of them combined. In a nutshell, Jesus knew He came from God and would return to God (John 13:1; 16:27–30). This meant His words carried divine weight.

THINK ABOUT IT" Jesus was speaking the language of God that He translated into Aramaic as He talked.

"The crowds were amazed at His teaching, because He taught them as one having authority, and not as the scribes" (Matthew 7:9 KJV). The contrast was glaring: these instructors of the Law, in their teaching, certainly did not possess even a smidgen of His anointing and absolute confidence.

This is the kind of certainty expressed in all of Jesus' discourses. In this particular case, the Master Teacher discerned why they were searching for Him. It comes to the surface in this situation because of Jesus' authority to perceive the thinking of a person or a crowd of people, and the attitudes that undergird their thinking. This same ability is referred to by the Apostle Paul as discerning of spirits, a gift of the Holy Spirit in the church (1 Corinthians 12:10).

Like these Galileans, we often think we are doing the searching and actually succeed in finding Jesus. The truth is the Holy Spirit motivates our very yearning to find Him so that we want to be in His presence. People who find Jesus, like these searchers, tend to stop short of recognizing Him as the Son of God. The people the Holy Spirit finds are those who are much more likely to confess Jesus as the Son of God and the Savior of the world (See John 6:65 MSG).

THINK ABOUT IT: The gift to discern spirits Jesus demonstrated here unveils the ability of the Holy Spirit to open up the hearts of individuals, and even large groups, displaying their attitudes and motives. This enables the Lord's servants to say just the right word guaranteed to touch the spiritual nerve in their lives that can result in new life with God. Have you ever had the experience of the Holy Spirit reading your mail; your heart?

The Father's Endorsement

6:27 "Do not work for food that spoils, but for food that endures to eternal life, which the Son of Man will give you. On him God the Father has placed his seal of approval."

Jesus discerned their motives were impure and challenged them to reach for the Father's "seal of approval." They probably had no concept God offered a "seal of approval." Therefore, they desperately needed to eat the food that does not decompose. This bread has only one source; it comes solely from the Son of Man.

The word picture here assumes the internal drive, or work ethic, that motivates a farmer to till the soil, and grow, and then harvest his crops, and of a dad who goes to work daily and labors to feed and clothe the hungry children in his family. It is quite natural to work for the food that spoils. But all too often we do not equally yearn to "grow" in the nourishing "food" that strengthens spiritual bones and muscles. The far greater need is for a strong faith in Jesus Christ who is indeed God's Son and gives eternal life.

The Labor God Demands

6:28 Then they asked him, "What must we do to do the works God requires?"

What an excellent question! It really is the key to the "seal of approval."

6:29 Jesus answered, "The work of God is this: to believe in the one he has sent."

Is this all God is after?

Yes, indeed it is; it is just this simple and the "seal of approval" comes with it. Yet for them, it was a tall order. The only way they could attain the Father's seal of approval, that Jesus fully enjoyed, was for them to be willing to go to the Father through Jesus.

In fact, this statement embodies the whole prophetic message of God's covenant with Abraham (Genesis 15:6), and its fulfillment in the death and resurrection of Jesus. Jesus showed here His ability to express a word of wisdom, an ability that became known in the church as the manifestation gift of wisdom (1 Corinthians 12:9). Jesus wisely summarized what God is looking for from each of His followers. What He said translates into English with fourteen simple words anyone can understand: *"The work of God is this, to believe in the one He has sent" (NIV).*

This understanding confronts Christian Universalists who claim the right to pick and choose between the attributes of God. They embrace the mercy and love of God, for example, but reject divine judgment. Religious pluralists make the same mistake, claiming all roads lead to God so long as a person is sincerely following his chosen path. But Jesus said the seal of approval goes to those who "believe in the *one* God has sent." No, Jesus is not one among many; He is *the* road to the Heavenly Father.

THINK ABOUT IT: Both universalists and pluralists digest only part of the teaching of God's Son and fall short of embracing everything Jesus taught. This picking and choosing seeks to diminish the standard of the gospel: believing the *one* God has sent, which includes all He said and did. Anything less cannot receive the Father's seal of approval; instead, it is grievous error.

A Miraculous Sign

6:30 So they asked him, "What miraculous sign then will you give that we may see it and believe you? What will you do?"

The reasoning seems to be this: *"Jesus, since that is your requirement—believe in the One the Father has sent—how do we know we are to place our trust in you? What sign will you give?"* The implication was they not only wanted a sign so far out of the ordinary as to be miraculous; they also wanted to choose the sign (see Matthew 12:39–40).

Now we're down to the bottom line. It is as if the many miracles Jesus had already performed, which were public knowledge, were inadequate. This included feeding the 5,000 to the full. Some might have already heard the story of Jesus walking on the waves of the Sea of Galilee in a storm not many hours earlier.

We are not told who the spokesmen were of this group. But what quickly becomes apparent is they came prepared to enter into a contract with Jesus if He would perform the one miracle they chose.

6:31 "Our forefathers ate the manna in the desert; as it is written:'He gave them bread from heaven to eat.'"

Ah, here it is. Give us more bread than Moses gave our forefathers. They also wanted proof He could and would keep His word. This meant they wanted a sign to go with the proof. Clearly they liked the meal to the fill, but at the same time did not trust Jesus to keep it up. So they reasoned they had to get a solid agreement with Him.

This thinking demonstrates their second response to Jesus. Simply put, they were operating in unbelief and mistrust. They showed it with their effort to get a tightly worded understanding with Jesus before they put the crown on His head. Achieving that meant they needed to maneuver Jesus into giving them the answer they sought. They even quoted Scripture to try to give their proposed contract authority.

Their statement in verse 31 is a poetic quotation from Asaph, one of David's outstanding tabernacle musicians (I Chronicles 16:5). God graciously fed the Israelites in the wilderness even though they had at best a weak faith in Jehovah and showed little confidence in Jehovah's power to liberate them (Psalm 78:22–24).

God's gracious provision of feeding the five thousand was a revelation of agape love. This God kind of love meets the needs of people as only God understands what their needs are (Isaiah 48:17). He does this even when He knows the receiver will not appreciate the provision. But God does it anyway, because this is how God loves.

The love of God for these people, and their offer of allegiance to Jesus were worlds apart. Their scheme said if He gives us more bread to eat than Moses furnished our fathers, and keeps furnishing bread, we'll know we should follow Him (see Psalm 78:17–25). The agape love of Jesus said, *I will allow myself to be nailed to a cross and die there in your place, doing it while you are sinners. I will give my very body to meet the deepest need of your life, becoming your Bread of eternal life. I will do it even though you do not believe you have this need.*

They were looking no further than their stomachs. Jesus was focused on the much deeper and far more serious need in their souls. He planned to offer them the gift of eternal life.

Asaph summarized this phase of Israel's history that so demonstrated agape love:

> They did not believe in God or trust in his deliverance. Yet he gave a command to the skies above and opened the doors of the heavens; he rained down manna for the people to eat, he gave them the grain of heaven. Men ate the bread of angels; he sent them all the food they could eat (Psalm 78:22–26).

Yes, they quoted part of what Asaph said, but not all. They left out verse 22, "They did not believe in God or trust in his deliverance." How ironic! History was repeating itself. The Israelites rejected God in the wilderness, and their descendants were doing it again, as their Messiah stood in front of them.

The second of the six reactions to Jesus in this chapter, therefore, is that they responded to the Lord with raw unbelief and refused to trust. They simply did not believe what He was telling them. They wanted bread for their stomachs, but they did not want Jesus, the Bread of Life!

6:32 Jesus said to them, "I tell you the truth, it is not Moses who has given you the bread from heaven, but it is my Father who gives you the true bread from heaven."

Moses "fed" the people for 40 years in the wilderness, or so the people thought. Moses, however, was not the source of the manna. When the Israelites looked at the manna the first time and did not know what it was, "Moses said to them, 'It is the bread the Lord has given you to eat.'" (Exodus 16:15). Moses is due credit as the intercessor who appealed to God's throne for the people's need for food, but God was the source and the giver.

THINK ABOUT IT: These Israelites were comparing the power of an intercessor who prayed for food, to the power of the Creator who both made the food and the delivery system for the food. The intercessor and the Creator must never be treated as equals.

In their twisted minds, they actually believed the intercessor was more important than the Creator who was the source of the bread.

After a great leader like Moses has deceased and time has passed, people tend to set the leader on a pedestal. When they do, it becomes difficult to delineate between the man who prayed in faith for the miracle, and the God who gave the miracle: "Moses gave us manna." Taken to extremes, this can lead to idolatrous worship of the servant the Lord empowered. Moses was God's instrument to give the Israelites manna, but only God fed them the manna from heaven.

These Jews seemed to be saying, "*You have given 5,000 men one meal; Moses gave manna to our whole nation for 40 years. Now if you will show you can match Moses, we will believe you and follow you. We have to see it before we can believe it.*" Or said another way, *Let's back Jesus into a corner to pressure Him into feeding us for 40 years!*

Is this not the classic example of what Moses meant when he said to the nation, "Why do you quarrel with me? Why do you put the Lord to the test?" (Exodus 17:2). At the end of his life, Moses described this testing of God as tempting God (Deuteronomy 6:16). Jesus quoted precisely this statement to the devil in His temptation in the wilderness (Matthew 4:7; Luke 4:12).

Paul later summarized the DNA of the sons of Abraham in a simple sentence: "The Jews require a sign" (1 Corinthians 1:22). Given man's fallen nature, it was a predictable expectation. Some Jews believed when Messiah came, He would duplicate Moses' miracle of 40 years of free bread (see Exodus 16). *So, let's put Him to the test: if Jesus really is the Messiah sent by God, then let Him prove it by raining manna from heaven* (see John 6:29, 38, 57). It was the third of the six reactions.

Because it was not Moses, but God, who gave the manna, Jesus could honor Moses without feeling any need to compete with him. The original manna was indeed a type of the true bread to come. In contrast, Jesus offered Israel bread to stop the hunger pains of the soul for all eternity. Jesus Himself in His own person is this nourishment from heaven regarding which Moses prophesied. Jesus is the Bread of Life.

Said another way, the distinction between Jesus and Moses is Moses prayed and God gave manna that had to be picked up six days a week for forty years. Jesus is the Living Bread come down from heaven who gives the bread of *eternal life* to those who believe in Him and demonstrate their faith in repentance. This makes a quantum difference between Jesus and Moses. The superiority of Jesus is so much greater as to make comparison nonsensical.

See, then Believe, or Believe, then See?

The Jewish DNA was locked into the "see and then believe" mindset. But "see and believe" has a major flaw. When faith is based on what can be seen, and not on Jesus who is the living Word as presented in the Scriptures, questions always follow, like:

- When has a person seen enough? and,
- Did I see correctly? and
- Did I see what I needed to see? and
- Did I see with proper discernment? This requires extra caution because Satan can do "lying wonders" (2 Thessalonians 2:8–10; John 2:18–25; 4:48).

For faith to have a strong and solid anchor, it must be grounded in Jesus, the "living Word" who is unveiled in the written Scriptures.

When we disregard the study of the Triune God, we go through life wearing blinders, never discovering our eternal purpose.

It is a one-way ticket to losing our souls.

Jesus alone is this Living Word, the Son of God who "changes not" (Malachi 3:6; Hebrews 13:8). Because the Holy Spirit expressed the Living Word as the written Word in the Bible, every generation has access to the same standard. The Holy Spirit presents Jesus to all people who hold fast to the Holy Scriptures as the revelation of the Living Word. And this is the cornerstone of the standard: "Anyone who wants to approach God must believe both that he exists and that he cares enough to respond to those who seek him" (Hebrews 11:6 MSG).

THINK ABOUT IT: "Faith does not operate in the realm of the possible," wrote George Mueller. "There is no glory for God in the humanly possible. Faith begins where man's power ends."[4]

Bread More Nutritious Than Manna

The Apostle John was an eye witness: Jesus could not be boxed into a corner. Neither could He be made to prove He could make more manna than the miracle God gave to Moses. John understood why:

1. Moses foretold the Messiah would come. Jesus was Moses' Messiah too. "The Lord your God will raise up for you a Prophet like me, an Israeli, a man to whom you must listen and whom you must obey" (Deuteronomy 18:15 TLB).

2. Moses did not create any manna. The heavenly Father gave the manna. Moses only believed for it and announced it. A big limitation was also on Moses' manna—it satisfied

the stomach for the day, and then it had to be repeated. This limitation was huge.

"When the dew was gone, thin flakes like frost on the ground appeared on the desert floor. When the Israelites saw it, they said to each other, "What is it?" For they did not know what it was.

Moses said to them, "It is the bread the Lord has given you to eat. This is what the Lord has commanded: 'Each one is to gather as much as he needs. Take an omer for each person you have in your tent'" (Exodus 16:14–16).

3. Jesus came to offer bread far more nutritious than the manna for which Moses prayed. Jesus' bread is good both for time and eternity.

THINK ABOUT IT: Jesus is the Bread of Life who quenches the hunger of the soul, day after day, after day. He keeps doing it, as the hymn proclaims, "just as long as eternity rolls."

Yes, Jesus is the Bread of Life who ended the need for repetitious sacrifices, over, and over, and over again.

The Bread from Heaven

6:33 "For the bread of God is he who comes down from heaven and gives life to the world."

By showing He Himself is the true bread from heaven, Jesus demonstrated *He* is the eternity-lasting nourishment of the soul. Anyone who wants to feast on the nourishment He provides must come to Jesus by faith, experiencing a new birth.

Jesus actually gave His body to save "whosoever will." Barley and wheat are ground so small each becomes the flour that is the staff of earthly life. But it must be eaten over, and over, and over, and over again. Jesus' very broken and mangled body, beaten to pieces in Pilate's judgment hall, is living bread. He preserves our souls unto eternal life.

Instead of choosing to feast on this living bread, these Jews demanded Jesus show them a sign like Moses did—forty years of free wheat and barley bread—it was *seeing* and then *believing.* Their "contract" was totally self-centered and based on what they hoped to *get.* These leaders had not learned the power of love is a far superior motivator; *agape* is love selflessly anchored on what can one *give to meet a true need.*

THINK ABOUT IT: Is your relationship with Jesus self-centered, serving Him for what you *get*? Or is it love-centered, serving Jesus with a heart to become a *giver* like Him?

Traveling on the King's highway to heaven always calls for *believing* first, then *seeing* follows. On this requirement, the Lord never budged. "The work of God is this: to believe in the one he has sent" (John 6:29). Abraham, the father of the nation, modeled this kind of faith: "Abraham believed the Lord and he credited it to him as righteousness" (Genesis 15:6; 2 Corinthians 5:21).

6:34 "Sir," they said, "from now on give us this bread."

They did not comprehend what they were asking. They wanted barley for the stomach, but Jesus came to offer His body and His blood for their eternal souls. They could have this eternal bread if they chose to "believe in the one [God] has sent."

6:35 Then Jesus declared, "I am the bread of life. He who comes to me will never go hungry, and he who believes in me will never be thirsty."

This is the first of Jesus' seven "I AM" statements recorded in John's gospel. The word picture shows the manna in the wilderness was but a foreshadowing of the true Messianic manna to come. Moses' manna had nothing eternal about it. Jesus, however, offers eternal life to each individual who comes to Him in repentance and accepts this gift for himself. No one can be born again for someone else; God has no grandchildren.

This *I am* statement links Jesus inseparably with Jehovah, the God who is revealed in the Old Testament as the "I AM." Moses received this revelation at the burning bush:

> Indeed, when I come to the children of Israel and say to them, "the God of your fathers has sent me to you," and they say to me, "What is His name?" What shall I say to them?
>
> God said to Moses, "I AM WHO I AM. Thus you shall say to the children of Israel, I AM has sent me to you" (Exodus 3:13–14).

The Prophet Isaiah spoke to this great revelation when he quoted Jehovah: "I am the Lord [Jehovah]; that is my name! I will not give my glory to another or my praise to idols" (Isaiah 42:8).

Chase After Me!

Uncle Billy was known as the "nickel uncle." Every time he came to visit, young Timmy, a very intelligent junior, got another nickel. He followed Billy around the house. Every time they were together for even a few seconds, Uncle Billy gave Timmy another nickel.

One day Billy took Timmy to see his trunk, filled with an almost unlimited supply of nickels. "Every time I'm with you, Timmy," he told his young buddy, "I'll give you another nickel."

After that, Timmy rarely left Uncle Billy's side.

A few days passed and Timmy had come up with what he thought was a good proposal. "Uncle Billy," the lad said. "Every time I'm with you, you give me another nickel. One day I'll have all your nickels. So why not hand them over to me now?"

"That would be a problem, Timmy," Uncle Billy responded. "In fact, that's precisely why I don't give you all the nickels now. I want to bless you with nickels, but I'm more interested in enjoying your company."

Like these Israelites, most of us have been guilty of chasing after a "nickel God." But the Lord says to us, I'd much rather you chase after me than my nickels."[5]

Jesus Faces Willful Unbelief

6:36 But as I told you, you have seen me and still you do not believe.

It is difficult to comprehend a spiritual blindness that did not want intimacy with Jesus. Indeed! They persisted in their unwillingness to believe even while...

> ...looking straight into the eyes of God's Son, incarnate as the Son of Man, and
> ...witnessing His miracles only God can do, and
> ...listening to teaching only God can give.

The way the Lord used the phrase, "and still," suggests He too was amazed at their unbelief.

The Heavenly Father as Evangelist

6:37 All that the Father gives me will come to me, and whoever comes to me I will never drive away. 38 For I have come down from heaven not to do my will but to do the will of him who sent me. 39 And this is the will of him who sent me that I shall lose none of all that he has given me, but raise them up at the last day. 40 For my Father's will is that everyone who looks to the Son and believes in him shall have eternal life, and I will raise him up at the last day."

Jesus stated the followers who come to Him are those "the Father gives" Him. This disclosure reveals the heavenly Father as the lead evangelist in the Tri-Unity of God. The Father does the work of evangelism, God's Son does the work of evangelism, and the Holy Spirit does the work of evangelism. The Trinity is totally committed to spreading the good news.

These elements are fundamental to all evangelism:

- "I came down from heaven not to do my will but to do the will of him who sent me." Calvary was the ultimate expression of the Father's plan for Jesus.

- "All that the Father gives me will come to me."

- The Father's will is that "I lose none of all he has given me." Hence, "Whoever comes to me I will never drive away."

- "Everyone who looks to the Son and believes in Him shall have eternal life, and I will raise him up at the last day." This is another of Jesus' specific claims to be the Son of God.

To achieve this, the heavenly Father sent His Son to die on the cross because of the compelling love in the heart of God for lost people (John 3:16).

This is the whole message of grace, the unmerited favor of God. The Apostle Paul later described "the incomparable riches of his grace, expressed in his kindness to us in Christ Jesus." Paul went on to say, "It is by grace you have been saved, through faith—and this not from yourselves, it is the gift of God—not by works, so that no one can boast" (Ephesians 2:7–10).

Jesus built a strong element of accountability into the gospel: "I told you that you would die in your sins; if you do not believe that I am [the one I claim to be], you will indeed die in your sins" (John 8:24).

For a person to repent assumes he accepts responsibility for his choices. If he "owns up" to his sins, as did the prodigal son, then he can repent with godly sorrow, and he will receive forgiveness (Luke 15: 18, 21; 2 Corinthians 7:10).

If a person does not accept his accountability and repent, he will be held responsible at the judgment to come (John 8:40; Luke 1:3–5; 16:22–26; Matthew 12:36; Acts 17:30; Romans 2:3; Hebrews 9:27).

THINK ABOUT IT: Do you perceive your heavenly Father as the ultimate evangelist?

Indeed, the highest authority in the universe, the Trinity itself, is vitally interested in drawing people to Jesus Christ.

The Apostle John shows later in his gospel the Holy Spirit's role in evangelism. The Spirit convinces unbelievers of the great sin of not believing in Jesus (John 16:9). This is sometimes referred to as the convicting grace of God that causes people to feel guilt for their sins. Even in the face of their raw unbelief, Jesus knew His life, climaxing with His death and resurrection, would produce a worldwide harvest based on these values. To guarantee this ingathering, objective number one in Jesus' life was obeying His Father. Jesus expressed His mission statement, in fact, amid this tough criticism. This summary affirmed what His purpose in His incarnation *was* and *was not*. He "came down from heaven," He said, not to change one iota the plan of redemption framed in eternity, but to "do the will of Him who sent me."

THINK ABOUT IT: "Christ became what we are that He might make us what He is."—Athanasius of Alexandria (296–376 AD).

Jesus clearly had a strong sense of His divine origin and His destiny. He knew where He came from—(from heaven)—and where He was going (back to His Father by way of the cross), and the path to accomplish it all.

The bond between Jesus and His Father to achieve this was stronger than steel, and this relationship has produced the Lord's truly international family. This also guarantees in the resurrection of the last day not one person "who looks to the Son and believes in Him" will be left behind—not even one. All will be resurrected and "shall have eternal life!"

During His ministry, Jesus did not make a single change to the Father's plan. He expressed to His Father in His High Priestly prayer, "I have brought you glory on earth by completing the work you gave me to do," and a few hours later from the cross said, "It is finished" (John 17:4; 19:30).

The Bible in this context establishes we are not human beings hoping for an eternal experience. Instead, we are eternal beings having a human experience (Ecclesiastes 3:11). The significance of this understanding is huge.

Eternity Sanctions Values

It is precisely because of the eternity outside time that everything in time becomes valuable and important and meaningful. Therefore, Christianity…makes it of urgent importance that everything we do here (whether individually or as a society) should be rightly related to what we eternally are.

"Eternal life" is the sole sanction for the values of this life.[6]

Our Sins Hurt God—God Has Feelings Too

After his sin with Bathsheba, David prayed, "Against you, you only, have I sinned and done what is evil in your sight" (Psalm 51:4). Many mistakenly see their sins as hurting people only. Sin is wicked, first and foremost, because it violates the heart and character of God (Genesis 6:6). For example, adultery is a grievous sin because fidelity is a fundamental attribute of the nature of God. David's sin, therefore, broke faith with God. Secondarily, his violating God also meant he wounded his family, Bathsheba's family, the people in his government, and the nation at large.

Agape Love Never Manipulates

Because the *agape* love of God is unconditional and always acts in the best interests of others, the concept of "taking advantage" has no place in the Trinity. Precisely because *agape* love never manipulates to get its way, King David violated God when he used Bathsheba and took advantage of her in the tryst (they were not equals). If David had acted in the love of God toward Bathsheba, he would have made a choice based on the character of God and what was best for her. Instead, his motivation was to get what he wanted at her expense. In doing so, he disregarded the character of God. This meant he knowingly rebelled against God. He also violated Uriah, Bathsheba's husband, and her grandfather, Ahithophel (David's most trusted counselor).

THINK ABOUT IT: It is imperative that parents teach their children, and pastors teach their parishioners, sin is evil and wicked primarily because it offends God and breaks His heart. Secondarily, because sin has offended God, it also wounds people.

Even though grossly violated, God the heavenly Father held David accountable. The king ultimately accepted responsibility and responded to God with the genuine repentance that always leads to forgiveness. In every generation, God has done the same.

Because the Father's heart beats to bring people to Jesus, it naturally follows the role of an evangelist in the church is to live out the Father's heart. Hence, the ministry gift of evangelist is one of the gifts of the Holy Spirit in the New Testament church (Ephesians 4:11–12). The gospel invitation is meant for all.

The heavenly Father's goal is to hold every person accountable and bring them to Jesus in repentance. Indeed, the gospel invitation is meant for all. In fact, this understanding of personal accountability before God, followed by repentance and then forgiveness has distinctly marked the worldwide spread of the gospel from its beginning (Romans 3:19).

Even though our sins truly hurt Him, the heavenly Father has always acted in the best interests of lost humanity. In every generation, God has reached out to Adam's fallen race with the offer that forgiveness will follow repentance. The ultimate expression of the Father's love is sending His dear Son Jesus as our redeemer. In fact, the Lord Jesus personifies the gift of evangelist. Students of Scripture also commonly recognize the role of the Holy Spirit in evangelism. But this passage shows the heavenly Father as an evangelist (vs. 37–40). Jesus expressed it, "All that the Father gives me…"

The Holy Spirit, without violating anyone's free will, bonds to every person the Father gives to Jesus. The goal is to bring each believer to maturity in Christ. In fact, this understanding from the beginning has distinctly marked the worldwide spread of the gospel. Jesus never drives away anyone His Father gives to Him, no matter his culture or ethnicity. Isaiah foretold Jesus' mission would be to restore bruised reeds; He certainly does not finish breaking them off (Isaiah 42:3).

The concept of evangelizing the nations was foreign to the Jewish mindset, which had no vision to bring all ethnicities to the God of Abraham. But it is a core Christian value. Peter learned early in the spread of the gospel "God is no respecter of persons," and he never forgot the lesson (Acts 10:34). Peter penned in his second epistle, for example: "The Lord is…not willing that any should perish, but that all should come to repentance" (2 Peter 3:9 KJV). Jesus has continued in every generation to receive whomever His Father gives Him (John 3:16). His ultimate reward for His followers' faithfulness is the gift of resurrection and eternal life (John 3:16; Revelation 22:17).

Grumbling Misses the Free Gift of God

6:41 At this the Jews began to grumble about him because he said, "I am the bread that came down from heaven." 42 They said, "Is this not Jesus, the son of Joseph, whose father and mother we know? How can he now say, 'I came down from heaven'?"

Making the transition from *Moses giving them bread,* to *Jesus as both the Son of God and the Bread of Life who gave Moses the manna* was a huge transition for people who knew well where Jesus grew up. Squarely they walked by sight and not by faith, placing the facts as they perceived them ahead of believing in Jesus' message and His miracles.

John here records the fourth of the six reactions to Jesus: the Jews stumbled over Jesus' birthplace. The result was they tried to quarrel with Him, and then grumble behind His back. With only a little imagination, although two millennia removed, we can hear it: "Who does Jesus think He is? We know He is only "the son of Joseph, whose father and mother we know."

This is a classic case of the clearly *obvious* being totally incorrect. Joseph was not Baby Jesus' father; the Holy Spirit was, so the Jews stumbled over their understanding of His parentage. Therefore, this passage lays down a marker in the journey of faith:

THINK ABOUT IT: If a person rejects the incarnation story, it is unlikely he will exercise faith to believe Jesus is the Son of God.

A pattern is emerging in these reactions to Jesus. First, they respond to Him as a respected rabbi. This was followed by raw unbelief, rejecting His claim to Deity as the bread from heaven. Then they put Him to the test, trying to goad him and trap Him into getting what they wanted. When that did not work, they turned to griping. The grumbling was justified in their minds because they knew all about his parentage, or so they thought. Some of them in the crowd might have known Joseph and Mary, and a few might have even seen Jesus working with Joseph in his carpentry shop.

Their fathers had done the same thing in the wilderness. Their murmuring made life miserable for Moses and brought judgment on themselves (see Exodus 16:4–36; Deuteronomy 8:2–16; Psalm 78:18, 41, 56; 106:14; Hebrews 3:8, 17). They did not perceive the intervention of God for their good in the desert, because they focused on their natural surroundings.

A grumbling tongue routinely fixates on partial truth and normally makes incorrect conclusions. Invariably, the result is painful discipline, whatever the focus of the murmuring—be it the church, a family, or a job. For example, nobody enjoys the company for long of a negative person who can look at a rainbow and find imperfections. These Jews' grumbling blinded them so that they could not see the gift of eternal life right in front of them!

6:43 "Stop grumbling among yourselves," Jesus answered.

The consequences can be serious when a driver disobeys red lights. But this was a case in which murmuring had been bred into the *DNA* of a people over centuries. In this account, it was not one person but a crowd involved in rejecting the Son of God. The Lord's statement commands them to see the red lights on the highway of the soul and "Stop grumbling!"

Grumbling is a choice. Repeated choices to grumble form an attitude, which springs out of deeply rooted mistrust. Grumblers are trying to get *what they want* from God even when God knows He has something better for them. Hence, grumblers are always trying to box God into a corner to get their way.

These grumblers rejected the revelation of God, although Messiah was standing before them face to face. They wanted free bread for their stomachs but God was blessing them with the immeasurably greater gift of His Son. If they accepted Him, they could have eternal bread.

Since grumbling is a choice, the solution to murmuring is the repentance that makes a new choice and walks away from that sinful lifestyle. Grumblers, however, usually find making such a lifestyle change hard to do.

Murmuring always gets a red light in the Lord's church—"STOP IT!"

6:44 "No one can come to me unless the Father who sent me draws him, and I will raise him up at the last day."

This statement links to verse 37 and expands on the Father's role in evangelism. The great attribute of Messiah's amazing mercy includes His death on the cross in our place. This compassion also embraces the resurrection of the Good Shepherd who comes hunting those whom *the Father* "draws."

THINK ABOUT IT: The Father loves us so much He sent His Son to die as our substitute. The portrait of the Father hunting us, searching us out, is very heartwarming indeed.

Although our sins violate the Father's heart, He continues to extend His hand to redeem us. The Father's goal is to draw us to His Son. He also adopts us as His children and gives us the rights of heirs. Yes, Jesus is the living bread who gives life everlasting. It behooves us, therefore, to "be diligent that [we] may be *found of him* in peace, without spot, and blameless" (2 Peter 3:14; see Romans 8:16–18).

How important to realize the role of the Trinity in evangelism. We do not of our own volition reach out and search for God. Instead the Holy Spirit motivates us as an act of the Father's grace to desire God's help.

It should also be noted King David looked through the lens of prophecy and discovered the ministry of the Holy Spirit. In fact, David was a prophet even as he expressed his repentant plea: "Do not cast me from your presence or take your Holy Spirit from me" (Psalm 51:11).

The Courtship that Saves

The gospel of the Lord Jesus Christ is a ministry of courtship. The Holy Spirit woos and draws people one by one to the heart of the Father through Jesus Christ. Because of this magnetic love, people recognize their desperate need. "*My life is not on the right path and I know it. I am living in rebellion against God and will never be able to get on the right road unless the Man on the middle cross helps me.*"

Many have trouble believing Jesus will forgive them—especially *them*. Hence, it is the work of the Holy Spirit to whet a person's appetite and convince him if he will repent, Jesus will forgive him. Blessing of blessings! When we decide to believe God's Word, accept the offer of His grace, and then repent, we will be forgiven. This is the essence of the grace that saves.

> "If we confess our sins, he is faithful and just to forgive us our sins, and to cleanse us from all unrighteousness" (1 John 1:9).

> "For by grace are ye saved through faith; and that not of yourselves: it is the gift of God; not of works, lest any man should boast" (Ephesians 2:8–9, KJV).

The heavenly Father chose us in Christ "before the foundation of the world" (Ephesians 1:4). The result is the very goodness of the Father draws us to Jesus (Romans 2:4). In fact, "[the Father] made us accepted in the Beloved" to the "praise of the glory of His grace" (Ephesians 1:6).

Jesus' Love—the Agent of Change

At Calvary, we look into the face of pure love expressed in the sinless countenance of Jesus Christ.

Please, dear reader, look at Him. Please look at Him. He is hanging on His bloody cross for you. Everything about the crucifixion of

72

Jesus says He suffered this shame and agony *for you* because *He loves you.* As our eyes meet His, we discover the strength to admit how wicked we really are. After all, it was these Jews' sins, and mine, and yours, dear reader, that nailed Jesus to the cross. Yes, as we look at the spectacle, we are filled with remorse and feel the pain of our guilt. That gaze is enough to motivate us desperately to want the help only God can give—forgiveness for the sins of yesterday, and an inoculation of grace never to do it again.

THINK ABOUT IT: God always meets repentance with forgiveness. Always. This reality is the crown jewel of Christian faith.

Augustine of Hippo (354–430 A.D.) wrote: "The grace of Christ without which neither infants nor adults can be saved, is not rendered for any merits, but is given gratis, on account of which it is also called grace."

The Heavenly Father as Teacher

6:45 It is written in the Prophets: "They will all be taught by God." Everyone who listens to the Father and learns from him comes to me. 46 No one has seen the Father except the one who is from God; only he has seen the Father. 47 I tell you the truth, he who believes has everlasting life.

We routinely recognize Jesus as the Master Teacher. In these verses, the Lord pulls the curtain back further, letting His followers look inside the working relationships in the Trinity. Jesus has already presented His Father as evangelist; now He portrays His Father as teacher. Jesus did this by demonstrating His mastery of the Old Testament prophetic writings. Isaiah wrote, "All your sons will be taught by the Lord [Jehovah] and great will be your children's peace" (54:13). Jesus the Master Teacher specifically makes the point Jehovah is a teacher. The grand theme of the Father's classroom is to reveal Jesus as His Son.

> "This is what the prophets meant when they wrote, '... they will all be personally taught by God.' Anyone who has spent any time at all listening to the Father, really listening and therefore learning, comes to me to be taught personally—to see it with his own eyes, hear it with his own ears, from me, since I have it firsthand from the Father" (John 6:45 MSG).

Many perceive Jehovah of the Old Testament as harsh and distant, but the revelation Isaiah received in 54:13 shows He is neither. Yahweh is a Father who is a very caring teacher, and Jesus Christ His Son is the great theme of His instruction (John 6:46; 14:9).

Special Delivery Pizza

Army National Guard Major, Shawn Faulkner, wanted to reach out from his post in Afghanistan and do something special for his wife's birthday, February 18, 2013. Since his wife loved Mellow Mushroom pizza, he contacted the corporate offices and asked them to deliver a pizza and a $50 gift card to their Jacksonville, Florida home.

Well, the local Mellow Mushroom franchise did better than that. Their chef made a heart-shaped pizza and even added heart-shaped pepperoni slices. Then their delivery guy dropped off the pizza, a bunch of flowers and balloons, and the $50 gift card—all for free.

"I was surprised and excited and overwhelmed and all of that," said Major Faulkner's wife Josephine. "It was so nice."

The general manager of Mellow Mushroom emailed Major Faulkner and told him, "We got you bro!"[7]

THINK ABOUT IT: As an evangelist the heavenly Father searches amid lost mankind even today, pointing people to Jesus. As He does so He performs a deed far, far better than the Mellow Mushroom general manager. He sent His only Son as our bread of eternal life. He is the one who really has "got you, bro!"

Moses longed to see God but was only permitted to view His back (Exodus 33:21–23). Jesus made the claim the only one who has ever seen the Father is His Son, "who is from God," and is "God the one and only" (John 1:14). And to be even more emphatic, Jesus actually repeated only He had "seen the Father." This teaching, of course, placed Jesus in a special class all by Himself as Deity in the flesh, a status no prophet could ever hope to achieve. Not only is He "the one who is from God," His uniqueness stands out because "only he has seen the Father."

Then one day, Oh! the blessed day; the intercessory ministry of Jesus will be completed and we "will see [the Father's] face" (Revelation 22:4; see also Romans 8:26–27, 34; 11:2; Hebrews 7:25).

THINK ABOUT IT: Is not the conclusion obvious? Jesus is *the* path to the Father. No one should ever seek to void the part of God's plan of redemption affirming Jesus as "the one and only."

Knowing Jesus is the only path to God places a heavy burden for evangelism on Jesus' followers at home and around the world. And, for evangelism to be effective, it must always be anchored in the humility and love of God revealed on Golgotha.

The responsibility for evangelism is all the greater when we assimilate that Jesus never taught anyone: *"If you reject me in this life, I will give you another chance in the afterlife."*

Jesus, Greater Than Moses

6:48 I am the bread of life. 49 Your forefathers ate the manna in the desert, yet they died. 50 But here is the bread that comes down from heaven, which a man may eat and not die. 51 I am the living bread that came down from heaven. If anyone eats of this bread, he will live forever. This bread is my flesh, which I will give for the life of the world."

Jesus is so superior to Moses the difference between them is clear and distinct. Moses fulfilled his job description as a servant who announced to the people of Israel God had given them manna from heaven (Hebrews 3:2, 5; Deuteronomy 8:3, 16). But the people who "ate the manna in the desert" ultimately died, as did Moses. Jesus, however, claimed to be "the bread of life." Jesus went on to explain:

> "This is the bread that comes from heaven so that whoever eats it won't die. I am the living bread that came from heaven. Whoever eats this bread will live forever. The bread I will give to bring life to the world is my flesh" (John 6:50–51 GW).

Hebrews 3 is the classic chapter in the New Testament that establishes the superiority of Jesus over Moses. At the same time it gives Moses his well-earned honor:

> Therefore, holy brothers, who share in the heavenly calling, fix your thoughts on Jesus, the apostle and high priest whom we confess.
> He [Jesus] was faithful to the one who appointed him, just as Moses was faithful in all God's house. Jesus has been found worthy of greater honor than Moses, just as the builder of a house has greater honor than the house

itself. For every house is built by someone, but God is the builder of everything.

Moses was faithful as a servant in all God's house, testifying to what would be said in the future. But Christ is faithful as a son over God's house. And we are his house, if we hold on to our courage and the hope of which we boast (Hebrews 3:1–6).

No one should put Moses up beside Jesus to imply Moses can compete with Him. Instead, the Mount of Transfiguration shows the proper relationship between them. Moses was chosen to visit with the Lord on the holy mountain because He was the great symbol of the exodus from Egypt and the revelation of the Law (Exodus 12; Hebrews 11:23–29). Elijah the prophet, who went to heaven in a chariot of fire pulled by horses of fire, symbolized the great exodus to come that will climax in the rapture of the church (2 Kings 2:11–14; 1 Thessalonians 4:13–18). Both Moses and Elijah, therefore, talked with Jesus about His "decease" [*exodon* = exodus] "he would accomplish at Jerusalem" (Luke 9:31). The term, *exodus*, communicates the thought of departure. They discussed Jesus' own exodus from this world and His return to His Father's right hand.

THINK ABOUT IT: When your time comes to leave this world, is it the deepest desire of your heart to be in the exodus Jesus leads?

Jesus, in His own person, is the ultimate exodus.

Because this is true, Jesus is the first fruits of the great exodus. One day He will take His followers from earth to heaven to spend eternity with Him. Knowing this was the subject of their conversation on the mountain, it is reasonable to believe Moses was very quick to affirm Jesus as His immeasurable superior, as he and Elijah talked with their Messiah on the Mount of Transfiguration.

Giving Moses his proper place does not diminish what he accomplished. Moses was a faithful servant in the house; he did his job well as emancipator and lawgiver. In fact, Jesus gave high honor to Moses. For example, the Lord used Moses' three great conclusions about life as His own three answers to Satan in the wilderness (Deuteronomy 6:13, 16; 8:3). In addition, the Spirit revealed to John on Patmos:

"I saw in heaven…what looked like a sea of glass mixed with fire, and standing beside the sea, those who had been victorious over the beast and his image and over the number of his name. They held harps given them by God and sang the song of Moses the servant of God and the song of the Lamb:

'Great and marvelous are your deeds, Lord God Almighty. Just and true are your ways, King of the ages. Who will not fear you, O Lord, and bring glory to your name? For you alone are holy. All nations will come and worship before you, for your righteous acts have been revealed'" (Revelation 15:1–4).

Jesus' Use of Symbolic Language

6:52 Then the Jews began to argue sharply among themselves, "How can this man give us his flesh to eat?"

This discourse unfolds the heartbreaking road Jesus, the man of sorrows, willingly walked to reveal Himself as the Son of God and Savior of all people. In doing this, Jesus also presented His Father to the world as both evangelist and teacher (Isaiah 53:3; John 1:18). Having done so, Jesus took the discourse to a new level by offering a word picture: "I am the bread come down from heaven" (verse 41) and "The bread…is my flesh" (verse 51).

From the point Jesus said, "The bread…is my flesh," nothing else He taught seemed to matter to His Jewish hearers. The bickering quickly became intense. Instead of grasping the word picture, they took it literally. This scene takes John's fourth record of the six reactions to Jesus to a higher level. Here their grumbling escalates to "arguing sharply," as the bickering quickly became intense.

The reactions started with a respectful greeting, rabbi, then advanced to raw unbelief, then to a callous effort to test Him. This is followed by grumbling over his birthplace that mushroomed into sharp arguing.

The Jews saw Jesus as "this man," as the son of Mary and Joseph. Jesus' encounter with Nicodemus showed the Lord might have been accepted as "a teacher come from God" (John 3:2). But such a job description would surely have degraded His mission and ministry as the Messiah who was God's unique, one and only Son, with an international vision to save the world.

THINK ABOUT IT: Jesus faced argument and contradiction every day of His ministry, or so it seems—even from His own brothers. It never stopped, but followed Him all the way to the cross, and it continues to this day.

The writer of Hebrews made the application, "Consider him who endured such opposition from sinful men, so that you will not grow weary and lose heart" (Hebrews 12:3).

"How can this man give us his flesh to eat?" the Jews asked. In their minds, when Jesus said, "The bread…is my flesh," the statement could have only one meaning, and it pointed to cannibalism.

After Noah came out of the Ark, God gave him a clear statement authorizing a very broad diet. It included wide varieties of meat, but eating the flesh of fellow humans made in the image of God was not on the list (Genesis 9:1–6). Jewish life and culture, therefore, has always condemned cannibalism. Hence, the thought of eating human flesh quickly became a stumbling block that was a huge boulder to Jesus' critics.

The problem here, of course, was these Jews were literalists who could not think outside their mental box and recognize the symbolisms in Jesus' teaching. Neither were they willing to adopt the attitude, *"I don't get His meaning, but I do get His miracles; therefore, I will trust Him to tell me more later about what He intends by those words."*

6:53 Jesus said to them, "I tell you the truth, unless you eat the flesh of the Son of Man and drink his blood, you have no life in you. 54 Whoever eats my flesh and drinks my blood has eternal life, and I will raise him up at the last day. 55 For my flesh is real food and my blood is real drink. 56 Whoever eats my flesh and drinks my blood remains in me, and I in him. 57 Just as the living Father sent me and I live because of the Father, so the one who feeds on me will live because of me. 58 This is the bread that came down from heaven. Your forefathers ate manna and died, but he who feeds on this bread will live forever."

The Lord's language is figurative here. Matthew records Jesus' explanation for using this form of speech. Jesus said:

> The knowledge about the mysteries of the kingdom of heaven has been given to you [the disciples]. But it has not been given to the crowd. Those who understand these mysteries will be given more knowledge, and they will excel in understanding them. However, some people don't understand these mysteries. Even what they understand will be taken away from them. This is why I speak to them this way. They see, but they're blind. They hear, but they don't listen. They don't even try to understand.

So they make Isaiah's prophecy come true: "You will hear clearly but never understand. You will see clearly but never comprehend. These people have become close-minded and hard of hearing. They have shut their eyes so that their eyes never see. Their ears never hear. Their minds never understand. And they never return to me for healing!" (Matthew 13:11–15 GW; see Isaiah 6:9–10).

The Lord showed people can choose a path of hardness of heart that enjoys grumbling and disputation, until it reaches a tipping point of no return: "They don't even try to understand." At this deepest level, according to Isaiah's prophecy, actually seeing the miraculous power of God and hearing the word of truth will not be persuasive. Isaiah also foretold the end result of their hard heartedness would be the ruin of their country. Their cities and houses would be left deserted, their fields ravaged, and the people sent into exile (Isaiah 6:11–12).

What Isaiah foretold was accurately fulfilled in the history of Israel in the Assyrian captivity (732 BC) and the Babylonian exile of Judah (606 BC). These historical events mark in history the beginning of the age of the *diaspora*, the era of the wandering Jew.

Jesus chose Isaiah's prophecy to explain what was happening in His own ministry some 750 years after Isaiah. This time God's Son, as Israel's Messiah, was on the scene in flesh and blood. This, of course, compounded the seriousness of their hard-hearted rejection. The end result four decades later was again ruined cities, deserted houses, ravaged fields, and exile. This dispersion among the nations lasted almost two millennia, from 70 AD to 1948 AD, when Israel was again born as a nation (Isaiah 66:8).

No, Jesus did not teach cannibalism in this discourse in the Capernaum synagogue. Instead, He used symbolic language to show salvation would come at the price of His broken and bleeding body. Jesus knew well His cruel death was ahead, to be followed by His glorious resurrection.

Do you, dear reader, eat this "manna"—the body of Jesus crushed for you and His blood freely poured to the ground for you? You can revel in this relationship with the greatest joy by walking in the Spirit, which includes love for Christ revealed in the Scriptures.

THINK ABOUT IT: Jesus' great love for the people of all ethnicities motivates humble obedience worldwide to the Lord's Great Commission.

It should not be missed while this language is symbolic, it is also emphatic. Unless people accept Jesus' love as it is revealed at His cross, they will never gain eternal life. But those who walk up the Hill of the Skull with Jesus will gain the ultimate reward: the bread of eternal life and resurrection from the dead. In this intimate identification with Jesus' cross, we can indeed symbolically eat His flesh and drink His blood, with the result His life remains in us.

This teaching, however, does not justify the conclusion the bread and wine, blessed in Holy Communion, miraculously become the body and blood of Jesus, actually conferring saving grace to believers. The church must hold firmly to the figurative meaning of the language the Lord used in this discourse.

The Apostle Paul did this very thing, teaching the church in Corinth: "The cup of blessing which we bless, is it not the communion of the blood of Christ? The bread which we break, is it not the communion of the body of Christ? (1 Corinthians 10:16 KJV). The word communion used here derives from the Greek word *koinonia*, which carries the idea of *fellowship*. The Holy Communion does not recreate the literal body and blood of Christ, but it surely does provide opportunity for fellowship with Jesus at His table as we remember His death in our place.

Wonderful News—Eternal Bread

As Jesus was sent by His Father and lived because of His Father, anyone who feeds in faith on this intimacy with Jesus will live because of Jesus' triumph over death. In this sense, Jesus is the living Bread from heaven. He gives eternal life, accomplishing what the bread in the wilderness was never able to do, because there was nothing eternal about it. All who ate the manna had to eat it again, and again, and again, until they died in the wilderness.

THINK ABOUT IT: This understanding of eternal bread also adds immeasurably to the gospel as good news.

Because of the death and resurrection of Jesus, any descendant of Adam who is dead in trespasses and sins against God can experience a new birth. For this to happen he must become accountable for his sins and repent, receiving Jesus as the true manna from heaven (John 3:16). Not only does he gain peace with God, but also the guarantee of a personal resurrection and eternal life.

This is a wonderful message in every generation. It is exciting news indeed for all people hungry for a restored relationship with God anywhere in the world.

Can You Be Offended by Jesus?

6:59 He said this while teaching in the synagogue in Capernaum. 60 On hearing it, many of his disciples said, "This is a hard teaching. Who can accept it?"
61 Aware that his disciples were grumbling about this, Jesus said to them, "Does this offend you?

Capturing the Lord's symbolic meaning when He used these very potent words (verses 53–61) was a challenge for many who were Jesus' followers, including His own disciples. They saw it as "tough teaching, too tough to swallow" (John 6:60 MSG), and continued to grumble.

THINK ABOUT IT: Has Jesus ever offended you? It is indeed possible to feel offended when Jesus does not answer our prayers the way we pray them, thereby not meeting our expectations.

No one can compel another person to be offended, however. We must willingly "take" an offense, or *choose* to be offended. Taking an offense presumes a decision, a choice to react with disappointment and hurt.

It is an interesting reality about our Lord that no one was able to offend him, not even the people who crucified him.

John the Baptist sent messengers to Jesus, for example, to ask if Jesus really was the Messiah. In the answer Jesus sent back to John, the Lord said, "Blessed is he who takes no offense because of me" (Matthew 11:6 RSV).

The gospel will stretch us, often further than we want to go, and keep on expanding us. Peter received specific revelation from God affirming the gospel is no respecter of persons (Acts 10:34). Even so, Peter stopped eating with the Gentile brethren and switched over to eat only with the representatives of James, who arrived in Antioch. The gospel had stretched Peter, but not enough. Peter had decided to hide his true beliefs and disguise his thoughts and intentions about the Good News while visiting and talking with these Jews. Peter did so because he wanted to be loyal to his Jewish brethren at the expense of the true message of the Cross (Galatians 2:11–21).

The Apostle Paul confronted Peter to his face because of his dishonesty.

Søren Kierkegaard: Admirers or Followers

If you have any knowledge at all of human nature, you know those who only admire the truth will, when danger appears, become traitors. The admirer is infatuated with the false security of greatness; but if there is any inconvenience or trouble, he pulls back. Admiring the truth, instead of following it, is just as dubious a fire as the fire of erotic love, which at the turn of the hand can be changed into exactly the opposite—to hate, jealousy, and revenge.

Christ, however, never asked for admirers, worshipers, or adherents. He consistently spoke of "followers" and "disciples."[8]

The Spirit, the Source of Life

65 He went on to say, "This is why I told you that no one can come to me unless the Father has enabled him." 6:62 What if you see the Son of Man ascend to where he was before! 63 The Spirit gives life; the flesh counts for nothing. The words I have spoken to you are spirit and they are life. 64 Yet there are some of you who do not believe." For Jesus had known from the beginning which of them did not believe and who would betray him.

If they were offended because Jesus presented Himself as the bread of eternal life, what would their response be when they saw "the Son of Man ascend to where He was before?" Notice the Apostle John records "the Son of Man" here, and not "the Son of God." It is easy to accept the Son of God would go back to His Father. But Jesus taught He would go back to His place with God as "the Son of Man."

Believers must comprehend the resurrected and glorified Son of Man ascended into the heavenly glory and took His seat at God's right hand. This births dynamic reason to rejoice because the Spirit who "raised Jesus from the dead" will also give life to our mortal bodies "through His Spirit who lives in [us]" (Romans 8:11; 12:12).

THINK ABOUT IT: No founder of any other world religion has made the claim He came from the presence of God in heaven and would return to His Father's right hand as the Son of Man (Luke 22:69; Acts 2:25). Jesus is very singular in asserting this. But the evidence backs Him up; His disciples saw him fulfill it at His ascension. The Apostle Peter said, "Now Christ is in heaven, sitting in the place of honor next to God the Father, with all the angels and powers of heaven bowing before him and obeying him" (1 Peter 3:22 TLB).

This is another evidence of Jesus as "the one and only Son of God."

Jesus gives another insight here into the Trinity. He emphatically asserted the Holy Spirit is the source of life too, a clear reference to the Deity of the Holy Spirit. Followers of the Lord, therefore, should make the mental adjustment that the flesh does not count for anything eternal. Jesus also asserted His own words have the status of both "spirit...and life," endowing His very words with eternal quality. The Apostle Paul later expounded on this theme saying, "If Christ dwells in you...the Spirit is life because of righteousness" (Romans 8:10).

THINK ABOUT IT: Jesus' followers, who walk in the Spirit, can also speak life-giving words and connect with their brethren on a spirit level. This turns people around. Have you accepted how *your* words can birth life?

The "word of God is living and active" and always cuts to the depth needed to get the job done; God's Word cannot be chained (Hebrews 4:12; 2 Timothy 2:9). In fact, "the sword of the Spirit...is the word of God" (Ephesians 6:17–18).

Jesus felt the resistance of "some of [them]" to His life-giving words as they refused "to have any part" in His teaching. Jesus also "knew from the start some were not going to risk themselves with Him," and He "knew...who would betray Him." John said this was the reason He told these unbelieving Jews, "no one is capable of coming to [Jesus] on his own. You get to [Jesus] only as a gift from the Father" (John 6:37, 44, 64–65 MSG).

Will You Walk Away Too?

6:66 From this time many of his disciples turned back and no longer followed him. 67 "You do not want to leave too, do you?" Jesus asked the Twelve.
68 Simon Peter answered him, "Lord, to whom shall we go? You have the words of eternal life. 69 We believe and know that you are the Holy One of God."
70 Then Jesus replied, "Have I not chosen you, the Twelve? Yet one of you is a devil!" 71 (He meant Judas, the son of Simon Iscariot, who, though one of the Twelve, was later to betray him.)

The words of Jesus are so life-giving they also motivate people to make free choices, but the Lord did not die to destroy free will. The Jews could say "Yes" or "No" to their incarnate Savior standing right in front of them. This explains the fifth of the six reactions of the Israelites in the synagogue who participated in this dialogue with Jesus: they simply walked away. Many of His followers made their choice to reject Jesus as they stumbled over the implications of His claim to be the Bread of Life. It is very sad when anyone walks away from the Lord, but it is also important to note Jesus made no effort to stop them.

THINK ABOUT IT: Jesus did not say, for example, "Don't leave; I'll lower the standard for you."

All pastors and teachers struggle here: should we weaken the standard to try to hold more people in the church?

Resolute in the face of these defections, He turned to the Twelve and asked them if they wanted to leave too. Peter's response is the sixth of the six reactions to Jesus in this discourse. It was at this point Peter made His first recorded confession of faith in John's record. It is all the more heartwarming when considered in the context of all the rejection Jesus faced: "Lord, to what person could we go? Your words give eternal life. Besides, we believe and know that you are the Holy One of God" (John 6:68–69 GW).

The Lord was surely pleased that His disciples had not been persuaded by all of the grumbling and bickering, refusing to accept Him as the Son of God. They had matured enough in the Good News to choose to stick with Jesus. In addition, Peter's statement demonstrated he had obviously stepped to the forefront as a leader among the twelve.

The Apostle John here shows the Lord balancing Peter's affirmation of faith with his own description of Judas as "a devil." Jesus knew Judas would betray Him (vs. 68–69). Yes, two themes were continuing to play out in the ministry of Jesus. He was making progress developing faith in the hearts of His disciples. He was also well aware the price ahead for Him was betrayal and crucifixion.

This brings to a close Chapter Six and the story of twenty-four dynamic hours with Jesus.

Filled with the Spirit beyond measure, Jesus, the Bread of Life, fed the 5,000 and walked on water for at least three miles, doing it in the dark of night in a deadly storm. Jesus superiority over the food chain and the turbulent elements showed He had the right to teach the people about His identity and mission. In doing so, Jesus revealed again He is "the one and only" who offers living bread, and has no equal or close rival.

Wow! so much happened in such a short time.

Skeptic Turns to Jesus

Lew Wallace (1827–1905), an agnostic lawyer, was governor of New Mexico over a century ago. Encouraged by his agnostic lawyer friend, the famous Robert Ingersoll (1833–1899), Wallace started out to write a book against Jesus Christ.

Instead, in the process of writing the book, Lew Wallace converted to Christianity. He told a friend how it happened:

"I went to Indianapolis, my home, and told my wife what I intended. She was a member of the Methodist Church and naturally did not like my plan. But I decided to do it and began to collect material in libraries here and in the old world...

"I had written nearly four chapters when it became clear to me Jesus Christ was just as real a personality as Socrates, Plato, or Caesar. The conviction became a certainty. I knew Jesus Christ had lived because of the facts connected with the period in which He lived.

I was in an uncomfortable position. I had begun to write a book to prove Jesus Christ had never lived…Now I was face to face with the fact He was just as historic a personage as Julius Caesar, Mark Antony, Virgil, Dante, and a host of other men who had lived in olden days. I asked myself candidly, "If He was a real person (and there was no doubt), was He not then also the Son of God and the Savior of the world?"

That question forced Lew Wallace to turn his life around.

"I fell on my knees to pray for the first time in my life, and I asked God to reveal himself to me, forgive my sins, and help me to become a follower of Christ. Towards morning the light broke into my soul. I went into my bedroom, woke my wife, and told her I had received Jesus Christ as my Lord and Savior.

"O Lew," she said, "I have prayed…you would find Him while you wrote it!"

Lew Wallace did write a very famous book. It was a masterpiece (published in 1880), but not the book he started out to write.

Now every time I watch the epic film made from Wallace's book (1959), I picture Charlton Heston racing those four magnificent white horses in that amazing chariot race. I also wonder how many who have seen *Ben Hur*, with its moving references to Jesus, know it was written by a man who wanted to disprove Jesus ever existed. Instead, he became convinced Jesus was the greatest man who ever lived![9]

In Chapter 7 we view another exciting dimension of Jesus' ministry: His mastery over time, expressed in His control of His hours and minutes as He kept walking the lonely road to Calvary.

John Chapter 7

JESUS
THE MASTER OF TIME

The Apostle John in this chapter brings to a conclusion a season of Jesus' ministry in Galilee. He does so with the story of Jesus' brothers goading Him as a show-off. This exchange between siblings brings to light how Jesus controlled the timeline of His life, down to the hours and minutes. The death threats alone required Jesus to make certain His sacrifice did not come prematurely, before He could fulfill all righteousness. Jesus did go back to Jerusalem on His own time line, this time for the Feast of Tabernacles. At this Feast Jesus gave one of His most important prophecies in His fifth discourse. He foretold the Holy Spirit would indwell all of His thirsty followers. Jesus' ministry in the second half of this one-week feast (John 7:10–10:21) marvelously demonstrates the miracle power of God, and so much more revelation of gospel truth about the Son of God. What a week!

JESUS: THE ULTIMATE TIME MANAGER

7:1 After this, Jesus went around in Galilee, purposely staying away from Judea because the Jews there were waiting to take his life.

Jesus lived with death threats throughout His incarnation. It started with King Herod when Baby Jesus was in the cradle (Matthew 2:13). Jesus' challenge in His maturity was to carry on His ministry amid the death threats, and successfully finish everything His Father assigned to Him, doing it exactly on the timeline. The Apostle John in this study demonstrates Jesus' control over the time necessary for Him to fulfill His mission.

THINK ABOUT IT: The overriding purpose of the incarnation was for Israel's Messiah, Jesus Christ, to die on a cross for the sins of the world as "our Passover lamb" (1 Corinthians 5:7).

Jewish "self-righteousness" viewed this kind of vision as the height of foolishness. The Apostle Paul wrote that Jesus' death and resurrection, however, revealed the power of God and the wisdom of God (1 Corinthians 1:21–25).

An important theme of this chapter, therefore, is Jesus' ability to stay in control of the timeline of His life. This motivated Him "purposely [to stay] away from Judea" for a season. The issue was not fear for His life, but controlling the time when He would climb Golgotha.

Jesus was in charge of His time at His Jordan baptism: "Let it be so *now*," Jesus said to John the Baptist when John protested His unworthiness to baptize Jesus. "Now" in this verse is a word of timing. Jesus knew at Jordan River His exact moment to begin His ministry had arrived. And Jesus added, "It is proper for us to do this to fulfill all righteousness." Then John consented (Matthew 3:15).

Jesus is the Creator of time as expressed by the word *chronos*: time as of extended duration, time as the big picture. It portrays the magnificent design of divine purposes—chronological time. Jesus is "the beginning and the end," who is "with [us] always, to the very end of the age." (Matthew 28:20; Revelation 21:6; 22:13). Since God is the author of time, He is also greater than the time He created. He will one day merge time into eternity so that "there should be time *[chronos]* no longer" (Revelation 10:6 KJV).

Kairos refers to minutes, hours, and days of time, the events and episodes so critical in a person's life. *Chronos* time is ultimately made up of these tens of thousands of units of *kairos* time. How important to slow down, and smell the roses of life.

Will Rogers on Managing Time

"Half our life is spent trying to find something to do with the time we have rushed through life trying to save."[1]

Jesus held to a grand universal vision to save the world. Achieving this goal required Him to be a masterful strategic thinker who could control the minutes, hours and days making up the timeline of His life. The Lord continued to do this until His death on the cross as the Passover Lamb, who died for the sins of the world. If His critics could have controlled the clock, they would have thwarted His mission in life, and would surely have killed Him prematurely. This meant He would not have fulfilled "all righteousness." Jesus was determined not to let that happen: "no weapon forged against" Him prevailed (Isaiah 54:17).

The Grand Stroke in Time Control

Jesus demonstrated the ultimate achievement in time management when He was nailed to the cross at the same time when the Passover lamb was slain in the temple (Matthew 3:15; 1 Corinthians 5:7). Controlling time was evidenced in many other aspects of the Lord's life as well. To name two: His resurrection came on the third day, fulfilling the prophecy of Jonah (Matthew 12:40). A second was His forty days of ministry before His ascension made room for ten days of intercession to follow in the Upper Room. This brought the disciples exactly to the Day of Pentecost (fifty days after Passover—Leviticus 23:15–16). The

Holy Spirit was given exactly on this timeline, and the church was born.

7:2 But when the Jewish Feast of Tabernacles was near...

This statement too is also about timing. The Feast of Tabernacles came in September-October and the Passover was a March-April feast, about six months later. [For a discussion of the significance of the Feast of Tabernacles, please refer to *Jesus Son of God*, (Chapter 1, John 1:14).] This verse about the upcoming Feast of Tabernacles in Jerusalem, therefore, frames the time of Jesus' stay in Galilee, about to come to an end.

Then, as the Feast came closer:

7:3 Jesus' brothers said to him, "You ought to leave here and go to Judea, so that your disciples may see the miracles you do. 4 No one who wants to become a public figure acts in secret. Since you are doing these things, show yourself to the world." 5 For even his own brothers did not believe in him.

Managing Kairos Time Amid Sibling Conflict

Two gospel writers, Matthew and Luke, describe Jesus as Mary's "firstborn" (Matthew 1:25 and Luke 2:7). *Firstborn*, by definition implies more than one. In Jesus' case, these siblings were His half-brothers, with Joseph as their father, but not Jesus' Father. The Biblical record states:

1. Jesus' brothers accompanied Jesus and His mother to the wedding in Cana of Galilee, and to Capernaum after the marriage at Cana (John 2:12).

2. During the Lord's ministry, Mary and Jesus' brothers sought an audience with Jesus (Matthew 12:46–50; Mark 3:31–35; Luke 8:19–21).

3. Matthew recorded the names of Jesus' four brothers, and stated He also had sisters.

> "Coming to his hometown, he began teaching the people in their synagogue, and they were amazed. 'Where did this man get this wisdom and these miraculous powers?' they asked. 'Isn't this the carpenter's son? Isn't his mother's name Mary, and aren't his brothers James, Joseph, Simon and Judas? Aren't all his sisters with us? Where then did this man get all these things?' And they took offense at him" (Matthew 13:54–57).

4. Jesus' "brothers" later converted and united with the disciples in "prayer and supplication" in the Upper Room prior to Pentecost (Acts 1:13–14).

5. Paul states "the Lord's brothers" married (1 Corinthians 9:5).

6. James, the Lord's brother, led the church in Jerusalem (Acts 15:13; 21:18; Galatians 1:19; 2:9, 12).

7. The author of the epistle of Jude identifies himself as the "brother of James," who was one of these brothers (Jude 1; see also Galatians 1:18–19).

8. The Jewish historian, Josephus, in his *Antiquities of the Jews*, recorded the Sanhedrin ordered James to be stoned to death. (This happened about AD 62.)[2]

John is emphatic Jesus' brothers at this early point did not believe in Jesus' ministry or mission. They used the upcoming Feast of Tabernacles in Jerusalem as their opportunity, therefore, to goad Him. They may have thought they were merely having a little fun, without appreciating they were following Satan's prodding. Jesus' brothers did indeed poke fun, saying to Him:

"Go where more people can see your miracles! You can't be famous when you hide like this! If you're so great, prove it to the world!" (John 7:3–4 LB).

It must have been heart-rending for His half-brothers to talk to Him in this way. At the same time it is well established Satan does use siblings to attack relatives, and their negative attitudes can feel devastating. In this instance their scoffing was Satanic to the core, the same kind of onslaught Jesus faced in the wilderness when the devil tried to tempt Him to act independently of His Father's guidance (Matthew 4:5–7). In this attack by Jesus' brothers, the devil wanted to get Jesus off His Father's timeline and motivate Him to do something that would break faith with His Father and His Father's plan. Jesus perceived His siblings' efforts for what they were—they "didn't believe in him" (John 7:3–5 TLB).

THINK ABOUT IT: Some of the hardest attacks of the devil can come from inside your own family, from people you love dearly.

God's children must indeed be sober and vigilant against Satan's schemes even in the relative safety of their own homes (1 Peter 5:8). Jesus' brothers had hearts like Joseph's brothers some seventeen hundred years earlier. They listened to Joseph's dreams, no doubt never thinking the day would come when they would bend their knee in petition before their own brother—but they did (Genesis 37:5).

After Jesus' resurrection, the Lord's brothers did come to place their trust in Jesus. We too have opportunity, like Jesus' brothers in the Upper Room, to cry out boldly to our Brother, seeking His aid (Acts 1:13–14; Hebrews 4:16; 13:6). This is true because each believer in Jesus Christ is adopted into the family of God, making Jesus our "elder brother" too! (Romans 8:15–17; 1 John 3:1–3).

7:6 Therefore Jesus told them, "The right time [*kairos*] for me has not yet come; for you any time [*kairos*] is right. 7 The world cannot hate you, but it hates me because I testify that what it does is evil. 8 You go to the Feast. I am not yet going up to this Feast, because for me the right time [*kairos*] has not yet come." 9 Having said this, he stayed in Galilee.

This story shows the unbelief in the hearts of Jesus' brothers. It also illustrates the Lord's marvelous ability to continue to manage His hours and minutes in the midst of His brothers' scoffing. In addition, it makes plain the hatred of the Jewish leadership toward Jesus. Jesus knew He needed to manage His time carefully. He also knew deep disdain awaited Him when He went back to Jerusalem.

Near to the Timeline, but Missing the Mark

Jesus' response to His brothers shows how watchfully Jesus did in fact manage His hour-to-hour and even minute-to-minute circumstances (*kairos* time).

Jesus' brothers were actually close to the Father's timetable for His Son. But a moon rocket with a trajectory only a fraction of a degree off course will miss the moon by thousands of miles. These brothers were off the timeline by only hours and minutes, at most a day or two, but not weeks. John faithfully shows here how important hours and minutes were to Jesus. He was determined to stay precisely on target.

THINK ABOUT IT: Minutes and hours must be important to all God's children. The choices of little minutes combine to define one's life. It is imperative, therefore, to redeem the time (Ephesians 5:16; Colossians 5:5).

The story about Jesus' relationship with His brothers further demonstrates the world system has its own timeline (*kairos*), and it is very different from the plan Jesus followed. With Jesus' unbelieving brothers, their goal was to get to Jerusalem for the start of the Feast of Tabernacles. They wanted to participate in the ritual celebrated over, and over again by their fathers for some fifteen hundred years. Jesus had a timeline for going to the celebration too, and told His brothers He was "not yet going up to the Feast." The statement meant He was indeed going to Jerusalem, but on a narrowly different, "not yet" timeline.

> Jesus came back at them. "Don't crowd me. This isn't my time. It's your time—it's always your time; you have nothing to lose. The world has nothing against you, but it's up in arms against me. It's against me because I expose the evil behind its pretensions. You go ahead, go up to the Feast. Don't wait for me. I'm not ready. It's not the right time for me" (John 7:6–8 MSG).

JESUS' MINISTRY AT THE FEAST OF TABERNACLES
–John 7:10–10:21

Hours and Minutes Critical to Jesus

7:10 However, after his brothers had left for the Feast, he went also, not publicly, but in secret.

Jesus kept time by His Father's clock. It meant God's Son would go to the Feast, not with His brothers, but incognito. Doing so would enable Him to arrive at Jerusalem at the midpoint of the Feast, on His Father's timeline. He would also escape listening to the negative conversations and attitudes of His unbelieving brothers. Further, staying on His timeline would help him guard against the death threats of His own people.

7:11 Now at the Feast the Jews were watching for him and asking, "Where is that man?"
12 Among the crowds there was widespread whispering about him. Some said, "He is a good man." Others replied, "No, he deceives the people." 13 But no one would say anything publicly about him for fear of the Jews.

The people described Jesus as "that man," and "a good man," and as a deceiver, but not as...

> ...God's only begotten Son,
>   ...The Bread of Life, and
>   ...The only path to God.

Theirs was Nicodemus' kind of thinking (John 3), repeated here by the common people in the streets of Jerusalem. This account shows the iron grip the religious leadership held in the land. The people talked in whispers, and would say nothing publicly "for fear of the Jews." Yes, religion can enslave, and religious slavery arguably is worse than political slavery. So the majority of these Jews concluded Jesus was a deceiver who "was selling snake oil" (7:12 MSG).

So many people today, like these Jews from long ago, are willing to recognize Jesus as "that man," and even as "a good man." C. S. Lewis hit the nail on the head when he wrote in *Mere Christianity*, we can make only three decisions about Jesus. "Either Jesus was, and is, the Son of God, or else a madman, or something worse."

THINK ABOUT IT: Three choices: a liar, a lunatic, or Lord. What is your choice?

We now turn our attention to the fifth of Jesus' seven discourses recorded in John's gospel.

Jesus' Teaching in His Kairos Moment

7:14 Not until halfway through the Feast did Jesus go up to the temple courts and begin to teach. 15 The Jews were amazed and asked, "How did this man get such learning without having studied?"
16 Jesus answered, "My teaching is not my own. It comes from him who sent me."

Jesus was there in Jerusalem for ministry at the Feast for only the second half of the week, but so much happened in those few days. Jesus' ministry during Tabernacles is remembered for many reasons, but one of the most outstanding is how Jesus revealed Himself and His heavenly Father. This means students of the gospel can thrill to the Christology that unfolds. Our understanding of Jesus Christ as the Son of God is immeasurably enriched by the Lord's teaching at Tabernacles.

THINK ABOUT IT: It is safe to say that no mere man, when choosing from the greatest geniuses of history, has been able even to conceptualize the teaching that poured out of Jesus at Tabernacles. And if such a genius could think the thoughts, he certainly would not be able to back them up with God-sized miracles as did the Nazarene. Neither would he be willing to die on a cross, knowing he was innocent.

Jesus, the *logos from God*, spoke the language of heaven translated into Aramaic as he opened up to mankind the fragrant roses of revelation after revelation.

No founder of any world religion known to man wrote or taught about Himself what Jesus expressed about God.

Hence, the instruction from Jesus, the Master Teacher, adds weighted evidence to the Apostle John's conclusion that Jesus of Nazareth truly is the Son of God. Jesus deserves to be believed for His teaching alone, even if He had not done the miracles (see Luke 11:20; John 14:10–11).

What a story follows! What a Messiah is about to be revealed! Yes, when Jesus comes on the scene, amazing things always start happening.

Jesus Was No Bore

The dogma we find so dull—this terrifying drama of which God is the victim and hero—if this is dull, then what, in Heaven's name, is worthy to be called exciting? The people who hanged Christ on a cross never, to do them justice, accused Him of being a bore. On the contrary, they thought Him too dynamic to be safe. It has been left for later generations to muffle up that shattering personality and surround Him with an atmosphere of tedium.

We have very efficiently pared the claws of the Lion of Judah, certified Him "meek and mild," and recommended Him as a fitting household pet for pale curates and pious old ladies. Those who knew Him, however...objected to Him as a dangerous firebrand.[3]

The people were amazed at the quality of His teaching. Many of them were aware He had never attended the elite educational institutions of the land; "our schools," is how they expressed it (7:15 TLB). This meant in their minds Jesus was not qualified to teach shoulder to shoulder with the best in the land. In the days leading up to His crucifixion, Jesus would demonstrate He had no equal among the doctors and scribes; He and He alone, par excellence, was Israel's Master Teacher (Matthew 22:46).

The issue to Jesus was not the titles and degrees He could have earned in the Jewish schools studying the Law of Moses. Instead, Jesus knew He came from the universe's fountain of all knowledge and wisdom (Ephesians 4:13; Colossians 2:3; 2 Peter 1:2; 3:18). "I'm not teaching you my own thoughts," Jesus told them, "but those of God who sent me" (vs. 16 TLB). Jesus flatly rejected the idea He was presenting a personal doctrine unique only to Him.

The Hallelujah Psalms in the book of Psalms (111–117) prophetically exalt the Messiah for His unfailing wisdom and righteousness. For example, "How can men be wise? The only way to begin is by reverence for [Jehovah]. For growth in wisdom comes from obeying his laws. Praise his name forever" (Psalm 111:10 TLB).

Jesus: Learning from His Father

In Jesus' humanity, the Master Teacher learned from His Father, Himself the Master Teacher. "My teaching...comes from him who sent me," Jesus said (John 7:16). This is classic *kenosis* thinking (describing how Jesus as the Son of Man in His incarnation emptied Himself of His divine attributes and was taught and received direction from His Father and the Holy Spirit). The prophet Isaiah gave a glimpse into how this worked. He foretold the Messiah, the Servant of the Father, would "open his ears like one listening; like one being taught" (Isaiah 50:4–5). The heavenly Father and His Son were in communication throughout His ministry. Jesus described this relationship in His great discourse following His healing the lame man at the Pool of Bethesda (John 5:19–20).

Believing, as a Choice

7:17 If anyone chooses to do God's will, he will find out whether my teaching comes from God or whether I speak

on my own. 18 He who speaks on his own does so to gain honor for himself, but he who works for the honor of the one who sent him is a man of truth; there is nothing false about him. 19 Has not Moses given you the law? Yet not one of you keeps the law. Why are you trying to kill me?"

THINK ABOUT IT: The first step in building a relationship with God is making a choice to believe the One God has sent (John 6:17, 29). We *choose*, then we *find out*. First comes faith, then the facts follow. When this choice is made, life becomes a great journey of discovry of the "infallible proofs" Jesus offers for the integrity of His claims (Acts 1:3).

Jesus also shows in this passage His great capacity to discern motives. When a person speaks on his own authority, Jesus said he is self-seeking, wanting "honor for himself." A primary way to judge the truthfulness of motives, then, is to discern if the person is truly working "for the honor of the one who sent him." If he is, his trustworthiness skyrockets, because a sent person will be much more likely to "stick to the facts" and not "tamper with reality" (vs. 18 MSG). As for Jesus, He came bringing a message to mankind from His Father and delivered it faithfully: "there [was] nothing false about Him."

None of the Lord's hearers in Jerusalem doubted Moses gave them the Law. But Jesus knew not a single one of the people listening to Him was honoring Moses' testimony by keeping the Law faithfully. In fact, they were all guilty of violating the Law. What could be a worse violation of the Law of Moses than their desire to kill the Messianic Messenger Moses wrote about in the Law? Jesus had brought them the good news from God the Father showing how they could have peace with God and everlasting life (Deuteronomy 18:15).

Jesus' Superb Understanding of the Law

7:20 "You are demon-possessed," the crowd answered. "Who is trying to kill you?"
21 Jesus said to them, "I did one miracle, and you are all astonished. 22 Yet, because Moses gave you circumcision (though actually it did not come from Moses, but from the patriarchs), you circumcise a child on the Sabbath. 23 Now if a child can be circumcised on the Sabbath so that the Law of Moses may not be broken, why are you angry with me for healing the whole man on the Sabbath? 24 Stop judging by mere appearances, and make a right judgment."

Jesus suffered verbal abuse almost every day of His ministry, or so it seems. One of the worst accusations leveled against him, must have been to tell the Son of God to His face He was demon possessed. Could rejection and loathing get any worse than this? [We must answer it could, and did.] Some of these same citizens of Jerusalem might have been among the crowd who shouted to Pilate, when Jesus was on trial for His life, "We have no king but Caesar" (John 19:15).

The people seemed to believe it was their leaders who were after Jesus, but not them. This explains the innocent sounding question, "Who is trying to kill you?" After all, *they* had no plans to kill Jesus, so they claimed their hands were clean. They did not admit they were actually an extension of their rulers. What their elders wanted, the majority of the people wanted. It is also true what the people wanted, their rulers wanted.

Jesus knew His miracle of healing the man at the Pool of Bethesda on the Sabbath, during His prior visit to Jerusalem, had been a tough pill for the lawyers and religious leaders to swallow (see *Jesus Son of God*, Book 1, John 5:1–18). Jesus was actually eroding their interpretation of the Law of Moses right before their eyes. As the Messiah and Son of God He had the authority to correct their interpretations of the law, even if it made them angry enough to want to kill Him. They reasoned correctly if Jesus could help people like this, and do it willingly and freely, it would not be long before their power would begin to weaken.

Conflicts like this established Jesus' divine authority as Messiah come from God. It also set His teaching apart, showing that the gospel would be characterized by love for God and love for one's neighbor. The Lord's message here is clear: it is always lawful to do good on the Sabbath.

As for them, they knew they could not attack Jesus for the obviously wonderful miracle, but they could and did charge the Lord with working on the Sabbath. After all, keeping the Sabbath holy was one of the Ten Commandments. In their minds they had all the justification they needed, as their sense of being threatened began to boil over into a murderous anger.

THINK ABOUT IT: In the minds of these leaders, enforcing the Law of Moses was a much higher moral value than giving the lame man the use of his limbs and a renewed mind.

In fact, these religious leaders did not care about this man who could not walk; he was expendable. But to Jesus, the man was of eternal worth and anything but a throw-away. For years his life had been bound up in the statement, "I have no man to help me get in the pool when the water is troubled." But Jesus helped him and in the seconds of this creative miracle, this man's attitude radically changed for the better. In doing so, Jesus established He was Lord over the Sabbath (Matthew 12:8–13; Luke 6:5).

What actually happened was Jesus healed "the whole man"— body, soul, mind and spirit (Mark 12:30). In the moment of the miracle, he actually had the energy in his muscles and the vigor in his mindset to go get a job and earn his livelihood.

What a miracle!

Jesus saw through their life-threatening anger and demonstrated in His response total recall of the Law. It is quite possible none of them had ever thought circumcision would be a defense for doing miracles on the Sabbath—but Jesus knew it was. He proceeded first to balance their understanding of the Law of Moses, showing circumcision started with Abraham, not Moses. Then Jesus made His application.

Jesus' hearers understood well the Law specified a child had to be circumcised on the eighth day (Exodus 22:30; Leviticus 12:3). This meant from time to time the eighth day invariably came on a Sabbath. The priests did the work of circumcision on the Sabbath in such cases, and considered it totally permissible (Exodus 31:15). Since it was not sinful to circumcise a baby on the eighth day, even if it was on the Sabbath, was it not also proper for Jesus to show mercy on the Sabbath? The conclusion follows: what was to hinder Jesus giving the man on the Sabbath his health as well as his livelihood, and a new attitude to go with it?

Inherent in Jesus' reasoning was a powerful indictment of the religious establishment: they were actually lawbreakers for refusing to show mercy on the Sabbath. In fact, according to the spirit of Moses' Law, any day is the right time to show mercy (Matthew 12:12; Luke 6:9; 14:5).

> The Lord descended in the form of a pillar of cloud and stood there with him, and passed in front of him and announced the meaning of his name. "I am Jehovah, the merciful and gracious God," he said, "slow to anger and rich in steadfast love and truth. I, Jehovah, show this steadfast love to many thousands by forgiving their sins (Exodus 34:6–7 TLB).

THINK ABOUT IT: Do you ever violate the heart of God by making the decision *not* to show mercy?

These elders obviously did not comprehend the point of the golden Mercy Seat that formed the lid atop the Ark of the Covenant in both Moses' tabernacle and Solomon's temple. But Jesus knew what it meant. In fact, He in His own person is the essence of the Mercy Seat (Exodus 25:17–22). Each of the character traits of God in its own way endears God to us. But mercy is truly one of the most special qualities showing who God is. All sons of Adam need the heavenly Father's mercy. As the Mercy Seat covered the Ark of the Covenant and sheltered the Israelites from the wrath of God, so the blood of Jesus is our Mercy Seat, the covering for our sins (Romans 3:24–25; 1 John 2:1; 4:10; Hebrews 9:5). Jesus showed just how unlimited the mercy of God really is when He went to the cross so that no one has to perish; instead all can come to repentance (John 3:16).

God said to Moses:

> The Guardian Angels [*on either end of the Mercy Seat*] shall be facing each other, looking down upon the place of mercy, and shall have wings spread out above the gold lid. 21 Install the lid upon the Ark, and place within the Ark the tablets of stone I shall give you. 22 And I will meet with you there and talk with you from above the place of mercy between the Guardian Angels" (Exodus 25:20–22 TLB).

The mercy of these elders, however, was far removed from the mercy in God's heart. They reasoned Jesus could have waited until the next day to help the man; after all, it would not hurt him to suffer one more day.

How callous!

In fact, Jesus' unwillingness to delay in their minds resulted in such egregious work it justified the rulers wanting to kill Him (Exodus 31:15; Numbers 15:32–36). But why make the man wait another day to receive a "whole man" miracle? After all, they did not wait an extra day to circumcise the babies in the land.

With them, the law did not permit work on the Sabbath day, and doing miracles, by their definition, was forbidden work. By their standard, Jesus' healing the man on the Sabbath also resulted in the man doing work—picking up his mat and carrying it. To them, any thinking person could see those were the facts!

Jesus saw through their reasoning, however. What about this fact: mercy trumped the fourth commandment of the law that prohibited work on the Sabbath. A follower of Moses' law certainly could get his child, his ox or his sheep out of a well on the Sabbath (Matthew 12:11; Luke 14:5–6; Deuteronomy 22:1–4). And another fact: a priest could do the work of circumcision of a baby on the eighth day even if it fell on the Sabbath. Why, then, could Jesus not show mercy and heal a man on the Sabbath? Was not this son of Abraham of greater value than a sheep, or equal in value to an infant? (Matthew 12:12). Little wonder Jesus said, "Stop judging by mere appearances, and make a right judgment" (vs. 24).

The Folly of False Assumptions

A traveler, between flights at an airport, went to a lounge and bought a small package of cookies. Then she sat down and began reading a newspaper. Gradually, she became aware of a rustling noise. From behind her paper, she was flabbergasted to see a neatly dressed man helping himself to her cookies. Not wanting to make a scene, she leaned over and took a cookie herself.

A minute or two passed, and then came more rustling. He was helping himself to another cookie! By this time, they had come to the end of the package, but she was so angry she didn't dare allow herself to say anything. Then, as if to add insult to injury, the man broke the remaining cookie in two, pushed half across to her, and ate the other half and left. Still fuming some time later when her flight was announced, the woman opened her handbag to get her ticket.

To her shock and embarrassment, there she found her pack of unopened cookies. How wrong our assumptions can be![4]

False assumptions, in fact, almost resulted in a civil war with nine tribes of Israel against the three tribes of Rueben, Gad, and the half tribe of Manasseh (see Joshua 22). The nine tribes assumed the altar the three tribes built meant they were in idolatrous rebellion against the Law of Moses—but they were not.

Jesus: From Both Bethlehem and Nazareth

7:25 At that point some of the people of Jerusalem began to ask, "Isn't this the man they are trying to kill?"

In this verse the people affirmed their awareness all along of the death threats, showing their protestations of innocence in verse 20 were false. Jesus' response in verse 21 had been totally appropriate.

7:26 Here he is, speaking publicly, and they are not saying a word to him. Have the authorities really concluded that he is the Christ? But we know where this man is from; when the Christ comes, no one will know where he is from."

The people obviously had enough knowledge of Jesus to understand He grew up in Nazareth. But their next statement showed just how skewed their understanding really was: "The

Messiah is going to come out of nowhere. Nobody is going to know where he comes from" (John 7:27 MSG).

What teacher had taught them this? Micah the prophet was clear: the Messiah would come out of Bethlehem (Micah 6:2; Matthew 2:6). The English poet Alexander Pope (1688–1744) was so right: "A little learning is a dangerous thing."

Jesus' Cry of Rejection

7:28 Then Jesus, still teaching in the temple courts, cried out, "Yes, you know me, and you know where I am from. I am not here on my own, but he who sent me is true. You do not know him, 29 but I know him because I am from him and he sent me."

Jesus felt their brutal rejection and "cried out" while teaching at the Feast in the courtyard of the temple. The term is *krazo*. The verb actually communicates a loud yell or even a scream. Jesus' voice no doubt dripped with passion in this exclamation as He loudly entreated His own people to receive what He was teaching.

The statement, "…you know me and you know where I am from," insightfully probes the condition of the human heart in its rebellion against God. Jesus is asserting His own people could not make the case they did not know Him. They even had good reason to accept He came from His Father. All the signs were there (John 3:2; 7:28). They also knew, with His saying and doing all these good things, He had not come among them on His own. The conclusion is obvious: their rejection was willful and deliberate, a decision made in the face of the overwhelming evidence (see Psalm 81).

Jesus could have defended Himself easily by explaining to them He was born in Bethlehem, thus fulfilling Micah's prophecy. But the Lord's bottom line was to bring them to recognize He came from His heavenly Father. Jesus knew if they would not accept His heavenly Father, they would not accept Him as their Messiah even if He absolutely proved to them He was born in Bethlehem (see Matthew 2:1, 5; Luke 16:19–31). To acknowledge Jesus as having come from the heavenly Father would require them to accept His Deity, and this they were not willing to do. A good man? "Yes," but absolutely not God's "only begotten Son" (John 3:16).

The Blessing of Divine Protection

7:30 At this they tried to seize him, but no one laid a hand on him, because his time had not yet come.

Here, the Greek word translated as "time" is not *kairos*, but *hora*, meaning *"hour,"* and the Authorized Version translates it as such: "They sought to take him: but no man laid hands on him, because his hour was not yet come." When John wrote about Jesus managing His *kairos* time, the apostle was pointing to one special and divinely appointed "hour"—His hour of crucifixion at the time of the Passover sacrifice.

This situation offers further insight, therefore, into how Jesus controlled the details in His timeline. Apparently, John and the other apostles saw no good reason to explain why they did not seize Jesus on the spot. All of the circumstances were there to make it a prime moment—all, except one: "his hour was not yet come."

This compels the conclusion: Jesus' Father and the Holy Spirit placed an umbrella of protection over the Lord. Elisha the prophet enjoyed this same kind of security when the king of Aram sent an army to Dothan to capture God's prophet (2 Kings 6:8–22). As for Jesus, the Jewish leaders wanted to arrest Him, but they could not. Moreover, if the eyes of the people in Jerusalem at the Feast of Tabernacles had been opened as was

Elisha's servant, they surely would have seen the protective shield around Jesus.

Jesus, the Miracle Worker

7:31 Still, many in the crowd put their faith in him. They said, "When the Christ comes, will he do more miraculous signs than this man?"

This really is an exciting admission. In the midst of all of the unbelief and rejection, people were turning their hearts to Jesus as their Messiah. The word is *many*, certainly not the majority, but not a handful either. The Lord's miracles were attracting them.

THINK ABOUT IT: Is the Lord's church today suffering from a famine of the gift of miracles action?

In the purposes of God, the long drought of no miracles for 400 years from Malachi to Christ made the miracles of Jesus stand out all the more. The Lord fulfilled Isaiah's prophecy foretelling Messiah's appearance:

"Be strong, do not fear; your God will come...,
  he will come to save you."
Then will the eyes of the blind be opened
  and the ears of the deaf unstopped.
Then will the lame leap like a deer,
  and the mute tongue shout for joy" (Isaiah 35:4–6).

Jesus' many miracles were cornerstone proofs He was God's Son, although only a few of them are recorded in the four Gospels (John 21:25). In fact, their own teachers had said a hallmark of the Messiah's appearance would be His miracles. So the people asked, "Will the Messiah, when he comes, provide better or more convincing evidence than this?" (John 7:31 MSG).

The Temple Guards Come for Jesus

7:32 The Pharisees heard the crowd whispering such things about him. Then the chief priests and the Pharisees sent temple guards to arrest him.

While ruled by Rome, the Jewish people wrested from their conquerors the right to practice their own religion. This was true even though Romans viewed Jewish monotheism as atheism, because they did not embrace Rome's gods. The Jews could not field an army, but they were permitted to have a contingent of guards to protect the temple and enforce the religious system on the people. When the Pharisees heard the "whisperings" of the crowd, it was more than they could handle. So the chief priests and the Pharisees set in motion a plan to arrest Jesus, sending the temple guards to do the job. Meanwhile, Jesus continued to teach.

7:33 Jesus said, "I am with you for only a short time, and then I go to the one who sent me. 34 You will look for me, but you will not find me; and where I am, you cannot come."

Jesus knew His ministry was approaching its end, and His time (*kairos*) was short. In just a few months, He would go back in triumph to the right hand of His Father who sent Him. But these words went sailing over their heads, and were like a riddle to them.

7:35 The Jews said to one another, "Where does this man intend to go that we cannot find him? Will he go where our people live scattered among the Greeks and teach the Greeks? 36 What did he mean when he said, 'You will

look for me, but you will not find me,' and 'Where I am, you cannot come'?"

In the hindsight of Golgotha, we can understand well what Jesus was talking about. No, He did not intend to go to the Greeks to become their teacher; although, after His resurrection this did happen in the ministry of the Lord's apostles. In fact, the first great Gentile city-wide revival was in Antioch in Syria. It was a spontaneous revival; the disciples at Jerusalem were not part of its beginning. The revival mushroomed primarily among the Greeks who lived there (see Acts 11).

Jesus' Prophecy of Pentecost

7:37 On the last and greatest day of the Feast, Jesus stood and said in a loud voice, "If anyone is thirsty, let him come to me and drink. 38 Whoever believes in me, as the Scripture has said, streams of living water will flow from within him." 39 By this he meant the Spirit, whom those who believed in him were later to receive. Up to that time the Spirit had not been given, since Jesus had not yet been glorified.

The word translated here as "Jesus stood and *cried,*" is the same *krazo* as in verse 28. It shows the burning passion the Lord felt about His mission. He yelled it out, as if to entreat with bold exclamation. In doing so He predicted a new era in *chronos* time (chronology). The age of the Spirit would be the new era of God's dealings with man. The Apostle John did not want anyone to miss its meaning. Hence, he interpreted the prophecy as the gift of the Holy Spirit that would be poured on thirsty people everywhere (see Isaiah 44:3).

When the Lord yelled it out at the feast, He was identifying a spiritual need in the life of each of His followers. Jesus intended to meet the need with "the Spirit poured upon [them] from on high" (Isaiah 32:15).

The prophet Joel had prophesied the day was coming when the Spirit would be poured out on "all flesh" (Joel 2:28–29). John the Baptist foresaw it too, and said the Messiah would baptize with the Holy Spirit and with fire" (Luke 3:16; John 1:33; Matthew 3:11). Jesus the prophet joined rank with these prophets and announced the exciting news at this Feast of Tabernacles that He intended to fulfill their prophecies.

What a privilege it would be to have Jesus physically present, living with each of His followers at all times. But this was not possible for the incarnate Messiah to do. What Jesus could not do in flesh and blood, He fulfilled by giving the Holy Spirit to indwell each thirsty believer.

Hungering for God

"Creatures are not born with desires unless satisfaction for those desires exists," said C. S. Lewis. "A baby feels hunger: well, there is such a thing as food. A duckling wants to swim: well, there is such a thing as water.

"If I find in myself a desire which no experience in this world can satisfy, the most probable explanation is that I was made for another world. If none of my earthly pleasures satisfy it, that does not prove the universe is a fraud. Probably, earthly pleasures were never meant to satisfy it, but only to arouse it, to suggest the real thing."[5]

When the Lord expressed this great truth about the Holy Spirit at the Jerusalem Feast of Tabernacles, it was only a prophecy. Jesus' atoning sacrifice on the cross followed by His glorification at His Father's right hand would be required to swing wide this open door in the heart of God.

Without question, bundled into this loud yell is one of the greatest predictions Jesus-*the*-Prophet made. It foretold a new era in which the temple switched from a structure of stone, ornate with gold and silver, to the fleshly tablet of the heart. The prophecy forecast a fresh-from-heaven paradigm change. It would move the Most Holy Place from the temple to the inner being of Spirit-filled believers. This was a huge strategic move made by the master of strategic thinkers, and it changed the whole focus of how God is to be worshipped. God is looking for people who will worship Him "in spirit and in truth;" this, in fact, is what worship is all about in the New Covenant (John 4:23).

To this day, Jesus' piercing cry pleads to be heard by all: "If any man thirsts…" This was the grand cry of Moses when he taught youthful Joshua an important life-lesson in the wilderness: "Would God that all of the Lord's people were prophets and that he would put His Spirit upon them" (Numbers 11:29). Surely Joshua never forgot how Moses longed for every person in the twelve tribes to receive the Spirit.

THINK ABOUT IT: Have you received the baptism with the Holy Spirit?

If not, are you thirsty, really thirsty?

John the Baptist made a bold, prophetic declaration about the gift of the Holy Spirit at Jordan River, saying, "[Jesus] will baptize you with the Holy Spirit" (Matthew 3:11; Mark 1:8; Luke 3:16 KJV). John specifically foretold Jesus would be the baptizer.

In *Book One* the author said a possible reason Jesus never baptized anyone in water (John 4:2) is because had He done so, people surely would have concluded water baptism held saving properties; e.g, baptismal regeneration.

In Jesus' great prophecy at the Feast of Tabernacles, an additional possibility emerges. John the Baptist's assignment was to baptize in water (and it is ours too). Jesus' mandate from His Father, however, was to baptize with the Holy Spirit (John

1:33–34; Matthew 28:16–20). John the Baptist could not give a person *the water*, the Holy Spirit baptism Jesus gives, neither can any other spiritual leader in the Lord's church.

> "If anyone is thirsty, let him come to me and drink. 38 For the Scriptures declare that rivers of living water shall flow from the inmost being of anyone who believes in me." 39 (He was speaking of the Holy Spirit, who would be given to everyone believing in him; but the Spirit had not yet been given, because Jesus had not yet returned to his glory in heaven (John 7:37 LB.)

This water from heaven, which is the Holy Spirit and the third Person of the Trinity, has an inward and outward flow. The Spirit streams first from God into the temple-of-the-heart of a thirsty person. The outward flow follows. The Lord said, "rivers of living water shall flow from the inmost being of anyone who believes in me" (John 7:38 LL). The great goal of these surging rivers is to make Jesus known worldwide (John 14:25).

THINK ABOUT IT: "If *any man* thirsts" embraces all people of every generation anywhere in the world, including the far flung islands of the seas (Acts 2:39; see Isaiah 41:1–4; 42:12; 49:1–6).

Jesus' prophecy given at the Feast of Tabernacles came true on the Day of Pentecost. It was a May/June festival, also known as the Feast of Weeks. Fifty days after the Lord's crucifixion, 120 believers were assembled in the Upper Room [*pentekostas* is the Greek term for the numeral 50]. It happened in a spectacular manifestation from heaven that sounded like a rushing, mighty wind. Cloven tongues "as of fire" sat on each of the 120 as the presence of the Spirit saturated the whole house (see Acts 2). They were all filled with the Holy Spirit and spoke with tongues.

The gift of the Holy Spirit completed the temple switch in the New Covenant. It also brought to fulfillment Joel's prophecy, promising in the last days God would pour out His Spirit on all flesh (Joel 2:28–29; Isaiah 59:21; Acts 2:16–21).

THINK ABOUT IT: Oh! To have the Lord's loud yell leap off the pages of Holy Writ and grip us. Sense the powerful anointing present that historic day in the courtyard. Then perceive in your own life the authority of this profound prophecy fulfilled at Pentecost that birthed the era of the Church in salvation history.

Moses' wish found its fulfillment after a fifteen hundred year wait, when the Holy Spirit indwelt the believers in the Upper Room (Numbers 11:29). This also meant the Most Holy Place in the temple had been replaced by the fleshly temple of the heart, and a new form and era of worship had begun (John 4:23–24). This divine act made it possible for the gospel to go around the world (Jeremiah 31:31–33; Joel 2:28–29; Acts 2:17; see *Jesus Son of God, Book One John 2:17–25* for further discussion of this great paradigm change).

The blessing of the Holy Spirit continues to be available to the Lord's thirsty followers. Jesus is as passionate about it now as when He yelled out the prophecy at the high point of the Feast of Tabernacles. To commemorate this world-changing Pentecostal outpouring, the name of the Feast of Weeks came to be identified in the church as the Feast of Pentecost. Pentecost Sunday is its name on the church calendar today. The paradigm change Jesus foretold that day birthed the church in the story of salvation history.

Jesus' promise also produced the Pentecostal outpouring at Azusa Street in Los Angeles at the start of the twentieth century. This revival has now spread around the world. The baptism with the Holy Spirit is this unstoppable flow of the "fountain" that continues to "pour out of the Lord's house" (Joel 3:18).

Jesus' Ministry Model

Jesus' method for doing ministry is described by the Apostle Peter: "God anointed Jesus of Nazareth with the Holy Spirit and power. He went about doing good, healing all who were oppressed of the devil, for God was with Him" (Acts 10:38). The Spirit does His work as the third Person of the Triune Godhead.

Jesus came in an incarnation as the God-man, and accepted the limitations of time and space. The Holy Spirit came as God-the-Spirit and knows no boundaries of time and space.

Blessing of blessings: the first priority in the job description of the Spirit is to make Jesus known.

All of Jesus' followers can be filled with this same Holy Spirit the Father poured into Jesus, in His case without measure. The promise also includes our sons and daughters (Acts 2:17).

The gospel makes the specific claim that God the Holy Spirit is working in the earth (e.g., Acts 2; 19:1–7; see John 5:27). This Spirit actually indwells Jesus' "thirsty" followers. They become warm, walking, talking temples who take the essence of the Most Holy Place to the nations in obedience to the Lord's Great Commission (Matthew 28:16–20; Acts 1:8).

Yes, the Feast of Tabernacles and the Feast of Weeks (or Pentecost) will be forever closely linked in the era of the Lord's church.

THINK ABOUT IT: Religious pluralists, in formulating their saying that all roads lead to God, make a huge error by not taking seriously the active ministry of the Holy Spirit in the earth. The Spirit is one of a kind too, and does not fit into a modern pantheon of gods. It simply cannot be done. This alone makes the conclusion obvious: Jesus Christ is in a league all by Himself that no other world religion can touch (Isaiah 45:5, 18, 21–24). The Lord who baptizes with the Holy Spirit is, in fact, "the one and only Son of God."

A New Form of Worship

This Spirit, also known by the Hebrew term, *shekinah*, took His abode first in the Most Holy Place of the Tabernacle in the Wilderness, dwelling between the cherubim on the mercy seat. Later the Spirit moved to the same location in Solomon's Temple. At the dedication of the Temple, this *shekinah*, or presence, actually took on a visible manifestation as the cloud that filled the temple (Exodus 40:34–38; 1 Kings 8:10). Hence, *shekinah* speaks to the manifestation of the majesty of the divine presence that moves in and settles down. This majestic revelation of God was a foretaste of the day when the Spirit would indwell people.

At Pentecost the Spirit moved into the hearts of the 120 in the Upper Room when cloven tongues like fire sat on them (Acts 2:1–4). This act of God completed the Temple Switch (Numbers 11:29; Isaiah 59:20–21; Jeremiah 31:33; Acts 11:15–16, 24).

Roman soldiers demolished the temple stone by stone in 70 AD, but the "temple" had already relocated; hence, the tide of the Spirit continued its uninterrupted penetration of the Roman Empire. This flow of the Spirit even found deep spiritual thirst in the hearts of the pagans in the Empire's hinterlands.

THINK ABOUT IT: Christians understand "God is spirit" (John 4:24). The Spirit of God in the Temple had a manifest Presence that could actually be felt. Worshipers perceived the Presence of the *Shekinah*. This manifest

Presence actually occurred at the dedication of Solomon's Temple, for example.

In the New Covenant, the *Shekinah*, the Presence, can manifest in worship services too, even as He dwells in the hearts of God's children. Jesus expressed it, "He dwelleth with you and shall be in you" (John 14:17).

As this new worship form developed, the practices of the Old Covenant soon vanished. Most notably, no longer was worship built around priests sacrificing animals, and the smell of blood and burning flesh disappeared. In the new order, worship was centralized in the heart of each worshiper.

Preaching the gospel became a principle form for teaching the masses the great values of the faith. Singing the scriptures gave opportunity for every worshiper to participate and made it easy for people to memorize gospel truths. Apostles, prophets, evangelists, pastors and teachers became the leaders of the new order.

The new Gentile believers began meeting on the first day of the week, commemorating the Lord's resurrection on the first day of the week. Places of worship quickly came to be identified by the Greek term, *ekklesia*, meaning people called out from the world and called to fellowship with Jesus Christ. The English translation for *ekklesia* is church.

These assemblies sprang up mostly in people's homes, beginning in Asia and spreading to Europe and North Africa. People also met to worship in caves and even in fields and forests, cemeteries, hired houses, and lecture halls (Acts 19:19; 28:30). People living in the metropolitan centers of the Roman Empire, and on the back side of the empire, as well as the most distant ocean islands could assemble in "churches" and worship in the Spirit as maturing disciples. Their worship practices included:

- Avidly studying the Scriptures.

- Intently receiving the preaching of the Word that is Jesus Christ.

- Communicating personally in prayer with their risen Lord.

- Singing with deep conviction the songs of Zion, and especially the psalms that foretold Messiah's coming (Isaiah 35:9–10; Ephesians 3:21) and

- Living out their faith by personally sharing Jesus' message in their cities, towns, and hamlets everywhere.

As they did so, they had an intense personal awareness Jesus was indeed with them, made real by the presence of the Holy Spirit among them. Because the Lord was present, the people could worship in spirit and in truth, offering to the heavenly Father the kind of worship He plainly said He seeks (John 4:23).

Ultimately, this living water that quenches a person's thirst for God will also result in the resurrection of the dead and life eternal with Jesus.

As for the unbelievers who rejected the gospel, the message was also clear: "There is no peace, says my God, for the wicked" (Isaiah 48:22; 57:21). Indeed, "it is appointed unto man once to die, but after this the judgment. So Christ was offered..." (Hebrews 9:27–28; 1 Thessalonians 1:10).

THINK ABOUT IT: The ultimate wickedness is to reject Jesus Christ as God's Son and our Savior, who baptizes with the Holy Spirit (Luke 3:16; John 6:29; 14:16, 26; 15:26; 16:7; Isaiah 57:21).

How important for all of the Lord's followers to learn just how valuable their minutes and hours really are, and

---

stay on the gospel timeline. This road will ultimately take them to the New Jerusalem, "world without end. Amen." (Isaiah 45:17; Ephesians 3:21).

Both Faith and Schism Because of Jesus

7:40 On hearing his words, some of the people said, "Surely this man is the Prophet."
41 Others said, "He is the Christ." Still others asked, "How can the Christ come from Galilee? 42 Does not the Scripture say that the Christ will come from David's family and from Bethlehem, the town where David lived?" 43 Thus the people were divided because of Jesus. 44 Some wanted to seize him, but no one laid a hand on him.

Several responses to Jesus are identified here. Apparently, some of the people believed Jesus fulfilled Moses' prophecy of the coming Messiah-Prophet (Deuteronomy 18:15). Others went so far as to make the grand confession, affirming Jesus was indeed the Messiah (the Anointed One). Still others wanted to believe Jesus, but were hung up with the Nazareth question. They knew the prophecy that Jesus would come out of Bethlehem as the seed of David, but they did not comprehend He could be born in Bethlehem and grow up in Nazareth. The result was division among the people "because of Jesus" (vs. 43). One other group "went so far as wanting to arrest him, but no one laid a hand on him" (John 7:44 MSG). In the sense that Jesus has always motivated people to make decisions and choose sides, the Messiah is indeed the great divider (Luke 12:49–53).

The Temple Guards Report Back

7:45 Finally the temple guards went back to the chief priests and Pharisees, who asked them, "Why didn't you bring him in?"
46 "No one ever spoke the way this man does," the guards declared.
47 "You mean he has deceived you also?" the Pharisees retorted. 48 "Have any of the rulers or of the Pharisees believed in him? 49 No! But this mob that knows nothing of the law—there is a curse on them."

The testimony of the temple guards is as refreshing as the demand of the Pharisees is callous: "Why didn't you bring him in?" To which the guards answered, "He says such wonderful things! We've never heard anything like it" (TLB). Their honesty was met by a cold come-back accusing them of having been tricked and led astray.

Inspired by His Presence

President Theodore Roosevelt was a charismatic figure who made quite an impression on people. One journalist, William Allen White, wrote of his first meeting with Roosevelt in 1897:

"He sounded in my heart the first trumpet call of the new time that was to be...I had never known such a man as he, and never shall again. He overcame me. And in the hour or two we spent that day at lunch, he poured into my heart such vision, such ideals, such hopes, such a new attitude toward life and patriotism and the meaning of things, as I had never dreamed men had...After that, I was his man."

If a mere mortal can have such an effect on another, how much more our Lord?

If we will spend time with him in prayer and in the Scriptures, we too will find our hearts filled with vision, with hopes, with a new attitude toward life and the meaning of things, and afterwards we too will say with thankfulness, "I am his."[6]

It understates reality to say the whole first century Jewish religious system, and especially the Pharisees, are remembered in history as feeling arrogantly superior. They could not believe the common people, whom they disdained as an ignorant and cursed mob, could recognize truth ahead of them. Sadly, the Law of Moses as they interpreted it was much more valuable to them than were the sons of Abraham. Arrogance does not get much worse than describing their fellow Israelites as a "cursed mob," who knew nothing about the law. (This disregard for the common man, showing no ability to feel their needs, will be illustrated further in Chapters 8 and 9.)

In their haughty pride, they could not entertain the thought of teachers being "judged more strictly" (James 3:1), or teachers "in their greed" exploiting their students "with stories they have made up" (2 Peter 2:3). Teachers can even frame their own righteousness (Romans 10:3). These religious leaders deeply resented the willingness of the common people to hear Jesus gladly (Mark 12:37). They certainly did not see the people as "harassed and helpless like sheep without a shepherd"—but Jesus did (Matthew 9:36). To them, the people were ignorant and stupid, but they proudly thought of themselves as the fountain of all truth and knowledge.

Faith and the Nazareth Question

7:50 Nicodemus, who had gone to Jesus earlier and who was one of their own number, asked, 51 "Does our law condemn anyone without first hearing him to find out what he is doing?"
52 They replied, "Are you from Galilee, too? Look into it, and you will find that a prophet does not come out of Galilee."
53 Then each went to his own home.

John pointedly recorded Nicodemus "was one of their own number" (John 7:50). He had recognized Jesus as a teacher come from God. But he was not at all willing to accept Jesus as Israel's Messiah and the Son of God, and become part of Jesus' number (John 3:2). Nicodemus made a feeble effort to intervene, but to no avail.

THINK ABOUT IT: Abraham, their natural father, *believed* before he *knew* (Genesis 15:6).

The religious leaders' made a sharp retort to Nicodemus: "a prophet does not come out of Galilee." It raises the question, did they know the Old Testament as well as they thought they did? If they had enjoyed better knowledge, Isaiah's messianic prophecy might have changed their minds about "Galilee of the Gentiles."

"Leaving Nazareth, [Jesus] went and lived in Capernaum, which was by the lake in the area of Zebulun and Naphtali—14 to fulfill what was said through the prophet Isaiah: 15 'Land of Zebulun and land of Naphtali, the way to the sea, along the Jordan, Galilee of the Gentiles— the people living in darkness have seen a great light; on those living in the land of the shadow of death a light has dawned'" (Matthew 4:12–16; Isaiah 9:1–2).

One is left to wonder if anyone in the religious leadership ever thought about asking Jesus for His actual birthplace. Surely He would have told them. They also could have checked His birth story themselves to see if it squared with the Old Testament prophecies (Micah 7:52; John 7:52). Had they done so with honest research, they could have learned the facts of His birth.

Some conclusions are now appropriate:

1. As the ultimate time manager, Jesus masterfully controlled the minutes and hours of His ministry (*kairos* time), based on His Father's clock. It meant He could not go to Jerusalem in the company of His own brothers, who made the journey on the clock of the world system. At this point in Jesus' ministry, His brothers shared neither His mission nor its timeline.

2. Jesus announced He came from God with the full backing of His Father, and His many miracles validated Him. The religious leaders rejected this outright as being blatantly false and unthinkable.

3. Jesus intended to establish a kingdom based on His sovereign reign, as King David's greater son, on the throne of radically changed hearts (Luke 1:32). Jesus' realm would be an international dominion of the heart. In the eyes of Jesus' detractors, this meant He was soft and weak, and no match for Rome.

4. Jesus did not consult and develop a contract with the Sanhedrin, go through their schools, and let them certify and define His ministry. Instead, He claimed God His Father was His validation. This too was simply anathema to them.

5. Jesus was not willing to fight Rome with the sword. Instead He showed *agape* love to Greeks and Romans alike, with no inclination at all to boot the foreigners out of Israel. Jesus' objective was to cure the rebellion against God in the hearts of all people. In that way He would save Jews and Greeks, Romans and pagans. But to the religious leaders, Jesus was downright naïve before the power of Rome's military machine.

6. Jesus came out of Nazareth, not Bethlehem (or so they thought). They knew well Messiah had to be born in Bethlehem to fulfill Micah's prophecy (Micah 5:2; Matthew 2:6). They must have thought if Jesus had been born in Bethlehem, He surely would have announced it publicly and bragged about it. His very silence in the face of their accusations about His birthplace might well have proved to them His cradle was not Bethlehem. Yet, so many times in life, the most obvious conclusion is not the correct conclusion. In contrast, Matthew and Luke searched out Jesus' true origin and easily established where He was born. Matthew wrote it emphatically: "Jesus was born in Bethlehem in Judea, during the time of King Herod" (Matthew 2:1; see also Micah 5:2; Luke 2:4–7).

7. Jesus did not view the common man in Israel as a cursed "mob that knows nothing of the law" (John 7:48). Instead, when ordinary people were around Jesus, He made them feel like they had the worth of kings—and they did! Little wonder the common people heard Him gladly (Mark 12:37).

8. In this chapter, Jesus gives one of His most famous prophecies—the baptism with the Holy Spirit available to anyone who is thirsty. The unfolding of the prophecy at Pentecost, completing the temple switch, opened up a whole new paradigm of heart-centered worship, in spirit

and in truth (John 4:23–24). This development was essential in paving the way for the gospel as good news to go around the world—and it has.

It can be better comprehended now the Pharisees had crafted their own righteousness based on false and incomplete evidence. Hence, they wanted no part in the good news Jesus represented. Instead, they were blindly committed to indict Jesus for blasphemy and eliminate Him. The Apostle Paul expressed it:

> "Since they did not know the righteousness of God and sought to establish their own, they did not submit to God's righteousness. Christ is the end of [the era of] the law so that there may be righteousness for everyone who believes" (Romans 10:3–4; see Ezekiel 28:1–24, showing this same spirit destroyed ancient Tyre, and is utterly Satanic; also 2 Corinthians 5:21).

Yes, this chapter demonstrates Jesus was the Master in control of His own timeline. He was in step with His divine clock on the road to the cross and determined to build this new form of worship. The Hill of the Skull was not far over the horizon.

THINK ABOUT IT: Jesus' holy journey down the sandy roads of Israel to His destiny at Calvary, teaches us, too, the great value of our minutes and hours.

The series of thousands of *kairos* choices over a lifetime, if made as a bond to Jesus Christ, will yield peace with God in this life and eternal life in the ages to come. One day, oh! The blessed day, when time as *kairos* or *chronos*, will be no more.

The Apostle John will continue in Chapter 8 to tell the story of Jesus' very short but highly productive stay in Jerusalem for the Feast of Tabernacles.

John Chapter 8

JESUS

DEFENDER OF THE WEAK

This chapter, a continuation of Jesus' ministry at the Feast of Tabernacles, tells the story of a woman on trial for her life for committing adultery. Then, in the afterglow of the Lord's verdict that is now world famous, Jesus presented Himself as the Light of the world (the second of His powerful "I AM" statements). This chapter also includes a new way to look at the faith of Abraham. Without this paradigm change, the international momentum of the gospel would have been severely hampered. Yes, all of this happened and so much more in the short time of only half a week while Jesus was in Jerusalem for the Feast of Tabernacles.

THE MOUNT OF OLIVES

8:1 But Jesus went to the Mount of Olives. 2 At dawn he appeared again in the temple courts where all the people gathered around him, and he sat down to teach them.

To reach the Mount of Olives from the temple, Jesus had to walk through the Eastern Gate, outside the city walls, down into the Kidron Valley, and then begin His ascent of the Mount of Olives. The hill peaks at 2,900 feet and actually rises higher than Mount Zion. The Mount of Olives gives visitors even today a panoramic view of the Old City of Jerusalem. In the time of the Lord, Olivet was famous for its olive trees—and still is.

The Mount of Olives is first mentioned in the Old Testament when King David, barefoot and weeping, fled the city during the insurrection led by his son Absalom (ca 1000 B.C., 2 Samuel 15:30). Part of the Mt. of Olives was the site referred to as "the hill east of Jerusalem" Solomon gave to his foreign wives to worship their pagan gods (1 Kings 11:7–8). This royal grant led over time to the unspeakably hideous practice of child sacrifices in Israelite worship. This evil hastened the death of the nation. Good King Josiah, in the years immediately preceding the Babylonian invasion of 606 B.C., destroyed the idols associated with child sacrifice and desecrated the pagan shrines with bones of the dead (see 2 Kings 23). But it was too little too late. The nation was headed for 70 years of captivity (Jeremiah 25:91–92; 29:10).

The Mount of Olives is most remembered in salvation history because of the ministry of David's greater Son. Jesus Christ gave Olivet its enduring fame that continues to this day (Matthew 26:30; Luke 22:39).

The story in Chapter 8 begins with Jesus rising before dawn. The Lord retraced His steps, this time making the walk westward, down Olivet, back into the Kidron Valley, and then up to the city wall, again passing through the Eastern Gate and on to the temple. Pilgrims in the city for the Feast of Tabernacles were already gathering in the outer courts when dawn broke. "Swarms of people came to [Jesus]. He sat down and taught them" (John 8:1–2 MSG). John does not record what Jesus said early that morning, but he certainly documented what happened there.

THE WOMAN CAUGHT IN ADULTERY

8:3 The teachers of the law and the Pharisees brought in a woman caught in adultery. They made her stand before the group 4 and said to Jesus, "Teacher, this woman was caught in the act of adultery. 5 In the Law Moses

commanded us to stone such women. Now what do you say?" 6 They were using this question as a trap, in order to have a basis for accusing him.

Jesus Values Society's Rejects

The conduct of these religious leaders was despicably cruel and heartless. They showed here the same attitude they had expressed a day or two earlier: "this mob that knows nothing of the law—there is a curse on them" (John 7:48). The poor woman fitted perfectly into their category of a person of no value who deserved the evil treatment they gave her.

THINK ABOUT IT: The people the Pharisees were powerless to help, they wrote off as accursed and impossible to help!

Arrogance can be very self-justifying.

These hypocrites compounded their sin by bringing only the woman caught in the act of adultery. Why did they not bring the man too? Moses' law was clear: "If a man commits adultery with another man's wife—with the wife of his neighbor—both the adulterer and the adulteress must be put to death" (Leviticus 20:10). These leaders were self-righteous lawbreakers in the way they dragged this vulnerable woman in and presented the case. They were also guilty of framing a massive deception—using the woman to try to trap Jesus with their interpretation of the law.

The goal of these Pharisees was to ambush Jesus before the gathered crowd, and then publicly discredit Him. If Jesus defended the woman in her sin, they would accuse Him of breaking a law given by Moses requiring a death penalty. If Jesus came down on the side of the letter of the law and advocated stoning her to death, they would accuse Him of being uncaring and unmerciful. It was a well sprung setup. If it had worked, the Law would be defended, Jesus would be exposed as an imposter and a fraud, and their smug, self-righteous hold on the people would be further cemented.

The usual assumption is these Pharisees had every intention to start throwing the rocks at this woman's head. John did write, however, they were primarily after Jesus and not her. This could have meant they did not intend to execute her.

The first of these two possibilities certainly squares with the pattern of these Pharisees; they were indeed capable of capital punishment in defense of their interpretation of the Law of Moses. As for the second, if they would have ultimately shown her mercy, the woman obviously did not know it. Everything about their mannerisms said they were ready to start hurling the stones. The woman certainly believed the threat on her life was a horrifying reality.

They "made her stand" publicly before the staring crowd, leaving her no scrap of dignity. It is abundantly obvious they did not care about her feelings or her needs, and had no desire at all to help her find a new life. She was scum to them, but they were *"righteous!"* Self-righteousness knows no boundaries.

Jesus: The Judge in an Outdoor Courtroom

This setting was an ancient, open air, courtroom scene. The prosecutors were these teachers and Pharisees. To a casual observer the defendant was this woman.

The attention of the crowd surrounding Jesus quickly riveted on Him and the woman. Tension rapidly filled the air as the people began to perceive what was happening.

How desperately this woman, who could not save herself, needed an attorney who would defend her. It was also essential for

Jesus to rely on His Father and the Holy Spirit in His response, so the deadly trap would not spring.

Chilean Miners Could Not Escape

In the fall of 2010, billions of people around the globe were captivated by the story of thirty-three Chilean miners trapped beneath two thousand feet of solid rock. The collapse of a main tunnel had sealed their exit and thrust them into survival mode.

These were desperate men. They lived in a black midnight, and ate two spoonfuls of tuna, a sip of milk, and a morsel of peaches every other day. For two months they prayed for someone to save them.

On the surface above, the Chilean rescue team worked around the clock, consulting NASA, and meeting with experts. They designed a thirteen-foot-tall capsule and drilled, first a communication hole, then an excavation tunnel. There was no guarantee of success. No one had ever been trapped underground this long and lived to tell about it.

Now someone has.

The men began to emerge on October 13, 2010, slapping high fives and leading victory chants. A great-grandfather came up. A forty-four-year-old who was planning a wedding. Then a nineteen-year-old.

All had different stories, but all had made the same decision. They trusted someone else to save them.

No one rejected the rescue offer with a declaration of independence saying, "I can get out of here on my own." They had stared at their stone tomb long enough to reach the unanimous opinion: "We must have help. We need someone to penetrate this world of darkness and pull us out."

And when the rescue capsule came down, they climbed in.[1]

These religious leaders were utterly unlike Jesus. He was motivated by the love of God. This *agape* love does what is best for people, whether or not they have earned it, or understand they need it. As for them, they did not have the love of God in their hearts— none at all (John 5:42). If they had, they would have recognized Jesus as the Son of God and perceived God's love could give this woman a new life. No doubt about it; the guilty woman was actually more righteous than her self-righteous accusers.

THINK ABOUT IT: Why, we ask, is it so hard for people to respond to the gospel invitation by willingly stepping into the "saving capsule" that is the cross of Jesus Christ?

Jesus As Her Defense Attorney

The woman quite possibly grew up with an absentee dad, which meant she did not have a positive male role model in her childhood. One is left to wonder if she ever witnessed her own mother being cherished by a husband who loved her mom. Consequently, she matured with no dad in her life to help her positively build her self-esteem as a young woman. She also most probably believed it was normal for women to receive cruel treatment from men.

It is entirely possible she had lived the life of an adulteress searching for a "dad" who would value her and care for her, all the while feeling condemned by the moral emptiness of the lifestyle she had chosen in her futile search. She had probably tried many times to repent and change her life, but never could get it done on her own.

She also no doubt had realized for some time the damage her lifestyle was causing her and others. She surely had thought about escaping the slavery binding her, but could not find the path to achieve it.

If she had not realized her need earlier, she certainly did when these Pharisees dragged her into court, charged her with a capital offense, and held the rocks in their hands.

The crisis nature of her situation was without question an aid to her transformation. She was caught in the act and was on trial for her life. This meant she was desperate for help. If she was ever going to change, this was the moment. She was in a now-or-never situation.

THINK ABOUT IT: The crises in peoples' lives always seem to have built into them special opportunities to make new beginnings.

Our crises can actually be our friends.

When these Pharisees forced her to go with them, it is easy to believe this poor woman yelled out to God, perhaps even screaming in her pain. From the bottom of her soul, with her eyes full of hot and salty tears, she no doubt prayed in those moments for the help of her Messiah she believed would come one day. She was a bruised reed Isaiah had foretold, the very kind of person Isaiah prophetically fitted into Messiah's job description (Isaiah 42:3; 53:5; Matthew 12:20). This daughter of Abraham was without doubt, one of the brokenhearted prisoners for whom Jesus came to open the doors of the jail that had locked her soul in its iron grip (Isaiah 61:1–4; Luke 4:17–19).

What she did not know was she was being dragged to her Messiah! These Pharisees did not understand it either.

When they made her stand in the temple courtyard, the very advocate whose help she wanted most was there in front of her in flesh and blood. The Son of God was willing to help her, and took her case without a fee (Proverbs 28:11; Isaiah 3:13–15).

THINK ABOUT IT: Jesus was standing right in the middle of her life-threatening crisis, but she had not yet recognized Him.

Have you ever detected Jesus standing in the center of a crisis of yours?

Jesus! Ah Jesus! As the sun was rising over the City of David, the light that is Jesus was about to illuminate the shadowy jail at the core of her being—lights up ours too!

Sin the Curse; Christ the Cure

The woman caught in the act of adultery had the same problem at the core of her soul as did her accusers. She (and they) were living in rebellion against God, rooted in the broken relationship with God that is true with all sons of Adam. This condition is identified by the term, the sin curse. She expressed that rebellion with choices that violated the character of God, which is at the heart of all sinning. Adultery is so grossly sinful because it first and foremost disregards and flouts the fidelity in the character of God. Interestingly, the opposite, or the antonym for the character trait of fidelity is infidelity, which is also a synonym for adultery.

The great love of God is revealed in Jesus' death on the cross, dying in our place to provide our cure. He died the death we should have died, "the righteous for the unrighteous" (1 Peter 3:9). This understanding is expressed in Jesus' nighttime meeting with Nicodemus: "God so loved the world that he gave his one and only Son, that whoever believes in him shall not perish but have eternal life" (John 3:16).

The path back to peace with God is always the same, and it is implicit in John 3:16.

Admit your condition, accepting responsibility for your rebellion against God. Admit your relationship with God is so shattered you cannot fix it, so make the choice to repent with deeply felt sorrow for how you have hurt the heart of God (Genesis 6:5–6). [To repent means to turn around the "car" that is your life, go back, and get on the right road, and Jesus is the road.]

Believe Jesus died on the cross to heal the breach by forgiving you and giving you a spiritual "heart transplant;" a new heart with a new inner core that can love and obey God.

Confess your brokenness to God, ask for His pardon, and accept in good faith and with heartfelt gratitude that He has forgiven you.

THINK ABOUT IT: Jesus always responds to repentance with forgiveness. Always.

The road back to fellowship with God never changes, but the time line required routinely varies. With this woman it was quick, actually a matter of short moments. She knew she needed help and realized her very life was in the hands of the man they called Jesus.

With the thief on the cross it was only a sentence: "Jesus, remember me when you come into your kingdom" (Luke 23:42).

With the publican, it was a matter of a sincerely spoken sentence as well, expressed with real meaning and conviction, "God be merciful to me a sinner" (Luke 18:13–14 KJV). Interestingly, the publican stood afar off saying it, and kept beating on his breast while he spoke. Jesus responded that it was the sincere publican with the very short prayer and the very broken heart, and not the proud Pharisee who found peace with God. The woman caught in the act was the "publican" in Jesus's courtroom, and she went home justified that day—with a new heart and a new dignity.

8:6 But Jesus bent down and started to write on the ground with his finger.

If we only knew what Jesus wrote! Obviously, what He penned was significant. Everything Jesus did had importance; but the Holy Spirit did not inspire John to record these words in the sand.

Jesus' demeanor, in the minds of these religious leaders, gave the impression He was trying to ignore them. They thought it meant they had Him cornered, so "they kept on questioning him." The volume of their badgering probably increased as the seconds ticked off.

THINK ABOUT IT: When the Lord stood up, this woman who had no one to speak for her now had her Messiah as her defense attorney and judge (Psalm 68:5; Isaiah 18:20; 29:21). To Jesus, she certainly was not scum from the "cursed mob."

You, dear reader, are not scum either!

The delays of Jesus always have a purpose. In this case, the time Jesus used up writing in the sand permitted the tension to increase in the crowd, probably to fever pitch, as they waited to see what would happen next.

Jesus' View of Prostitutes

In his book, *What Good Is God?*, Philip Yancey writes about being invited to speak at a conference on ministry to women in prostitution. After some discussion with his wife, Yancey agreed to accept the invitation as long as he could have the opportunity to question the women and hear their stories.

"Did you know Jesus referred to your profession?" he asked the women. "Let me read you what He said: 'I tell you the truth, the tax collectors and the prostitutes are entering the kingdom of God ahead of you.'"

He was speaking to the religious authorities of His day. What do you think Jesus meant? Why did He single out prostitutes?"

After several minutes of silence a young woman from Eastern Europe spoke up in her broken English.

"Everyone, she has someone to look down on. Not us. We are at the low. Our families, they feel shame for us. No mother nowhere looks at her little girl and says, 'Honey, when you grow up I want you be good prostitute.' Most places, we are breaking the law. Believe me, we know how people feel about us. People call us names: whore, slut, hooker, harlot. We feel it too. We are the bottom. And sometimes when you are at the low, you cry for help. So when Jesus comes, we respond. Maybe Jesus meant that."[2]

Would Jesus be able to help this adulterous woman so desperately in need of help?

"Is anything too hard for the Lord?" (Genesis 18:13–14; Matthew 17:20; Mark 10:27; Luke 1:37).

Jesus Presents Her Defense

8:7 When they kept on questioning him, he straightened up and said to them, "If any one of you is without sin, let him be the first to throw a stone at her." 8 Again he stooped down and wrote on the ground.

Jesus defended her on a universal legal principle in the courtroom of God: every person is a guilty sinner in rebellion against God and without excuse (John 15:22; Romans 1:20; 2:1). In addition, every person knows he is, and is fully aware he needs mercy. This verdict nailed her accusers—these teachers and Pharisees. The Apostle Paul later summarized it: "All have sinned and come short of the glory of God," and "there is none righteous, no not one" (Romans 3:10, 23). That certainly included these self-righteous Pharisees.

It is important to consider the atmosphere in which the Lord expressed His verdict. The Holy Spirit came on Jesus beyond measure when He was baptized in Jordan River. The *shekinah* for centuries had dwelt in the Most Holy Place. Personified in Jesus Christ, the Presence at that moment was in the courtyard of the temple serving as the Advocate and Judge of a helpless and utterly humiliated woman. When Jesus stood up and spoke, His demeanor reflected His confidence; He was completely in charge of His open air courtroom with full authority to pass sentence.

Oh Yes, Jesus Cares!

Frank Graeff (1860–1919) was a Methodist pastor of Dutch descent who served some leading churches in the area of Philadelphia, Pennsylvania. Graeff was known as the "sunshine minister" because of his optimistic spirit. He also knew from personal experience deep despondency, pain and suffering, and struggled with spiritual doubt. In 1901, he wrote what is arguably his most famous poem that became a beloved hymn, "Does Jesus Care?" (1 Peter 5:7).

Does Jesus care when I've tried and failed
To resist some temptation strong;
When for my deep grief there is no relief,
Though my tears flow all the night long?

Chorus:
Oh yes, He cares, I know He cares,
His heart is touched with my grief;
When the days are weary, the long nights dreary,
I know my Savior cares.

The Spirit: Convicting of Sin

A vital dimension of the work of the Holy Spirit is to convince people of their sins, and the Spirit did it here. A sense of guilt from the Holy Spirit settled like a cloud over these accusers (John 16:18–20). Her brilliant attorney, speaking in the power of the Holy Spirit, boiled her case down to a simple statement: "All right, hurl the stones at her until she dies. But only he who never sinned may throw the first!" (John 8:7 TLB).

It was a verdict straight from the heart of God.

It is possible the woman actually *heard*, "hurl the stones." She was already tense all over, but in those seconds the stress multiplied, thinking the rocks would start bouncing off her head any instant.

What her accusers heard was, "Only he who never sinned may throw the first!" In fact, the Holy Spirit saw to it they heard Jesus correctly.

As for Jesus, He stooped down again and wrote in the sand a second time. One can wonder if this time Jesus scribbled the names of her accusers.

"Mercy and truth met together" as her Judge announced His verdict—not even the first rock took flight (Psalm 85:10). Instead, "grim justice and peace kissed" as Jesus ruled they could start throwing the stones *if they were sinless* (John 8:7 TLB).

Yes, "truth [rose] from the earth" in those highly charged seconds as righteousness "smiled down from heaven" (Psalm 85:10 TLB). This woman was "poor and weak;" yet, her Messiah was actually "thinking about [*her])*." She perceived herself a nobody, but as unworthy as she thought herself to be, *she* was the total focus of Jesus' concentration. He was *her* "helper." He had saved *her*. Yes, she had her Messiah's full attention (Psalm 40:17 TLB).

8:9 At this, those who heard began to go away one at a time, the older ones first, until only Jesus was left, with the woman still standing there.

Conviction, making a person feel his guilt, is in fact at the heart of the work of the Holy Spirit (John 16:8; Psalm 51:3). The Spirit causes people to face their shame and responsibility. These self-righteous prosecutors had to have a sickened, nagging feeling, even if they did think she was scum, as they listened to her screams while they dragged her into court. They knew they were taking advantage of this woman and abusing her (Psalm 82:1–5).

The Holy Spirit definitely compounded the inner sense of guilt in them. "One by one, beginning with the older men, the scribes and Pharisees departed. Jesus was left alone with the woman" (John 8:9–10 GW).

The message of Jesus Christ is a gospel of *agape* love. With no pre-conditions, Jesus will do what is best for you, as only God knows what is best for you. And He will do it, even if you do not realize your need or want His help. Jesus was full of the Holy Spirit beyond measure, and this anointing in His godly life was His magnetic drawing card. Hence, He owned no sword, compelled no one with threats, and never used force. Jesus operated His court exercising and manifesting Messianic authority to which these religious leaders who despised Him actually submitted. One by one the woman's accusers accepted His decision, dropped their rocks, and walked away.

Romans, Greeks and pagans in the Empire were pulled to the Lord by this kind of love that guided His life. Jesus also gave a Great Command to help perpetuate His love in His followers: "Love one another," He said. "As I have loved you, so you must love one another. By this all men will know that you are my disciples, if you love one another" (John 13:34–35).

THINK ABOUT IT: Can anyone dispute how the love of God guided the Judge the day of this open air trial? The Holy Spirit had kept the multitude orderly at the feeding of the five thousand, without pushing and shoving, as they awaited their turn to be served the bread and the fish (John 6:5–13). Jesus had no weapon and no temple guards on this day to enforce His ruling in the temple courtyard, but he was full of the Holy Spirit. The presence of the Holy Spirit in the outdoor courtroom was also the enforcer of Jesus' verdict when the adulterous woman was on trial for her life.

It is worthy of notice John did not record the woman spoke in her own defense, not even to say, "I'm sorry, please forgive me." No, she did not cry out with spoken words, but she certainly did with her expression and appearance, her demeanor.

Can a person come to Jesus in repentance without actually saying a word? We answer it may not be the norm, but this story says it can happen. Jesus knows our hearts, including our motivation (John 2:25; 1 John 3:20; Luke 16:15).

No safer place exists for your life, dear reader, indeed your eternal soul, than in the hands of Jesus.

It is also very obvious and easy to see—look again at her accusers as they walk out of Jesus' open air courtroom. They are still in their broken relationship with God, and feeling very guilty and enormously humiliated (Luke 18:14).

Jesus Balances Grace and Truth

8:10 Jesus straightened up and asked her, "Woman, where are they? Has no one condemned you?"
11 "No one, sir," she said.
"Then neither do I condemn you," Jesus declared. "Go now and leave your life of sin."

Jesus' verdict shows the classic power of the grace of God—the unearned and unmerited favors God does for people. John the Baptist was on target when he prophesied Jesus would be "full of grace and truth." The Lord Jesus has always been able to balance the two perfectly (John 1:14).

Jesus gave them permission to throw stones at her (meeting the demands of truth), but only on the condition each rock thrower was himself sinless (grace). When no one could measure up to this balanced standard, Jesus exercised the judicial authority to give the ruling that liberated the woman and opened the door to her new future: "Go now and leave your life of sin."

Ah! Jesus' goal has never been to destroy a sinner, but to put an end to the sinning. His mission is not to ruin but to redeem. Doing this requires truth to be faced. The woman *was* an adulteress. When she admitted the truth, then repentance could follow.

THINK ABOUT IT: Repentance is the fulcrum that brings grace and truth into balance.

With this adulteress, repentance quickly blossomed into deeply felt contrition as she faced her sin which she thought was about to get her executed. Can anyone doubt in those moments she truly wanted help to change her life and get on the right road? This genuine repentance meant she had changed on the inside, in her inner being. When repentance is genuine true change will occur in a person's soul (Isaiah 55:6–7). This godly sorrow meant she was a candidate for forgiveness, for grace in action, and Jesus gave it to her (Romans 10:9–11; Isaiah 30:19). In this case, the law (truth) was vindicated even as grace redeemed her. Yes, Jesus balances grace and truth! [See *Jesus Son of God God, Book One, John 1:14* for an expanded study on balancing grace and truth.]

Repentance is not based on how long a person prays, or even if the repentance is expressed aloud. Repentance involves changing on the inside, then turning around and getting on the right road. True repentance is judged by "meaning it"—and God knows our hearts. With the thief on the cross it was simple and gut-wrenching, "Jesus, remember me when you come into your kingdom" (Luke 23:42). With the publican, it was "God be merciful to me a sinner" (Luke 8:13).

> The adulteress' repentance was authentic.
> She was contrite.
> She desperately wanted to find a new moral freedom.
> She was certain if God did not help her, she would be stoned to death.

Jesus turned the tables on these vicious men. He showed them up to be imposters and charlatans. They were hireling shepherds of God's flock who clearly did not care for the sheep (Isaiah 56:11).

As for this woman, she left the courtroom a lady, a daughter of Abraham who had finally found the moral freedom she had wanted for so long. Standing in the temple courtyard in front of Jesus, feeling exposed and shamed, something very important changed inside her heart. On the spot she realized for the first time in her life, she had met a man who genuinely cared for her and saw worth in her. Jesus would not condemn her, use her, or abuse her.

She had met her Messiah.

Jesus showed the woman the heart of her heavenly Father. *Elohim* is supremely the "Father of orphans, [and] champion of widows...[He] makes homes for the homeless [and] leads prisoners to freedom..." (Psalm 68:5 MSG). As her prison door opened in those moments, Jesus revealed His own care for her, as the father figure for whom she had searched so long.

This nameless woman, as she walked out of the temple courtyard, also left behind the prison of her sinful choices, the slavery of immorality. Jesus took the Pharisee's evil intentions and transformed them into the greatest blessing of her life. Yes, Jesus gives "beauty for ashes" (Isaiah 61:3).

Jesus did not condemn her to a life of moral brokenness. Nor did He browbeat her, telling her sternly she had better learn to live with her weakness and manage it. And He certainly did not view her as part of the cursed mob knowing nothing about the Law of Moses. Instead, Jesus truly did care for her. He intended to love *her* enough to die on the cross as *her* substitute. In fact, Calvary was right up the road on Jesus' timeline.

This trapped woman could not help herself get out of her jail; she had certainly tried. Jesus' verdict, however, did what she could not do. He used her genuine repentance to balance grace and truth in offering her a new beginning: "Neither do I condemn you. Go and sin no more" (see Romans 10:9–11).

In those few minutes she was liberated from the shame and condemnation with which she had lived for so long. Jesus became the "dad" she never had. No man had ever stood up for her before like Jesus did, and He did it without condemnation. Her Messiah also poured dignity into her life and gave her a new sense of self-worth. In fact, the saving grace of God identified as the new birth, always endows a person with a new sense of worth (Isaiah 43:19).

We should not be surprised her attorney never sent her a bill! (Isaiah 55:1–3 KJV).

The Son of God forgave her without justifying her sins. Jesus gave her a brand-new future of moral purity. She was a changed woman; a new creation (2 Corinthians 5:17; Galatians 6:15). These teachers and Pharisees viewed her as trash; Jesus saw her as a bruised reed who would make beautiful music again. She had been a smoldering wick but Jesus brought her back to full light (Isaiah 42:3).

The grace Jesus showed this woman did more than forgive her. Jesus also adopted her as a daughter when He told her, "…go and sin no more" (see Romans 8:14, 23; 1 John 3:1–3). She would never commit adultery again. Truth was vindicated even as grace triumphed. Her Messiah, who is the essence of the "Spirit of wisdom and understanding, of counsel and power, and the Spirit of knowledge and of the fear of the Lord," changed her from the inside out (see Isaiah 11:1–4).

THINK ABOUT IT: She went into court knowing she had been caught in the act and was without a defense. She walked out of court knowing she had found the grace for a fresh start in life, with new self-respect and the dignity that accompanied it. Jesus accepted her that day just as she was, but He did not leave her as she was. She was transformed into a daughter of God. From those very moments she would be able to grow and mature as a member of God's family. Wow! She felt "accepted in the beloved" (Ephesians 1:6; Isaiah 49:15–16). The great wisdom Jesus displayed in this case also justifies the conclusion He has the ability to serve as the Chief Judge of the universe.

This woman's gratitude had to be monumental (Luke 7:42, 47). When opportunity blossomed for the remainder of her life she surely never tired telling the story, how Jesus came to her rescue. He gave her "hope and a future" when her life was literally on the line (Jeremiah 29:11). As long as she lived in her "crooked and perverse generation," she no doubt shined as a reflection of Jesus' moral purity (Philippians 2:15). When she thought she was going to die, she was instead blessed with a new beginning that included eternal life. She had her day in court, and it ended with the overflowing joy of a new birth (Isaiah 55:12–13).

One can only wish the woman's accusers had brought the man, since he too was caught in the act. Jesus' ability to balance grace and truth could have given him a new birth with a new future too.

Only the Messiah can rise to the level of this kind of judge!

As for these religious leaders, they were walking in sin much deeper than the woman they dragged into court. Far and away, despising and rejecting Jesus was the greater offense. Hence, the Lord's verdict against them was they would die in their sins (John 8:24). Their many choices, like this one, also ultimately cost them their homeland and their temple, as well as their eternal souls.

This story also teaches us to expect the miracle power of God to be demonstrated amid persecution. It further shows the great wisdom Jesus displayed in this case also justifies the conclusion the Lord has the ability to serve as the supreme judge of the universe.

Our Judge: The One Who Loves Us Most Fully

Whenever we speak of the end times, our hearts often quicken—partly out of joy, yet also out of fear. To speak of end times is to speak of somewhat uncertain times. "No one knows about that day or hour," Christ said, "not even the angels in heaven, nor the Son."

But the uncertainty of calendars and dates isn't what troubles us most. It's the sure promise of final judgment. Perhaps these words from author and pastor Frederick Buechner can offer us a bit of comfort—words that both acknowledge the reality of coming judgment and the grace-filled love of the Judge.

The New Testament proclaims that God will ring down the final curtain on history. There will come a Day on which all our days, and all the judgments upon us, and all our judgments upon each other will themselves be judged. The judge will be Christ. In other words, the one who judges us most finally will be the one who loves us most fully.[3]

This story of the woman caught in the act of adultery has established Jesus, for all generations, as the judge who is the friend of the helpless, the abused, the worthless, and the defenseless. The narrative also shows self-righteousness in all its ugliness. Little wonder Isaiah wrote, "…all our righteous acts are like filthy rags" (Isaiah 64:6).

Jesus' teaching at the Feast of Tabernacles follows up on this miracle and frames the fifth of the seven discourses. Now we discover:

Jesus: The Light of the World

8:12 When Jesus spoke again to the people, he said, "I am the light of the world. Whoever follows me will never walk in darkness, but will have the light of life."

Jesus speaks here in the shadow of His cross only a few months up the road. The hour was near for Him voluntarily to ascend the Hill of the Skull as the Lamb of God. Hanging on those crude nails He would offer the ultimate validation of His teaching and His miracles.

But for now, the Apostle John discloses in this dialogue truly profound insights about Jesus.

The court case was over in a few minutes. The morning was still very young. The people of Jerusalem were awakening to the warm sunlight just beginning to climb over the Judean hills. It was an apt setting for the teaching to follow. As for the *Son*light—the Light of the world—it had already reached full noonday warmth. In another bold claim to Deity, in that setting, Jesus claimed to be the "light of life," and "the light of the world."

Jesus: The Standard for Morality

Surely there cannot be a better illustration of what Jesus meant by proclaiming Himself the light of the world than His defense of the adulteress. He transformed her into a morally upright woman and did it in a matter of minutes. Jesus certainly shined the light of God into her life as He has for millions around the globe since then. Jesus Christ, *the* "I AM," is the essence of the gracious light come to transform "whosoever will" (John 3:16; Psalm 119:105).

THINK ABOUT IT: The splendor of Jesus' verdict is another demonstration the Messiah is the light of the world and the Son of God. He certainly set the standard for morality in this case, upholding fidelity as a moral principle in marriage, as well as in all of life's relationships. The Messiah did it by asserting the universal principle that all people are on common ground in their rebellion against God. Everyone needs the Messiah who has the authority to forgive sin and transform the heart, doing it from the inside out.

Religious pluralism says the shifting sands of culture identify right and wrong. Jesus' verdict shows He in His own holy person defines morality. His standards never change. They are true for all cultures and generations, and will even guide the final judgment (Revelation 20:11–15).

"I am the light of the world," affirms the essential core of the Lord's holy being. It is not a description of what He does but of who He is (see Isaiah 60:1, 19–20; Matthew 5:14–16; John 1:9). This light is the moral center of His holy life, and it illuminates the beauty of His pure character (Psalm 104:2; John 3:19; 2 Corinthians 4:6; Ephesians 5:8).

Because Jesus is the world's greatest luminary, His followers live as reflections of His light. The Lord spoke to this in His Sermon on the Mount: "Ye are the light of the world," and fidelity can be described as the electricity that empowers the "glow" (Matthew 5:14 KJV). It is the responsibility of all believers to "Let [their] light…shine" as the "children of light" (Matthew 5:16; John 12:36; Philippians 2:15; Proverbs 4:18).

The Apostle John expressed the application in his first epistle:

> This is the message we have heard from him and declare to you: God is light; in him there is no darkness at all. If we claim to have fellowship with him yet walk in the darkness, we lie and do not live by the truth. But if we walk in the light, as he is in the light, we have fellowship with one another, and the blood of Jesus, his Son, purifies us from all sin (1 John 1:5–7).

Defending Desperate People Results in Opposition

8:13 The Pharisees challenged him, "Here you are, appearing as your own witness; your testimony is not valid."

If Jesus' sworn critics had only absorbed the fair and balanced verdict Jesus had just shown to the adulterous woman, they would have validated Him as Israel's Messiah (Isaiah 42:1; Matthew 12:18). Before their very eyes Jesus had defended and vindicated the Law of Moses (truth) and at the same time mercifully given the woman a fresh start (grace, what grace!). The radiant new light of the gospel flooded into the depths of her soul. Yes, it was a verdict that had "Messiah" written all over it!

Why could these leaders not see the truth and make the choice to say, "*If He can render this kind of fair decision, we want to serve Him as long as we live!*"

THINK ABOUT IT: We can be sure the woman never ceased to be grateful for Jesus' verdict!

How grateful are you, dear reader, for the forgiveness your Lord gave you?

These lawyers realized they had lost a huge case; their trap had sprung on themselves. It left them embarrassed and humiliated. They could not deny the wisdom and power of Jesus' verdict, but they could attack Him. So they struck back and condescendingly challenged Him, "Here you are, appearing as your own witness; you are boasting and lying!" (John 8:13 TLB; see John 5:30–34, where Jesus faced this same charge in Jerusalem.)

Jesus: Offering Proof of His Identity

Wow! Calling the Son of God a liar! But Jesus did not answer in kind. He was already showing the traits of a lamb led to the slaughter (Isaiah 53:7; John 1:29, 36). Instead of slapping back:

8:14 Jesus answered, "Even if I testify on my own behalf, my testimony is valid, for I know where I came from and where I am going. But you have no idea where I come from or where I am going. 15 You judge by human standards; I pass judgment on no one. 16 But if I do

judge, my decisions are right, because I am not alone. I stand with the Father, who sent me. 17 In your own Law it is written that the testimony of two men is valid. 18 I am one who testifies for myself; my other witness is the Father, who sent me."

Jesus admitted He had testified on His own behalf (which was His right to do), but asserted His testimony was "valid" because His Father guided His life. His amazingly wise verdict rendered in the open air trial did not make Him the Son of God; He had been that from eternity. But the verdict surely illustrated His status as God's incarnate Son, and presupposed all of His verdicts would be equally convincing.

Jesus' relationship with His Father enabled Him to confront these Pharisees. Jesus would not compromise and negotiate with them by offering testimony they wanted to hear. He did not look to the Sanhedrin, for example, to validate His ministry. Instead, He offered no lesser affidavit than the word of His Father as His second witness. In Moses' Law a person could call corroborating witnesses. Jesus knew this and claimed Himself as one witness and His Father as the other (Deuteronomy 19:15).

> Jesus told them, "These claims are true even though I make them concerning myself. For I know where I came from and where I am going, but you don't know this about me. You pass judgment on me without knowing the facts. I am not judging you now; but if I were, it would be an absolutely correct judgment in every respect, for I have with me the Father who sent me. Your laws say that if two men agree on something that has happened, their witness is accepted as fact. Well, I am one witness, and my Father who sent me is the other" (John 8:14–18 TLB).

Jesus' courageous defense, that was sure to stir deep anger, has inspired so many thousands through the centuries to make their stand against those who oppose Him as the Son of God. Many of these defenders have done it at the price of their lives.

THINK ABOUT IT: Martin Luther, the father of the Protestant Reformation, lived some fifteen hundred years after Jesus' verdict. Luther refused to recant and reject his writings when on trial for his life. Instead, in the great tradition of his Lord, Luther offered his defense at Worms in Germany (1521 AD): "On this I take my stand. I can do no other. God help me."[4]

Jesus did not budge because He absolutely knew His origin, and it meant His Father was with Him. He also comprehended fully where He was going: He was on a journey to Calvary. Ultimately, the same road would also take Him back to His Father's right hand (Psalm 110:1; Matthew 22:44; Acts 2:33).

Jesus knew the Pharisees had their own system of passing judgment, and it was a very human standard (vs. 15). The sense of Jesus' response was that He would never pass judgment on anyone by their standard. Instead, Jesus followed His Father's principles of judgment. God's standard is based on *agape* love which cares for all people and does what is best for them. It is also accompanied by a divine ability to discern motives accurately. [In the church this capability is identified as a "word of knowledge" (1 Corinthians 12:8).]

Jesus knew He was going back to His Father's side, and understood His critics had no idea what He was talking about (vs. 14). But before He returned to His Father, up ahead in a few short months and just around the bend in the road, a cruel cross awaited the "the Lamb of God who takes away the sin of the world!" (John 1:29, 36; Genesis 22:8).

Jesus' Unique Relationship with His Father

**8:19 Then they asked him, "Where is your father?"
"You do not know me or my Father," Jesus replied. "If
you knew me, you would know my Father also."**

Jesus kept dropping all around them jewels of wisdom about
His relationship with His Father, but they did not pick up a single
one of these pearls "of great price" (Matthew 13:46). Instead, they
sneered at Him, "Where is this so-called Father of yours?" (John
8:19 MSG).

"Where is your father?" is the question, and Jesus answered
it. As a child is identified by his father, they would know clearly
who Jesus is if they acknowledged His Father. Jesus' teaching and
miracles, however, demanded a conclusion that His true Father
was far greater than Joseph, His supposed dad. Feeding some
ten thousand people with five barley loaves and two small fish,
walking on water, and the verdict in the court case of the woman
caught in the act of adultery—just those three miraculous signs
shined such a bright new light in the world it demanded another
conclusion regarding Jesus' true Father.

Jesus responded to their self-righteousness that so callously
rejected Him as their Messiah, by giving another absolutely
correct verdict. "You know my Father as little as you know me. If
you knew me, you would know my Father also" (John 8:19 WNT;
Mark 8:18).

This is the reasoning: if you accept my teaching and my
miracles, you will know they are acts of God, and that will
naturally lead you to discover my Father who backs me up.

Jesus' close relationship with His Father stands out in this
chapter. Jesus lived with an awareness so keen He knew His
Father was right there beside him. Jesus talked about His Father
as though He could reach out and touch Him, and converse
regularly with Him.

Jesus then responded to their depraved self-righteousness that so callously rejected Him as their Messiah, by giving another absolutely correct verdict. "You know my Father as little as you know me. If you knew me, you would know my Father also" (John 8:19 WNT; see also Mark 8:18). To know Jesus meant acknowledging God as His Father, and to know Jesus' Father meant acknowledging Jesus' identity as well. Either required admitting Jesus was God's Son. But this they would never admit (see the discussion at vs. 25–29).

Jesus: Master of His Hours and Minutes

8:20 He spoke these words while teaching in the temple area near the place where the offerings were put. Yet no one seized him, because his time had not yet come.

The Apostle John offered only one explanation for their not arresting Him then and there: "his time wasn't yet up" (John 8:20 MSG). The word rendered as "time" here too is *hora*, best translated as *hour*.

Jesus was speaking in the shadow of His cross only about six months up the road. The hour was near for Him voluntarily to ascend the Hill of the Skull as the Lamb of God. Hanging on those crude nails He would offer the ultimate validation of His teaching and His miracles.

But for now, the Apostle John disclosed in this dialogue some more truly profound insights about Jesus.

THINK ABOUT IT: In the broad sweep of time, including its millions of hours, one hour was appointed from eternity for the sacrifice of Jesus Christ. Jesus was perfectly in charge of this timeline.

Jesus: Looking Beyond the Cross

8:21 Once more Jesus said to them, "I am going away, and you will look for me, and you will die in your sin. Where I go, you cannot come."
22 This made the Jews ask, "Will he kill himself? Is that why he says, 'Where I go, you cannot come'?"

While teaching in the area of the temple treasury, Jesus dropped two prophetic facts, and another verdict:

1. He was about to depart (referring to His ascension), and they would not be able to go where He was going.

2. The day would indeed come when they would earnestly search for their Messiah but would not be able to find Him.

3. The chilling verdict followed, "You will die in your sin." By using the phrase, "in your sin," Jesus was saying you will die in your sinful condition. How scary! Their inner nature or condition inherited from Adam so dominated their lives they were bound and ruled by it. These people lived in the darkness of their smug self-righteousness all the way to their graves.

Unbelief so ruled these Judean leaders all they could imagine was to speculate: "Is [Jesus] going to commit suicide? Is this what he means when he says, 'Where I am going, you cannot come'?" (John 8:22 CJB).

Jesus' Stern Warning

8:23 But he continued, "You are from below; I am from above. You are of this world; I am not of this world. 24 I told you that you would die in your sins; if you do not

believe I am the one I claim to be you will indeed die in your sins."

This admonition from the Lord comes through as a serious word of caution from the Chief Judge of the universe. Hence it is both a warning and a verdict.

Universalists do not believe and embrace all of Jesus' teaching, especially His teaching about eternal punishment (John 3:36; Matthew 5:22, 29–30; 23:33; Mark 9:45; Luke 12:5). Yet, Jesus actually gave more teaching about hell than He did about heaven. The student of the Scriptures must conclude Jesus provided with His own blood a way so that all who repent and believe will not die in their sins, Neither will they experience unending punishment (Matthew 18:18).

Jesus was crystal clear in verses 23–24:

> "The difference between us," Jesus said to them, "is you come from below and I am from above. You belong to this world but I do not. That is why I told you will die in your sins. For unless you believe that I am who I am, you will die in your sins" (Phillips).

THINK ABOUT IT: Christian universalism maintains all who die outside of Christ will ultimately be saved in the afterlife. If this is true, it means Jesus gave a meaningless warning and verdict in verse 21, even though He repeated it twice (verses 23 and 24; see also Matthew 12:32; 25:41–46). But why would Jesus warn Israel's spiritual guides of the danger of dying in their sins in this solemn way, if there is nothing to dread?

Jesus' admonition was only shadow-boxing if in the next life there is a way to avoid the wrath to come (see Psalm 9:17, KJV; Proverbs 9:10; Matthew 25:31–46; 2 Thessalonians 1:7–10).

Christian pluralists maintain all sincerely held paths lead to God. But Jesus' warning and verdict are very specific: "If you do not believe I am the one I claim to be you will indeed die in your sins." This is an explicit claim that Jesus is the only path to God (see 1 Thessalonians 2:16).

Jesus also demonstrated in verses 23–24 qualities that belong only to God. He did this with the declaration, "You are from below; I am from above. You are of this world; I am not of this world."

Jesus affirmed His *eternality,* having come from heaven. He personified the *wisdom* of God [omniscience] just by giving this profound teaching. He declared His unchanging nature [immutability] by applying "I am" to himself three times in verses 23 and 24. The "I am" never changes. By asserting He is the Chief Judge of the universe, Jesus was also claiming He held the power and possessed the character to make universal judgments and to enforce His edicts [the attributes of omnipotence and holiness] (Matthew 28:18).

In short, Jesus came from the home of God and lived with the character traits and values that belong to His heavenly abode. He was "from above."

THINK ABOUT IT: How much wiser on our part to fear God and heed Jesus' stark warning: "If you do not believe I am the one I claim to be you will indeed die in your sins." (See Psalm 9:17 KJV; Proverbs 9:10; Matthew 25:31–46).

Jesus followed up on this verdict by drawing a sharp contrast between His accusers and Himself. Sin (the condition) breeds sins (acts of rebellion against God). The condition of their hearts dictated they were "from below" and wholeheartedly part of the world system. In their sinful condition they defended their power and position at all costs. This included using the world's ultimate weapon—they would kill Jesus to retain their hold on the people.

[At Jesus' trial even Pilate knew the chief priests had delivered Jesus to him for envy (Mark 15:10).] This meant the sin principle in their hearts kept on producing the sins which in due time took them to eternal separation from God (Romans 1:28–32; Revelation 21:8).

In contrast, Jesus was "from above." He was not controlled by the sinful condition binding them to the world's system and its way of doing things (1 John 2:15–17 KJV). This also meant Jesus never committed an individual act of sin (John 8:46).

At His inner core Jesus was guided by what He is: "God is love" (1 John 4:8, 16 KJV). From eternity this love has been the essence of the Tri-Unity of the God who is One. This reality made Jesus the Light of the world. Jesus was willing to die on a cross to prove the supremacy of "the true Light, which lighteth every man." The light had indeed come into the world (John 1:9; Matthew 10:27–28, KJV).

These leaders did not accept Jesus' solution to redeem all who become accountable before God and repent. Nor did they believe in Him as the Son of God and Savior of the world. Instead, these sons of Abraham after the flesh crafted their own religious system based on the good works they thought they could do to earn their salvation (Romans 10:3–4). It was totally predictable to the Lord where their plan ultimately would end.

> "Jerusalem, Jerusalem, you kill the prophets and stone to death those sent to you! How often I wanted to gather your children together the way a hen gathers her chicks under her wings! But you were not willing! Your house will be abandoned, deserted. I can guarantee that you will not see me again until you say, 'Blessed is the one who comes in the name of the Lord!'" (Matthew 23:37–39 GW).

THINK ABOUT IT: Many say the greatest danger in the world today is a nuclear holocaust. Not so. The sinful condition in the hearts of people who would make the decision to explode the bomb is a far greater issue. Many say guns are a great evil in a civilized society. But the greater evil is the sinful condition in people who make the decisions to use guns to harm others. The Law of Moses could do nothing to cure this evil core inside all mankind. But Jesus' death on the cross can and does change the heart—changes people from the inside out—and gives them the reward of eternal life in the process.

Abraham's natural seed made a deliberate choice to reject the walk of faith. This journey is anchored in the love of God revealed in the Law of Moses and especially in Jesus' ministry, and ultimately expressed in His death at Calvary (Deuteronomy 6:5) The indictment was not they did not know better, but they "were not willing" (Matthew 23:37; John 7:28). Instead of accepting their Messiah they killed Him. Stephen accused the members of the Sanhedrin of just this crime: "betrayal" and "murder" in crucifying Jesus (Acts 7:52).

Four decades after Jesus' resurrection Israel drew the sword and faced the Roman legions under General Titus (70 AD). During the insurrection, they yearned for the aid of their Messiah, but could not find Him because they refused to search for Him at the foot of Jesus' cross. The result was disaster for the Jewish people (Isaiah 6:11–12). The tragedy included great loss of life and the total destruction of their beloved temple, stone by stone (Luke 21:6). The rebellion ended in a mass suicide at Masada (72 AD).

THINK ABOUT IT: What would the world be like today, if Jesus' disciples had said, "Since all roads lead to God, why should we pay the price in our own blood to take the gospel across the empire?"

Ah! they did indeed take the good news, because they knew Jesus was alive and the one and only Son of God. No amount of persecution stopped them.

The love Jesus demonstrated at Calvary, kept moving them forward without owning a single sword, a sharp contrast to the methods of Rome. Ultimately it overcame all the persecution Rome could exert, and converted the Empire to the redeeming message of Jesus' cross, the Light of the world.

Jesus' Identity Revealed Best at Calvary

8:25 "Who are you?" they asked.
"Just what I have been claiming all along," Jesus replied.
26 "I have much to say in judgment of you. But he who sent me is reliable, and what I have heard from him I tell the world."
27 They did not understand that he was telling them about his Father.
28 So Jesus said, "When you have lifted up the Son of Man, then you will know that I am [the one I claim to be] and that I do nothing on my own but speak just what the Father has taught me. 29 The one who sent me is with me; he has not left me alone, for I always do what pleases him."
30 Even as he spoke, many put their faith in him.

"Where is your Father?" is the question of Jesus' critics in verse 19. In verse 25 the demand is, "Who are you?" The answer to both questions is basically the same. A person can learn much about a child, even if an adult, by visiting with his father. And, the more they learned about the Son of God, the greater would be their understanding of His heavenly Father.

Strange indeed! These leaders "still didn't get it, didn't realize Jesus was referring to His heavenly Father, because they saw Him as having only an earthly father. So He tried again. 'When you raise up the Son of Man, then you will know who I am—that I'm not making this up…'" (John 8:28 MSG).

No amount of pressure from men or devils, not even Jesus' cross, was ever able to penetrate the bond of unity in the Trinity between the Father, His Son Jesus, and the Holy Spirit. Jesus knew He was telling them the truth.

What spiritual blindness! All of His teaching, backed by His many miracles had gone over these Pharisees' heads. They had absorbed nothing. These leaders missed Jesus' meaning, but we should not. The statement goes to the heart of how the Father and the Holy Spirit guided the very words of the Son of Man in His humanity.

Jesus answered their question again by reaffirming He was their Messiah. This meant He was also their Judge. Hence, Jesus stated to them again the evidence for His trustworthiness: He had been sent into the world as the mouthpiece of His altogether reliable Father. His mission was to honor His Father. Jesus fulfilled His mission, telling the world what He had heard from His Father and then illustrating it at Calvary.

Sununu: Pleasing Only the President

In the early 1990s when President George Bush had fiery John Sununu as his White House Chief of Staff, a reporter asked Sununu if his job was difficult. He quickly answered, "No."

The reporter thought Sununu had misunderstood the question, so he asked again, and got the same reply.

Sununu, a former governor of New Hampshire, then explained why he felt his job was easy: "I have only one constituent."

He knew his job was to please the President.[5]

Jesus lived to please only His Father, and did it with "much joy" (John 8:28 MSG).

THINK ABOUT IT: The founder of no other world religion claims to be the Messiah, except Jesus.

In this temple discourse, the Lord of the temple prophesied He, the Son of Man, would be "lifted up"—crucified. Even though Jesus knew this was ahead, no amount of opposition ever motivated Jesus to stop honoring His Father and following His plan.

THINK ABOUT IT: So many in the Lord's church do not think it important to reflect on Jesus "lifted up" on His cross. But Jesus certainly remembers it. To this day, even though exalted in heaven with His Father, He carries the scars of crucifixion in His hands and His side (Zechariah 13:6; Isaiah 53:5; 1 Peter 2:24; Revelation 1:18).

It will always be a huge mistake to remember the resurrected Lord while at the same time diminishing the bloody sight of the Christ of the cross. In fact, both must be celebrated, in balance.

Without question, Jesus faced major opposition for His teaching about the tight bond between Himself and His Father. At the same time "many put their faith in Him." Jesus' message was beginning to get through (John 8:20).

The Lord's Standard: Walking in the Spirit

King David described his own relationship with God saying, "I foresaw the Lord always before my face, for he is on my right hand, that I should not be moved" (Acts 2:25 KJV). Jesus promised His followers, "I am with you always, even unto the end of the world" (Matthew 28:20 KJV). This warmth of intimacy in the church is described as walking in the Spirit (Galatians 5:25; Ezekiel 36:27 KJV).

How important for all of God's children to live by the Lord's pattern in His relationship with His Father. Jesus is the first fruits of Spirit-filled believers who walk in the Spirit. He is the Living Word who depended on the Holy Spirit to guide His choices and decisions in His ministry. In fact, the Father who sent His Son was always with Him (Philippians 2:1–13; Acts 10:38; Galatians 5:16; 1 John 3:1; Matthew 28:20). We too, anchored in the written Word, must depend for guidance on the heavenly Father and the Holy Spirit. We do it with our faith anchored in the Messiah who died on the cross and then came out of the grave (Acts 10:38; 2 Corinthians 2:2; Galatians 5:16).

A Child's Source of Truth

My eight-year-old embraces some interesting sources of truth. We were coming home from the grocery store recently when he asked, "Dad, do you believe in the Bermuda Triangle?"

"Jack," I replied, "if you're asking me if I believe that this place exists, my answer is yes. If you're asking me if I believe all the mysterious stories about ships and planes disappearing, no: I think that's all baloney."

"Well, Dad," Jack said with a note of defensiveness, "I believe in it. And I bet you want to know why."

"Yes, Jack. I do."

"Well, I was watching *Scooby Doo...*"[6]

While we rejoice in the heart of a child who finds it so easy to believe, Jesus (and not Scooby Doo!) is the correct source of truth. One highly important life lesson this reveals includes schooling ourselves never to act solo, but always to depend on the Word of God in the power of the Spirit (Psalm 119:9, 11, 16, 89, 105). The ultimate fruit of this lifestyle is living like Jesus did: with unwavering, joyful commitment to please our heavenly Father (John 8:29).

It is worthy of reaffirmation: the result of this teaching was "many" of the Jews made the choice to "put their faith in Him." They were beginning to see the new bright light—the light of the world—that was shining out of Jesus (Isaiah 60:1; Matthew 4:16; John 3:19).

Jesus Liberates with the Truth

8:31 To the Jews who had believed him, Jesus said, "If you hold to my teaching, you are really my disciples. 32 Then you will know the truth, and the truth will set you free."

When Adam and Eve rebelled against God in the Garden, corruption was introduced in the earth, identified by the term, the sin curse. This penalty touched every living thing in the creation, ultimately ending in death for all people, including the whole of nature (Genesis 3:14–19; see also 6:5–8).

Adam and Eve were each affected in the totality of their being by this penalty, and through them each of their descendants. In fact, all people are "wired" in their inner self from birth to revolt against God. This corruption explains sickness, disease, pain, and the abnormalities and birth defects of the human body. It is also portrayed in the reign of death in the plant and animal kingdoms, including all insects and reptiles, all life in the waters of the earth, and the microscopic world with all of its bacteria and viruses.

"The wages of sin is death" in the whole sphere of life (Genesis 3:13–19; Romans 6:23; 8:19–22; Hebrews 9:27).

THINK ABOUT IT: Each of the evils in society has sprung up out of the core evil—man's rebellion against God. Evils such as drug abuse and sexual abuse, to name only two, are indeed evils that spring from this rotten moral condition in the hearts of all people.

Truth liberates because it follows the heavenly Father's blueprint for integrity in all things.

Millions of people live out their lives thinking this dreadful condition at man's core is normal, and no one should even expect anything different. Obviously, this was the case with these religious leaders who fought Jesus so hard. Unfortunately, the majority of the people stood with their leaders.

Growing numbers, however, began to see the light Jesus was bringing into the world and started placing their faith in Him. Jesus admonished these new believers to hold steadfastly to His teaching; they were to make His character their blueprint for living. The proof they really were His disciples would be their continuing choice to live out His values. The result of this kind of lifestyle, Jesus promised, was they would know the truth, and the truth would set them free. Yes, it is true "the wages of sin is death." But, thank God, "the gift of God is eternal life through Jesus Christ our Lord" (Romans 6:23).

Trying to Use the Wrong Blueprints

Have you heard about the man who asked a mail-order company to send plans for a birdhouse? Instead of getting a birdhouse blueprint, they sent him drawings for a sailboat.

He tried to put it together, but it just wouldn't work. He couldn't figure what kind of bird was going to live in that dumb birdhouse. So he wrote a letter and sent the parts back. They wrote a letter of apology and added this post script: "If you think it was difficult for you, you should have seen the man who got your plans trying to sail a birdhouse."[7]

Jesus carried out His Father's design and timeline to the point He could say, "It is finished" (John 19:30). Indeed! the gospel message fits perfectly the need of all mankind, forming the marvelous plan of redemption.

Jesus Illustrates Sin with Slavery

8:33 They answered him, "We are Abraham's descendants and have never been slaves of anyone. How can you say that we shall be set free?"

It is true the Jews during the Roman occupation held the freedom to worship according to the Law of Moses, but they did not win political liberty, including freedom to establish their own taxation laws. And they certainly could not martial an army. Their assertion, therefore, was only partially truthful: "We are Abraham's descendants and have never been slaves to anyone." Obviously, the Jewish people told themselves they had more freedom than they possessed. Therefore, their question, "How can you say we shall be set free?"

Jesus was speaking about ending the rebellion against God which so reflects the corrupt condition of the heart of every person (see vs. 21).

8:34 Jesus replied, "I tell you the truth, everyone who sins is a slave to sin. 35 Now a slave has no permanent place in the family, but a son belongs to it forever."

Slave labor was the economic engine of the empire. Almost anywhere in the Roman world, on any given day, slaves would be present, carrying out their duties for masters who legally owned and totally controlled them.

Leprosy provided a vivid word picture in the Old Testament for the effects of sin (Numbers 12:10–15). It was a bacterial disease of the nerves at the surface of the skin that destroyed the ability to feel, and was incurable. Skin lesions were the primary external sign. Leprosy caused permanent damage to the skin and nerves, including limbs and eyes. The disease so destroyed lives, lepers were required to live outside the city, away from people (Exodus 13:45–46; 2 Kings 7:3; 15:5).

Nobody ever hugged a leper; people would not even touch them for fear of contracting the disease. But Jesus was compassionate toward them. He laid His hands on them freely, healed them, and gave them their lives back (Matthew 8:3; Mark 1:41; Luke 5:13).

What leprosy does to a person's body, sin does to his soul. In fact, sin is the ultimate killer—the wages of sin is death (Romans 6:23).

Jesus chose slavery instead of leprosy, however, as a word picture to explain His diagnosis of the core problem holding such a stranglehold on every son of Adam. Slavery is a good portrait of the effects of sin because it costs a person his freedom. Slavery was a legally accepted and enforced economic system in the empire. It painted a vivid, easily understood picture of man's rebellion against God. "Everyone who sins," Jesus said, does so because he "is a slave to sin." The control of sin reaches into the essence of man's being, so that he naturally resists God. This understanding links to the Lord's affirmations about *sin* and *sins* in verses 21–24.

Masters bought and sold, and legally owned their fellow human beings. In a similar way, it is the nature of sin to dominate people, including all of Adam's descendants. Jesus viewed sin as a very harsh and demanding taskmaster. Masters held slaves as their legal property. They told them:

When to get up and when to go to sleep.
What to eat, and drink, and how much.
What to wear.
When to speak, what to say and how to say it.
How many hours in the day to work, and
The list goes on and on.

It was a corrupt societal condition, and it so possessed people, slaves had no way to escape. The control was total to the extent a slave owner could kill a slave at will, and fear no punishment for the murder.

THINK ABOUT IT: Sin owns and controls the soul and moves outward to destroy the body too (Genesis 3:14–19). It is a cruel taskmaster. Sin *beats* and *whips* as it keeps people separated from their God who loves them.

Sin does it by corrupting the legitimate desires of the flesh, turning them into lusts—the lust of the flesh, the lust of the eyes and the pride of life (1 John 2:16; see Genesis 6:5–8). Sin molds a person's attitudes, controls what he eats and drinks, how he thinks, where he goes, what he does, what he says, and how he says it.

The Lord's point is clear that slaves could not "come and go at will" and certainly were not able to break out of the Roman legal system, freeing themselves. This understanding applied to the woman caught in the act of adultery. She was bound, corrupted in her heart, a slave to a very destructive way of life and it held her in its dark dungeon.

The Hardness That Doesn't Care About God

In his book *The Stranger*, Albert Camus tells of a man living his life without caring about anyone or anything.

Just before he was executed, the chaplain said to him, "Don't you believe in God?"

The man said, "No."

The chaplain said, "How do you know God doesn't exist?"

The man replied, "Whether he exists, I don't know. I do know I don't care either way."[8]

While many do not care, this bitterness of spirit is often only a façade. Deep down they do care. They are like the completely traumatized woman caught in the act of adultery, and the woman at the well, who had lived with five husbands, and her current relationship was a live-in arrangement. Both of these women had no doubt yearned for their Messiah to come and help them escape the prison in their souls.

In the Roman legal system, the only way out of slavery was if the owner granted the slave his freedom. This is exactly what Jesus the Son of God did for this adulterous woman. Suddenly she realized her chains had fallen off and she was free. The power which had led her to adultery was no longer her master. She was finally set apart from that old lifestyle. Blessing of blessings—she had her free will back and could make the choice to "sin no more!" At the moment of this great discovery, she became a daughter in the family of God.

THINK ABOUT IT: Jesus truly was the light of the world to her! He is for His followers today too.

Jesus' Gospel Breaks the Curse of Sin

8:36 So if the Son sets you free, you will be free indeed."

The gospel achieves this freedom. It breaks the stranglehold of the sin curse that produces a destructive lifestyle so at odds with God. We then as sons of God have "an established position, the run of the house" (John 8:35–36 MSG). The transformation leaves the old bondage behind. The liberation is so complete we become sons of God and joint heirs with Christ (John 8:35–36 MSG; Romans 8:14, 17; Philemon 1; 1 John 3:1–2).

"If the Son sets you free, you are free through and through" (John 8:36 MSG).

> As for you, you were dead in your transgressions and sins, in which you used to live when you followed the ways of this world and of the ruler of the kingdom of the air, the spirit who is now at work in those who are disobedient. All of us also lived among them at one time, gratifying the cravings of our sinful nature and following its desires and thoughts. Like the rest, we were by nature objects of wrath. But because of his great love for us, God, who is rich in mercy, made us alive with Christ even when we were dead in transgressions—it is by grace you have been saved (Ephesians 2:1–6; see Genesis 3:8).

What We Don't Want To Hear

> The truth that makes men free is for the most part the truth men prefer not to hear.[9]

Jesus' death and resurrection is the Father's antidote for the curse of sin, and His triumph cures the core condition in the heart. It does so for all who choose to respond to Jesus in repentance, taking Him at His word.

Jesus both forgives the sins we commit and conquers our natural disposition to sin, so that we again gain possession of our free will. We are fundamentally changed from the inside out.

Now we can make the decision not to sin and stick to it (Romans 6:5–18).

THINK ABOUT IT: This woman caught in the act wanted help and she got it, "without money and without price" (Isaiah 55:1).

Ah! the grace in the blood of Jesus: "if the Son sets you free, you will be free indeed."

John Wesley (1703–1791) expressed this great truth in the hymn, "O for a Thousand Tongues to Sing" (1739):

He breaks the power of canceled sin,
He sets the prisoner free;
His blood can make the foulest clean,
His blood availed for me.
Hear Him, ye deaf; His praise, ye dumb,
Your loosened tongues employ;
Ye blind, behold your Savior come,
And leap, ye lame, for joy.

Jesus' New Paradigm— The True Sons of Abraham

In revealing this great paradigm change, Jesus demonstrated His amazing ability as a strategic thinker. He showed how the faith of Abraham fitted perfectly with His sacrifice on the cross that was coming ever closer. If people were to find the gospel believable, they had to see how the two testaments, the old and the new, were inseparably linked. This is true because the gospel of Jesus Christ was born in a Jewish cradle. Jesus Himself honored the authority of the Old Testament in His teaching.

To achieve that goal, the writers of the New Testament gave much attention to how the Old Testament and the ministry of Jesus are intertwined. Jesus opened up a new way of thinking that did just this and swung the door wide for the warm light of the *Son* to shine into the hearts of all people everywhere.

In the gospel of Jesus Christ, Jews and Gentiles alike hold common ground, living under the curse of sin that keeps growing in the inner chamber of each person's heart. But there is a way out. It comes not by works of righteousness but by transforming faith in God—Abraham's kind of faith. "The Son sets you free."

8:37 "I know you are Abraham's descendants. Yet you are ready to kill me, because you have no room for my word. 38 I am telling you what I have seen in the Father's presence, and you do what you have heard from your father."
39 "Abraham is our father," they answered.
"If you were Abraham's children," said Jesus, "then you would do the things Abraham did. 40 As it is, you are determined to kill me, a man who has told you the truth that I heard from God. Abraham did not do such things. 41 You are doing the things your own father does."
"We are not illegitimate children," they protested. "The only Father we have is God himself."
42 Jesus said to them, "If God were your Father, you would love me, for I came from God and now am here. I have not come on my own; but he sent me. 43 Why is my language not clear to you? Because you are unable to hear what I say."

As has been discussed earlier in this chapter (verses 19, 25–29, if you know a person's father, you will have a reasonable understanding of his son. The principle applies here. To know Jesus' heavenly Father is to love Him. The issue with these

Pharisees, however, was if they admitted Jesus was the heavenly Father's Son, they had to accept and love Jesus as the Son of God too, and this they were not willing to do.

Jesus acknowledged physically they were "Abraham's descendants" [Greek: *sperma* =seed or descendants; the English word sperm is a transliteration of this Greek word]. These leaders had Abraham's blood in their veins, but they did not have Abraham's faith in their hearts.

That conclusion is obvious. Abraham had been quick to believe and obey God. For example, he responded "early the next morning," when God called on him to offer Isaac as a sacrifice (Genesis 22:2–3). The result was Abraham met his Messiah on Moriah. With deep gratitude Abraham embraced his Messiah when the pre-incarnate Christ spared Isaac's life (Genesis 22:8).

If Abraham had been living at the time of Jesus' incarnation, would he have joined the plot to kill his Messiah? It is simply unthinkable.

Abraham's blood descendants were doing the unimaginable in Jerusalem. Jesus even explained to them why they wanted Him dead—because "you have no room for my word." Accepting Jesus as their Messiah would have required them to tear down their entire system of self-righteousness.

THINK ABOUT IT: Jesus' Father simply could not be the Father of these religious leaders, no matter how much they claimed Abraham's blood flowed in their veins. Simply put, Abraham's faith was missing in their lives.

In their sinful condition, they did not want a message that shined the light of God into the deepest inner chambers of their souls. The progression of the reasoning went like this:

1. Jesus explained the Word He was giving them came from His being in the presence of His heavenly Father.

2. The fact they were rejecting this Word meant Jesus' Father was not their Father. You are doing, Jesus said, "what you have heard from your father."

3. When they indignantly responded, "Abraham is our father," Jesus was very straightforward: "No! for if he were, you would follow his good example. But instead you are trying to kill me—and all because I told you the truth I heard from God. Abraham wouldn't do such a thing! No, you are obeying your real father when you act that way " (John 8:39–41 TLB).

4. These religious leaders protested again, "We are not illegitimate children!"

5. To which Jesus answered: "I came out from God; and now I have arrived here. I did not come on my own; he sent me. Why don't you understand what I'm saying?"

6. Jesus answered His own question. They did not reject Him out of ignorance. Instead, they understood the choice they were making: to accept Jesus they would have to change their basic spiritual foundation. But that they would not do; even the very thought was too much for them. Hence, Jesus told them, "you can't bear to listen to my message" (John 8:43, CJB).

In a nutshell, the Son of God was the *logos,* the Word sent by the heavenly Father. He brought these Jewish leaders a message they refused to consider. In their self-righteous pride, they believed the system they had built was correctly based on the Law of Moses, and was right for the Jewish nation. Said another way, the price was too high for them. Instead, they shut their ears to the truth and closed their eyes to the light. They could not even "bear to listen to [Jesus'] message."

In the Jewish mindset, the true sons of Abraham were the Israelite people who were Abraham's blood descendants. It was an understanding steeped in their heritage, and it had marked them as a people for some 1800 years. But "God looks at the heart" (1 Samuel 16:7). This conclusion was made very plain when the Holy Spirit instructed the Prophet Samuel to anoint Jesse's youngest son as Israel's next king. The Lord was looking for a ruler with a heart willing to believe Him and practice the faith of God in the governmental, religious, and socio-economic life of the nation (Romans 3:3).

Who Is Truly in Bondage?

None are more hopelessly enslaved than those who falsely believe they are free.[10]

People with Abraham's Faith Recognize Jesus

We have already noted in this study that Jesus dared to change a centuries old paradigm the author has identified as the "temple switch." Jesus himself, the sovereign *logos, the* Word, moved the dwelling place of God from the Most Holy Place in the temple to the new temple of the heart. It meant the Spirit of God indwells believers and goes with them wherever they go, anywhere in the world (John 14:17 KJV). [See the discussion about the temple switch in *Jesus Son of God Book One, Chapter 2.*]

Jesus paved the way for a second new paradigm when he laid down the guiding principle regarding relationships in the body of Christ. He expressed it one day when Jesus' family visited Him and wanted to talk with Him. Jesus responded: "Who are my mother and my brother?" Then the Lord answered His own question: "Whoever does God's will is my brother, and sister and mother" (Mark 3:33–35).

Jesus applied this principle (in John 8) when He redefined the sons of Abraham. Obviously, a person could have Abraham's blood in his veins but not Abraham's faith in his heart. True sons of Abraham manifest Abraham's faith in God. Jesus said the true right to claim Abraham as father goes to those who have his faith. The litmus test here sets the starting place as personal relationship with God: does a person take God at His word and recognize the heavenly Father's Son? Jesus could not be more explicit: "The work of God is this," He said, "to believe the one God has sent" (John 6:29).

True sons of Abraham were those who welcomed Jesus the Messiah standing physically on Mt. Moriah, the home of their beloved temple. It was the same spot where Abraham had welcomed his Messiah on Moriah some eighteen centuries earlier (John 8:56; Genesis 22:8). This Messiah became the sacrificial lamb God provided to redeem all who believe in Him.

In a nutshell, Abraham's true descendants anywhere in the world are the people who *choose* to live out in their lives Abraham's faith in his Messiah, Jesus Christ (Genesis 22:11).

Jesus, the Son of God and Israel's Messiah paid the price with His own blood to make this huge paradigm change.

The conclusion is clear: those who exercise the faith of Abraham to believe what God says will also recognize Jesus as the Messiah. *They* are the true children of Abraham. And they are "free indeed!" (John 8:36). But those who rejected Jesus were not Abraham's seed at all, but slaves bound by their own self-righteousness.

In this exchange, Jesus' new definition of the spiritual sons of Abraham had a telling application. True sons with Abraham's faith would accept the Messiah on the streets of Israel, just as Abraham welcomed Him on Moriah (John 8:56; Genesis 22:8).

The Apostle Paul a few years later, with the benefit of Jesus' cross in his hindsight, understood the contribution Jesus' new paradigm makes and the light it brings to the world. Paul made this revelation the cornerstone of Galatians and Romans, two of his most important New Testament epistles.

"Understand, then, those who believe are children of Abraham. The Scripture foresaw God would justify the Gentiles by faith, and announced the gospel in advance to Abraham: "All nations will be blessed through you." So those who have faith are blessed along with Abraham, the man of faith" (Galatians 3:7–9).

"The promise comes by faith, so that it may be by grace and may be guaranteed to all Abraham's offspring—not only to those who are of the law but also to those who are of the faith of Abraham. He is the father of us all" (Romans 4:16).

In summary, Jesus laid the foundation for this understanding when He asked the question, "Who are my mother and my brother?" Jesus answered His own question saying, "Whoever does God's will is my brother, and sister and mother" (Mark 3:33–35).

This principle, when applied to the definition of the true sons of Abraham, served to connect inseparably the Old Testament and the New Testament scriptures. In doing so, it opened the door wide for people all over the world to come to Jesus Christ in faith.

God's plan has always been that salvation comes by grace through faith (Genesis 15:6). It was true with the revelation that came to Abraham, and Jesus taught the same message. Each person who comes to Jesus has the opportunity to become and mature as a warm, walking, talking temple of the Holy Spirit, who "dwells with you" and "lives in you" (John 14:17–18). The good news of the gospel is all about "Christ in you, the hope of glory" (Colossians 1:27).

Believers in the New Covenant live anchored with one foot at Jesus' cross where He gave His blood to the last drop for our salvation. The other foot is fixed at the Lord's empty tomb that shows Jesus arose from the grave for our justification (Romans 4:25). Hence, followers of Jesus, Jews and Gentiles, are also fully connected with their Old Testament roots in Abraham, "the father of us all" (Romans 4:11).

Yes, the message of the scriptures in the Old Covenant and the New Covenant merged into one redemptive stream at Calvary. It happened even as Jesus' blood splattered on the rocks and quickly soaked into the dry ground. In this new relationship, each follower of Christ walks in faith as a true son of Abraham, and becomes a dwelling place of the Spirit in the new temple of the heart (1 Corinthians 3:16; 2 Corinthians 6:16).

The good news of the gospel is that anyone who comes to Christ is adopted into the family of God, and no one is left an orphan. "I will come to you" is Jesus' personal promise (John 14:18).

These two new paradigms also meant the gospel would begin to break free of its Jewish cradle in the decades following Pentecost. The process was largely completed by the time Jerusalem was wiped out by the Romans in 70 AD. The result was the young church continued its march to the ends of the earth.

THINK ABOUT IT: The Testaments are joined by the crimson stream that began in Eden with the blood of the animals God sacrificed, and continued its flow past Moriah in its journey to Golgotha (Genesis 3:21; 22:1–13; 1 Peter 1:19; 1 John 1:7; Revelation 1:5; 5:9; 12:11; 19:13).

Jesus' own holy blood on Mt. Calvary sanctified the long river carved over the millennia by quite possibly more than a million lambs and rams, turtledoves and pigeons.

Jesus offered himself as the perfect sacrifice. In doing so He ended permanently animal sacrifices as atonement for the sins people commit against God (Hebrews 10:10–18).

Yes, Abraham's Messiah spared Abraham's "only son" atop Moriah (Genesis 22:2, 11–13). But the heavenly Father provided His own Son as His sacrificial lamb (Genesis 22:8, 14). God "spared not his own Son" at Skull Hill; instead, He "gave him up for us all" (Matthew 27:33; Romans 8:32).

Followers of Jesus Christ embrace two covenants, the Old and the New Testament. Jesus is concealed in the Old Testament and revealed in the New Testament. The cross of Jesus ties the two covenants together. The people who follow Jesus are happy to claim Abraham as the father of of the faithful, and Jesus is Himself the bridge who pulls the two covenants into His embrace. Jesus is the essence of the New Covenant.

With these two new paradigms—the temple switch and the true seed of Abraham—the gospel began its march to every ethnicity and tongue worldwide.

Two Paths: Man's Way and God's Way

The Apostle John in Chapter 1 names four people who took the all-important step of professing faith in Jesus as the Son of God. John the Baptist, Andrew, Phillip, and Nathaniel each accepted and confessed Jesus' Deity. None of these men at the time had witnessed a single one of the seven Deity-proving miracles John records. Neither had they enjoyed opportunity to learn from Jesus' teaching. Even so, they were as quick to believe God as Abraham had been some eighteen centuries earlier when the nation was being birthed.

In contrast, Israel's religious rulers had the additional benefit of Jesus' miracles and did not dispute they happened (John 11:47–48). They also heard Jesus teach. Even in the face of all the evidence, they made a choice not to believe Jesus was the Son of God (John 5:47; 6:29, 36; 7:28; 8:24, 44; 11:48; 1 John 3:23; Matthew 23:37). They fulfilled, in fact, what Isaiah described when he penned, "All we like sheep have gone astray.

We have turned every man to *his own way*. But the Lord has laid on him the iniquity of us all" (Isaiah 53:6). The Apostle Paul used a different term for "his own way" when he wrote the Israelites rejected God's plan and "sought to establish their own" righteousness (Romans 10:3).

These two realities—man's way and God's way—frame the glaring differences between faith and unbelief. They show the depths to which spiritual blindness and hardness can plunge the souls of unbelievers. In rejecting Jesus as the Son of God, they were also rejecting Jehovah God, who revealed Himself to Abraham, and to whom Abraham speedily gave full obedience and devotion.

Abraham had been quick to believe and obey God. He responded "early the next morning," for example, when God called on him to offer Isaac as a sacrifice (Genesis 22:2–3). The result was Abraham met his Messiah on Moriah. "[Abraham] knew I was coming," Jesus said, "and was glad" (Genesis 22:9–13; John 8:56 TLB).

THINK ABOUT IT: What greater demonstration of faith could Abraham make than his willingness to offer his only son Isaac as a sacrifice to God? This is all the more true when one considers Jehovah had promised Abraham nations of people would come through Isaac and that "All nations would be blessed through Abraham's seed, "which is Christ" (Genesis 17:5–6; 22:18; Galatians 3:16).

Framing their own righteousness largely took shape in the turbulent, 400-year era from Malachi to Christ. In those centuries, Judaism found it necessary to confront and withstand the all too real threat from the philosophy, idolatry, and immorality of Greek culture. The Hellenistic way of life was followed in the last hundred years of these four centuries by the equally polytheistic power of Roman administrative genius, backed by its military machine. Jerusalem fell to the Roman general Pompey in 63 BC.

In the ongoing effort to meet these Hellenistic and Roman threats, the Israelites crafted a substitute righteousness built on two anchors: Abraham's bloodline and a strict application of Moses Law that included a dogmatized monotheism. It allowed no room at all for the later revelation God gave to King David that God has a Son (Psalm 2:7; Romans 9:30–33; 10:3). In doing so, perpetuating Abraham's personal faith in Jehovah God and Moses' understanding of love for God and neighbor were not significant parts of the equation as it ultimately developed (Deuteronomy 6:4–5; Leviticus 19:18).

Diminishing the importance of Abraham's faith and the ethic of love for God and neighbor was destined to be very costly, however. It took the anointing of the Spirit out of the new Judaism they crafted. The monotheistic dogmatism ultimately meant when Messiah came, neither the people nor their leaders would be quick to recognize and welcome Him, as Abraham had at Moriah. In fact, the majority of the population would not recognize Messiah at all. Instead, they would crucify Him.

Instead of turning to God in faith, the descendants of Abraham increasingly believed they had to defend the system to preserve their way of life. They were aware of the promises of a coming Messiah and most had some expectation He would appear one day. However, they viewed His arrival in the context of their self-righteousness. This meant He would come as a brilliant warrior, another King David armed and ready to go forth "conquering and to conquer" (Acts 1:6–7; Revelation 6:2 KJV).

As this process of building their own self-righteousness evolved over those many decades, the result was a stiff legalism based on individual works of righteousness. Keeping the Law of Moses became the cornerstone of the system. Achieving this legalism even eclipsed the importance of Abraham's and Moses' encounters with the Messiah. One result was the development of the Pharisees' checklists of do's and do not's based on their interpretation of the Law. Violations were easily measurable; hence, punishment for lawbreakers could be swift.

The big problem with this approach to righteousness was what the Apostle Paul later identified when he wrote to the believers at Galatia. "If a law had been given that could impart life," he penned, "then righteousness would certainly have come by the law" (Galatians 3:21). Said another way, it is not possible for law to produce righteousness; it can only yield fear of punishment for breaking its mandates.

After Pentecost, as the church began to grow, "they of the circumcision" were among its primary adversaries (Acts 13:50; Titus 1:10). These Judaizers (people who believed the Law of Moses was prerequisite for coming to Christ) taught the death and resurrection of Jesus were not enough to be a follower of Christ. People must first accept circumcision and keep the law (see Romans 11:6; Galatians 2:14–16; 5:1; 1 Timothy 4:1–5; Titus 3:3–7).

In contrast, the love of God highly motivates a changed heart precisely because, the Apostle Paul wrote, it is based on gratitude, not fear: "God commendeth his love toward us, in that, while we were yet sinners, Christ died for us" (Romans 5:8 KJV). This striking kindness "is meant "to lead...to repentance" (Romans 2:4 TLB). The Apostle John added, "There is no fear in love. But perfect love drives out fear, because fear has to do with punishment. The one who fears is not made perfect in love. We love because he first loved us" (1 John 4:18–20).

Law can define right and wrong and motivate with fear for not doing the right (Romans 7:7). But no law has ever been written that can birth life (Galatians 3:21). The love of God is superior because it *can* and does impart life. Yes, the love of God can accomplish in the soul of man what the legalisms in the Law of Moses never could—a heart changed from the inside out.

It must be admitted freely and not minimized—the challenge of Hellenistic thinking and Roman power was all-pervasive in their pagan efforts to force fundamental change in Israelite religion and culture. Greeks and Romans had developed their own "righteousness" too that reeked of polytheism and the massive immorality associated with it. The monumental task of preserving Judaism, these religious leaders believed, was based on preserving the Law of Moses as both the standard and the fire wall against the influence of the Greek way of life and the Roman occupation.

THINK ABOUT IT: Salvation, Jesus taught, comes by believing "the one God has sent" (John 8:24). Jesus added no other requirement; the Lord did not make circumcision and the law prerequisite for believing "the one God has sent." Paul followed Jesus' teaching when he penned: "It is by grace you have been saved, through faith [in Jesus]—and this not from yourselves, it is the gift of God—not by works, so that no one can boast" (Ephesians 2:8–10).

God's Massive Intervention in History

Looking back at the cross, Paul summarized the significance of the era when he wrote "the fullness of the time" finally came (Galatians 4:4). Jehovah mightily went into action during the time when Rome occupied Israel and Augustus Caesar was emperor of the empire. In fact, it was God's greatest act of intervention in all human history (Luke 2:1). Before their eyes Jesus broke into time with an incarnation through a virgin birth. "The Holy Spirit will come upon you," the angel Gabriel said to Mary, "and the power of the Most High will overshadow you. So the holy one to be born will be called the Son of God" (Luke 1:35–36).

That achievement was on a scale far, far greater than their fathers experienced crossing the Red Sea and possessing the Promised Land. The birth of Jesus showcased to the world that

God's only Son and Israel's Messiah had arrived, a mammoth revelation of truly massive proportions (Isaiah 7:14; Matthew 1:23). The angel Gabriel expressed to Mary, "Nothing is impossible with God" (Luke 1:37).

By the time Jesus had grown up and launched His ministry, however, perpetuating the Law of Moses and saving the Jewish way of life from Roman military might and Greek culture had become Israel's highest priority (John 11:48; Luke 23:1–2).

As Jesus began doing His mighty miracles and winning a following, in the eyes of the national leaders, Jesus quickly became an enemy of the state. Accepting Jesus as the Messiah whom Abraham and Moses had worshipped, simply put, was not going to happen.

To achieve their goals, they were certain, required the path of the sword, in regards both to Rome and to dealing with what they thought was their "Messiah problem."

Jesus Christ came offering another track—the journey of faith grounded in the love of God best revealed in Jesus' sacrificial death on the cross. This strategy proved it could change people in their hearts. Without wielding a single sword, the love of God ultimately transformed the Roman Empire by changing people one at a time.

This understanding also shows the bloodline sons of Abraham missed seeing in their generation how Jehovah God of their Fathers was indeed active in their history. The intervention of God was bold. Just two examples among so many is how the influence of Jesus' life, death and resurrection actually won the empire. It even redefined the calendar worldwide, with time counted as "BC" (before Christ) and "AD" (*Anno Domini—after Jesus' birth*).

As regards Jesus' way of life, He lived humbly. His demeanor was meek and lowly (Zechariah 9:9; Matthew 11:28–30; 20:26–28; 21:5). Unthinkably, He did not even own a sword, and in the minds of the religious leaders He talked far too much about love.

The common expectation was when Messiah came, he would repeat Israel's glorious past and restore David's literal kingdom again to Israel.

THINK ABOUT IT: Because national Israel was living in "yesterday," they could not see their future. The new thing springing up that God was doing sailed past them like ships silently passing in the night (Isaiah 43:19).

The heavenly Father chose for His Son:
The path of a virgin's womb by a young girl with no social standing in Israel.
A cold stable as Jesus' birthplace in Bethlehem,
A cattle trough for His bed and
A cross on which He suffered and died.

Yes, the most humble of people can identify with the Savior of the world.

Jesus freely made Himself the sacrifice that would change the hearts of Jews and Gentiles alike. He planned to achieve this monumental task by establishing the righteousness of God as His kingdom in people's hearts worldwide (Acts 1:6; John 1:29, 36; Romans 3:21–23). It meant He did not even consider letting them make Him *their* king, because they would have done so by their definition and on their terms (John 6:15). Yet, He was a king, but on His Father's terms—an invisible kingdom not of this world that includes all who believe Jesus is the one the Father sent, the Son of God (Luke 17:21; John 6:29; 18:36; Romans 14:7).

All the armies in the world, for example, could not change the malady of the human heart; instead, the sinful condition in the inner being of all mankind produces wars. Greed, for just one example, is a powerful killer that walks the corridors of every capitol, no matter the system of government.

Jesus' Solution—Inside Out

A Messiah who came as God's only Son to provide a cure for this problem of the heart was so foreign to Jewish expectations they rejected Him out of hand. They actually saw such a Savior as a threat to Israel's national survival (John 11:48).

THINK ABOUT IT: To these leaders, the love Jesus showed would never convert the Roman Empire. But Jesus knew it would, and it did. Overpowered Greek culture and learning too.

"There is no God apart from Him" (Isaiah 45:18, 21–24).

It is striking that no Roman emperor and no Jewish priest or doctor of the law has impacted history and the individual lives of millions like Jesus of Nazareth, and His influence has never stopped. Caesar Augustus, for example, claimed to be a god, but who worship's him today? As for Caiaphas, his name was actually lost to secular history until the modern era, when the Caiaphas ossuary (bone box) was discovered in1990.

Jesus the Messiah shined the light of God on the needs of people, doing miracles explained only as acts of God, but to no avail (Luke 23:2; John 11:48). The people and their leaders had made the choice to embrace and follow their belief system. Their downward spiral actually took them to the bottom of the well, into the depths of depravity. At this level their system enslaved them and their self-righteousness dictated to them. It is in this context Isaiah's prophecy, that both Jesus and Paul quoted, can be understood.

> "They were ever hearing but never understanding,
> Ever seeing but never perceiving."
> Their hearts were "calloused,"
> Their ears were "dull," and
> "Their eyes" closed to what God's Son was doing among them (Isaiah 6:9–10; Matthew 13:15; Acts 28:27).

The end result of their sinful condition led these leaders to kill even their Messiah sent from God, who is the Light of the world (Romans 1:18–32). They had moved in the downward spiral of unbelief from *would not believe* to *could not believe* (John 12:37–40; 47–50; Isaiah 6:9–10; 53:1).

In their thinking, Judaism's survival required two things: they would have to fight for it, and keep the letter of their Law.

Time proved neither was possible (Ecclesiastes 2:17; 5:13, 16; 6:2; see also Matthew 23:4; Luke 11:46). But man's own way is always an impossible task (Daniel 4:37; see Ezekiel 28:2). It is actually an either/or of the two choices below:

- Either a person will believe in the one God has sent and walk before Him in faith, as did Abraham. He will also, as Moses taught, live by the ethic that loves God and one's neighbor (Deuteronomy 6:5; Leviticus 19:8).

- Or, secondly, he will go "his own way," crafting his own righteousness (Genesis 15:6; 21:21; Galatians 4:24–25; Romans 10:3).

THINK ABOUT IT: The latter is exactly the path the Apostle Paul said the nation of Israel selected (Romans

10:3). The result was they turned the truth of God into a lie (Romans 25).

These first-century Jews believed in their system strongly enough to kill trying to preserve it, even as they wrapped their robes of self-righteousness in Abraham and Moses.

False religion can be equally deadly in the twenty-first century.

Jesus Helps People Discover Their True Father

When God's Son was born as Israel's Messiah, the choice had already been made. They boldly protested to Jesus: "The only Father we have is God himself," not comprehending their choice had deceived them so that they could not see the light Jesus was bringing into the world (2 Thessalonians 2:11–12). Neither the God of Abraham nor of Moses was their heavenly Father. This meant the faith of Abraham was not their guiding star, although it would have led them to Bethlehem's manger (Matthew 2:1–2).

The truth is the leadership of Israel was on the path of raw rebellion. [So are all people who have not humbled their hearts in repentance at Jesus' cross.] Spiritual hardness had pitted them against God's revelation to Abraham and to Moses. In their gross pride they had become God's enemies, and they showed it very clearly to the Father's only begotten Son. If they had believed Abraham, they would have also believed Jesus. This made them spiritual brothers, not with Abel, Isaac, or Jacob, but with Cain, Ishmael and Esau, with Hagar as their spiritual sister (1 John 3:12; Jude 11; Genesis 16:11–12; 21:9–10; Ezekiel 28:17; Galatians 4:24–25).

Descendants of Abraham, who enjoyed a personal relationship with God and walked in faith as did their forefather, understood the Law of Moses was anchored in love for God and for one's neighbor (Deuteronomy 6:5; 30:16,20; Leviticus 19:18; Luke 10:29). These believers freely, of their own choice, became God's instruments to facilitate Messiah's coming into the world. In modern culture believers like them also take the gospel to the ends of the earth.

Yes, the Law was the schoolmaster intended to lead Israel to Christ (Galatians 3:24–25). With this in mind we can understand why Paul said Christ "is the end of the [era of the] law so that there may be righteousness for every one who believes" (Romans 10:4). But those who took the other path and rejected Jesus acted in their own free will to despise God's Son, the Messiah, when he came. In fact, they joined Rome that wielded the power of the state, and actually nailed Jesus to a cross. But God raised Him from the dead.

Jesus did find in His ministry the remnant who held to the true faith of Abraham, although the self-righteous group was much larger (John 1:35–51; 2:23; 4:39–41; 7:31; 8:30; see also Jeremiah 23:3–4; Micah 5:7; Acts 15:17; Romans 9:27; 11:5). The people with hearts like Abraham's were indeed Israelites who believed what Jesus said and the miracles He did. Many of them accepted Jesus as quickly as had been true with Abraham, the father of the faithful. Jesus also knew He would find people by the tens of thousands among the Gentiles who would vest implicit faith in God, loving Him with all their hearts and their neighbors too (Matthew 21:42–46; John 12:20–30). They would reject the proud self-righteousness that defies God and His dear Son, Jesus the Messiah.

THINK ABOUT IT: Jesus said it very clearly: those who have Abraham's faith are the true sons of Abraham.

As for the second group, Jesus made crystal clear who their father was.

Jesus Shows the Origin of the Curse of Sin

8:44 You belong to your father, the devil, and you want to carry out your father's desire. He was a murderer from the beginning, not holding to the truth, for there is no truth in him. When he lies, he speaks his native language, for he is a liar and the father of lies."

Jesus identifies the devil as being a living spirit, personal and real (Genesis 3:1–4). He is the source and fountain head of lies, and the thief who comes to steal, kill and destroy (John 10:10). The Lord also described him as a "father," meaning he has a family of followers. His skill at deception is so effective he always has a fresh supply of recruits. Jesus prophesied "false Christ's and false prophets will appear and perform great signs and miracles to deceive even the elect—if that were possible" (Matthew 24:24–25). Many of the misled will actually think they are following God (John 15:20; Acts 22:3–5; 2 Corinthians 11:13–15; Philippians 3:6).

Jesus' question in John 8:43 and restated in 8:46 is penetrating: "Why can't you understand what I am saying?" His answer to His own question reveals His ability to discern and judge what motivates people: "It is because you are prevented from doing so" (TLB).

The follow-up question is obvious: Who was the source of this kind of mind control that prevented these leaders from accepting their own Messiah? After all, they had seen the light He brought into the world demonstrated with many signs and wonders. This was particularly obvious with His verdict in the case of the woman taken in the act of adultery.

The Lord's answer was not what they wanted to hear: "You are the children of your father the devil, and you love to do the evil things he does" (John 8:44 TLB). Isaiah's prophecy had come true: "If you do not stand firm in your faith, you will not stand at all" (Isaiah 7:9).

Jesus' response links to the Lord's teaching in verses 21–23 and 34. It describes the source of sin as man's inner condition, his DNA that produces acts of sin. This condition of a sinful soul is in continual opposition to God and has no independent power to escape (see Isaiah 1:5–6; Romans 3:10–18). Jesus came to change this stark reality.

Jesus did more than tell these leaders His heavenly Father was not their father. He also forthrightly identified their father—*the devil*, to whom they had surrendered their freedom of choice. In establishing to whom they belonged, Jesus revealed information about the devil not told in this specific way anywhere else in Holy Scripture.

1. Because these elders had made this huge surrender, Satan had the power to control their motivating wishes. This meant: "[you want] to carry out your father's desire." Slaves quickly learn to do what the master tells them, even when they know he is wrong. After all, he feeds them, clothes them, and gives them shelter. The longer a person obeys the devil, the more it becomes second nature to do what he directs, all the while knowing it is evil. Jesus said Satan was a murderer from the beginning—and the leopard has never changed his spots (Jeremiah 13:23; See John 10:10). He does his most deadly work by destroying the soul.

2. Satan did not hold to the truth because he could not—there was no truth inside him.

3. When he lies, he speaks what is normal and natural for him, his native tongue. He *is* a liar and the father of lies.

Little wonder Jesus told His disciples after He sent the seventy out to minister: "I saw Satan fall like lightning from heaven" (Luke 10:18; see Isaiah 14; Ezekiel 28:1–19; Revelation 12:1–9).

How scary! This process of evil starts in a person's downward spiral of repeated surrender to Satan. An individual makes the choice "here and there" to reject the evidence that Jesus is God's Son. It begins one small step at a time. But soon the rejection includes bigger and bigger decisions. What ultimately follows is a person chooses to believe a lie and actually reaches the point of loss of control over his own decisions and destiny (Romans 1:25). The outcome on this slippery slope is Satan controls a person's free will to the extent he *will* carry out the devil's desires, even while knowing better. He has long ago surrendered his power of choice to the point he no longer controls his decision making (Isaiah 6:9–10).

Addictive drugs have basically the same effect. What might start with a euphoric thrill soon turns into the addiction that controls a person's will. Addicts have been known to steal and even kill to try to satisfy their drug habit that controls them.

What is the final outcome of this God-rejecting thinking:

> "...the cities [will] lie ruined and without inhabitant,
> ...the houses [will be] left deserted and the fields ruined and ravaged, until the LORD has sent everyone far away and the land is utterly forsaken. And though a tenth remains in the land, it will again be laid waste.
> ...[but] the holy seed will be the stump in the land" (Isaiah 6:11–12).

THINK ABOUT IT: A person who is bonded to Satan to this degree can be in the presence of his Messiah, yet consider his Savior demon possessed and a Samaritan, and worthy of the death penalty (Isaiah 5:20). Yes, self-righteousness will kill trying to prevent the rule of righteousness in the earth.

John 8:44–47 is best understood as having its roots in Eden. Eve gave the devil control of her desire as she gazed on the forbidden fruit; it looked so pleasing to her. Then, the devil proceeded to take control of her will power (See Genesis 3:1–4; James 1:14–15).

Satan's goal was to destroy both her and Adam, and the result was devastating. First, the light of God went out of their lives immediately (Genesis 1:8–20). Sin's first bitter fruit was to destroy their souls. The curse of physical death also possessed each of them, and the death of the body followed in its time. Eternal separation from God is the second and ultimate death to result from the curse of sin (Revelation 2:11; 20:6, 14; 21:8).

Adam and Eve had been cathedrals of innocence, brilliantly luminous with the presence of the Holy Spirit. But the temple of the soul went midnight black in the rebellion and the devil himself moved into the darkness. Adam and Eve and all their descendants since then have lived in this rebellion against God. All have been ruled by this murderer, who is also a liar and the father of lies. He did not hold to the truth in his deliberate deception in the Garden of Eden because he had no truth in him to which to cling. Lies were his native language even in paradise. This has been his character from the beginning, and it has never changed to this day.

"Unless Something—or Someone—Intervenes"

A cargo ship left Hong Kong in 1992, bound for the U.S. While in route, the ship hit rough seas, and several shipping containers were washed overboard and lost at sea. One of the lost shipping containers held 28,000 plastic bath toys—rubber ducks, turtles, and frogs. The container broke open, and the toys were henceforward in the total control of the ocean currents.

The ducks were never able to set themselves free and reach their intended destination. Instead, they were controlled by the whims of the currents.

A few ducks landed in Hawaii, some made shore in Alaska, others beached in South America, Australia and the Pacific Northwest. The plastic toys have been found frozen in Arctic ice. Others made their way to Scotland and Newfoundland, in the Atlantic. Even 20 years later, some of the rubber ducks were coming ashore.

None ever reached the original intended destination.

We, too, are trapped in our human condition, lost and circling in the clutches of sin. Left to ourselves, we are doomed to float around in this state until something—or Someone—intervenes to set us free.[11]

The first prophecy in the Bible of the all-important intervention by the Messiah was expressed by God in Eden: "I will put enmity between you and the woman, and between your offspring and hers; he will crush your head, and you will strike his heel" (Genesis 3:15).

The devil maliciously used the natural sons of Abraham as his agents to strike at the "heel" of Abraham's Messiah. But Satan did not prevail. The Son of God, who was also the Son of Man and Israel's Messiah, crushed the "head" of the serpent on Golgotha and then victoriously arose from the dead on the third day (Revelation 1:18; 4:10; 5:14).

The story line of the Bible is all about the triumph of the Father's plan carried out fully by Jesus, the Messiah and Son of God. He redeems people who repent and ultimately destroys this great deceiver (1 John 3:8). Jesus went to Calvary to pull God and man into loving embrace, thus opening the temple of the soul again to the Savior who is the light of the world.

Satan's power as "the ruler of the kingdom of the air" must not be minimized, however. His is "the spirit who is now at work in those who are disobedient" (Ephesians 2:2). God's solution is His Messiah, Jesus Christ. He boldly claimed, "the prince of this world has no power over me" (John 14:30 TLB).

The Apostle Paul later framed it: "Although they knew God" they made the decision not to glorify Him as God or to be thankful. Following this destructive choice, the downward spiral

198

continued unabated into the depths of spiritual slavery (Romans 1:21–28).

The Apostle Paul is clear: the claim of lack of knowledge is inadmissible as evidence in the universal court of divine justice, because it is based on a falsehood. Paul explained this to the believers in Rome, saying that while knowing better they made the choice anyway to "exchange the truth of God for a lie." The result was they developed their own religion, making "mortal man" and "birds, and animals, and reptiles" their idols of choice (Romans 1:18–23; 10:18). Even the testimony of man's conscience demonstrates this insurrection. The rebellion was deliberate in Adam and it is intentional in all of Adam's children.

THINK ABOUT IT: The Bible teaches man cannot plead ignorance regarding his rebellion against God. Adam's children do know better (John 6:36; 7:28–29; 8:44; Matthew 23:37; Romans 1:20; 10:18, 21).

Jesus: The Guiltless Savior

8:45 Yet because I tell the truth, you do not believe me! 46 Can any of you prove me guilty of sin? If I am telling the truth, why don't you believe me? 47 He who belongs to God hears what God says. The reason you do not hear is you do not belong to God."

In their deeply rooted stubbornness and corruption they simply were not *willing* to listen to the truth Jesus was teaching because it did not complement the righteousness they had crafted (Matthew 13:34). The problem was not a lack of clarity in Jesus' message. The indictment was, "because I tell the truth, you do not believe me." Jesus' teaching contradicted what they believed so they rejected it on the spot. Yes, they had exchanged the truth of God for a lie.

Then the Lord challenged them with this question: "Can any one of you convict me of a single misleading word, a single sinful act?" (John 8:46 MSG; Isaiah 50:8–9).

Good question, this. It is a bold claim to Deity, because only God can make it with integrity. Indeed! No mere man can, not with a straight face. Instead, "all" of Adam's children "have sinned and come short of the glory of God," and know they have (Romans 3:23).

Jesus' point is transparent. Since none of them could, should this not have been compelling evidence for the truthfulness of His identity and His message—that He was indeed the Son of God and their Messiah?

Jesus faced argument and contention throughout His ministry. But stand if you will with the Lord at His empty tomb where there is no one to dispute Him. The religious establishment, when the soldiers reported Jesus was missing from His tomb, did not go searching for Jesus to check out the news face to face. Their hearts were committed to protecting themselves and the value system by which they lived (Matthew 28:11–15; Luke 16:19–31).

As for the soldiers, the Sanhedrin leaders bribed them to change their testimony. Yes! The religious leaders tried to cover their tracks with lies. It should never be forgotten that religion will lie when its self-interests are at stake, even though the ninth commandment of the Law they were so zealous about upholding forbade bearing false witness. Consider the deception the religious leaders crafted to explain the resurrection: "His disciples came by night, and stole him away while we slept" (Matthew 28:12–13).

THINK ABOUT IT: Can anyone believe the disciples stole the body of Jesus? It would have meant each of the Roman guards risked execution by falling asleep. Then, the disciples whisked Jesus' body away for another secret burial. Then, knowing it was a lie, they created a series of lies about the resurrection sightings. Then, one of the disciples crafted the Great Commission as another lie. Then, Pentecost was only a hoax. Then the disciples dedicated the remainder of their lives, amid great persecution, to telling passionately the story of Jesus' bodily resurrection that they knew was a lie.

In addition, is it credible the disciples cheerfully faced martyrdom for a lie, with no disciple breaking down and spilling the truth to save his life?

Like father like son; they were indeed sons of the devil. Indeed! self-righteous religion will stubbornly reject God in every generation, in all cultures, and in each ethnicity, including American life (Isaiah 48:1–11). This reality shows the depth of human sinfulness (see Jeremiah 29:30–32).

Even after Jesus' resurrection, these elders of Israel continued to say a bold and categorical "No" to God's Son and their Messiah. Their hearts were as hard as Esau's, and Pharaoh's, and Hagar's (Hebrews 12:16; Romans 9:17; Exodus 9:16–17).

All people, not just these rulers, desperately need an honest defense attorney and a fair judge. We have both in the sinless Messiah who always judges knowing the facts and the motives: "It is the Sovereign Lord who helps me. Who is he that will condemn me?" (Isaiah 50:9; Mark 14:56–59).

Yes, wonderful things happen when the Messiah is on our side.

THINK ABOUT IT: Jesus' personal purity transformed the cross from the symbol of pain and shame to the ultimate sign of triumph.

Ah! "Bring forth the royal diadem and crown Him Lord of all."[12]

This analysis of self-righteous religion leaves no room for haughtiness in Jesus' followers, however. Our security against the wiles of the devil is solely to stand humbly under the cross of Jesus and trust completely in His righteousness for our salvation and in His Word as our defense (Romans 3:21–26; Deuteronomy 8:3; Matthew 4:4).

"Where then is boasting? It is excluded" (Romans 3:10, 21–24, 27).

The God of Exodus and Easter

The gospel message says: "You don't live in a mechanistic world ruled by necessity; you don't live in a random world ruled by chance.

You live in a world ruled by the God of Exodus and Easter. He will do things in you that neither you nor your friends would have supposed possible."[13]

Jesus: Rejected with Racial Slurs

8:48 The Jews answered him, "Aren't we right in saying you are a Samaritan and demon-possessed?"
49 "I am not possessed by a demon," said Jesus, "but I honor my Father and you dishonor me. 50 I am not seeking glory for myself; but there is one who seeks it,

and he is the judge. 51 I tell you the truth, if anyone keeps my word, he will never see death."

The blindness and rejection continued, this time with racial slurs. Calling Jesus a Samaritan was like saying He lacked all credibility. Accusing Him of being demon-possessed dishonored Him by labeling Him a bizarre and deranged man. They had to despise Jesus in their hearts to be willing to say these kinds of things to His face. So when they had no facts with which to charge Jesus, they turned to slander to try to defame His good name.

The Lord did not slap back in kind on this occasion either (1 Corinthians 4:12–13). Instead, He calmly denied He was demon-possessed and remained committed to honoring His Father even as they were callously contradicting Him. He also asserted He sought no personal honor, but added His Father does seek honor for Him. No doubt about it, to reject Jesus is also to reject His Father. This is a huge mistake. After all, Jesus sits as the Judge on the bench of the highest tribunal of the universe. This Judge cannot be deceived, because He knows the facts and our motives.

The Devil's Strategy

One is left to wonder how the Lord emotionally handled such bombs bursting in His face. Surely part of Lucifer's strategy was to make the fire so hot Jesus would do something in anger. Push Him until He did any solo act, independent of His Father and the Holy Spirit (1 Peter 2:23).

THINK ABOUT IT: If only Jesus could be made to say, "I don't have to take this!"

How important to realize the devil regularly springs this same trap on God's children.

Part of the reason the bond held between Jesus, His Father, and the Holy Spirit in confrontations like this was Jesus did not expect any better treatment from them (John 2:25). Nor did He seek personal glory. He simply intended to honor His Father. This fact of His motivation was an additional proof He did indeed come from God. If He were seeking His own honor, He surely would have taken matters into His own hands. Instead, He left the judgment of these fierce and determined critics to His Father. Amid the horror of being called a Samaritan, demon-possessed and raving mad, Jesus actually responded with a gracious promise: "I say this with absolute confidence. If you practice what I'm telling you, you'll never have to look death in the face" (John 8:51 MSG; 1 Corinthians 4:12).

Nothing they tried flustered Jesus. If only that bond between Jesus and His Father could be broken. But they never could do it. In fact, it held, even on His cross.

Jesus: Greater than Abraham and the Prophets

8:52 At this the Jews exclaimed, "Now we know you are demon-possessed! Abraham died and so did the prophets, yet you say if anyone keeps your word, he will never taste death. 53 Are you greater than our father Abraham? He died, and so did the prophets. Who do you think you are?"

Since these depraved leaders refused to believe—they made the choice to reject Jesus as their Messiah and God's Son. This included rejecting that Jesus held the power to give eternal life to His followers. They had already slandered Him, now they sought to diminish Him further. This explains the verbal slap, saying He was not greater than Abraham, who had died centuries earlier.

Nor was He greater than the prophets, because they had died too. And so the demeaning retort, "Who do you think you are?" This kind of put-down—"who do you think you are?"—has motivated millions through the centuries to strike back in kind. Add the charges of demon-possession and raving mad and this satanic technique never seems to fail. But it did on Jesus! The Lord remained calm.

> To this you were called, because Christ suffered for you, leaving you an example that you should follow in his steps. He committed no sin, and no deceit was found in his mouth. When they hurled their insults at him, he did not retaliate; when he suffered, he made no threats. Instead, he entrusted himself to him who judges justly. He himself bore our sins in his body on the cross, so that we might die to sins and live for righteousness; by his wounds you have been healed. For you were like sheep going astray," but now you have returned to the Shepherd and Overseer of your souls (2 Peter 2:23–25; Isaiah 53:4–6, 9).

Jesus: Abraham Saw My Day and Rejoiced

8:54 Jesus replied, "If I glorify myself, my glory means nothing. My Father, whom you claim as your God, is the one who glorifies me. 55 Though you do not know him, I know him. If I said I did not, I would be a liar like you, but I do know him and keep his word. 56 Your father Abraham rejoiced at the thought of seeing my day; he saw it and was glad."

Jesus was not trying to honor Himself by making this declaration. Instead, He knew His praise would come from His Father in due time. He proceeded to tell them candidly they were falsely claiming His own Father as their Father; but truthfully, they did not even know Him. Then Jesus affirmed He did indeed know His Father, and had no intention to be a liar like them and deny the truth about His Father. Not only did Jesus know Him, but He also kept "His word."

They had just told Jesus they did not view Him as being any greater than the prophets, and certainly not greater than Abraham. Now the Lord puts the capstone on this exchange by saying some eighteen hundred years before Jesus' birth in Bethlehem, "Your father Abraham rejoiced as he looked forward to my coming. He saw it and was glad" (John 8:56 NLT).

The Greek word translated "rejoiced," suggests a word picture of a rural dad and mom anxiously waiting for a son to come home from war. When the time has arrived, the whole family is looking out the window, with the children actually jumping with excitement, and then running down their lane to welcome their brother. That's rejoicing!

Psalm 24 sets in poetry the grand processional after Jesus' ascension, when His Father and the hosts of heaven welcomed back home God's Son and the second Person of the Trinity. The prophet David foretold what His Father said to Him: "Sit at my right hand until I make your enemies a footstool for your feet" (Psalm 110:1; Acts 2:34; Hebrews 1:13).

THINK ABOUT IT: Abraham "with jubilant faith looked down the corridors of history and saw my day coming. He saw it and cheered" (John 8:56, MSG; see Genesis 22:2–18; John 1:29, 36).

It is worthy of repeating Abraham had met his pre-incarnate Messiah on the same mountain where Jesus the Messiah was physically standing in this confrontation. In fact, it was a warm memory to Jesus.

The Lord said Abraham saw that Messiah was coming, and actually "rejoiced." The King James renders it as Abraham "was glad" (KJV). The Message paraphrase uses the word *cheered*.

The Apostle John is the only gospel writer to record this expressive scene. The pre-incarnate Christ had been on Moriah with Abraham and witnessed his reaction.

Jesus certainly had the right on Moriah as He faced His critics to describe Abraham's emotions that long ago day so historic in salvation history.

THINK ABOUT IT: One can imagine the Lord on Moriah breaking into a big smile as He watched Abraham start dancing, and laughing and crying, all at the same time, when his Messiah spared Isaac's life.

On this occasion, however, some nineteen hundred years later, the Messiah is standing in the same place on Moriah again. But this time things are very different. Rejection is so thick it is like an ugly mudslide picking up speed as it skids down a mountain, leaving nothing but pain of heart and destruction of soul in its wake. Nobody is praising God with crying and laughing and dancing in this setting with Jesus on Moriah.

Several themes are at play as these two Messianic stories blend:

- The angel of the Lord miraculously spared Isaac's life.

- A spin-off meaning of this act was that Judaism never adopted the ancient hideous practice of child sacrifices. God nipped that in the bud at Moriah. To this day, the gift of a child is a highly prized treasure in Judaism. This principle also speaks to the modern evil of abortion on demand.

- Abraham met the Lord as Jehovah-Jireh, the God who provides. "And to this day it is said, 'On the mountain of the Lord it will be provided'" (Genesis 22:14).

- The occasion also marked a red letter prophecy: "My son, God himself will provide the lamb" (Genesis 22:8). The ram caught in the thicket was the immediate answer, so that Abraham sacrificed that ram. The ultimate meaning of Abraham's prophecy was fulfilled some eighteen hundred years later. People offered tens of thousands of lambs down the long road of history from Abraham to Christ. But God offered only one lamb. John the Baptist described Him as "the Lamb of God who takes away the sin of the world" (John 1:29, 36). Jesus of Nazareth is His name. "[Abraham] knew I was coming," Jesus said, "and was glad" (John 8:56, TLB; see Genesis 22:1–18).

- God spared Isaac with a divine intervention, but the heavenly Father "did not spare his own Son, but gave him up for us all" (Romans 8:32).

Jesus: The "I Am"

8:57 "You are not yet fifty years old," the Jews said to him, "and you have seen Abraham!"
58 "I tell you the truth," Jesus answered, "before Abraham was born, I am!"

John wrote his gospel to convince his readers Jesus is the Son of God. Part of John's plan to achieve this was to tell the stories of people who refused to accept Jesus' Deity; his readers could then judge for themselves their God-rejecting words and motivations. A diamond always sparkles brightest on a backdrop of black velvet!

Jesus answered these unbelieving critics truthfully, speaking out of the context of His claim to be the Son of God. He asserted He was:

God's equal, and
Jehovah God (the I AM) of the Old Testament, and
The eternal God who lives in the present sphere of "is," with no past and no future, and
The author of the New Covenant.

Instead of seeing Jesus as the light of the world, this was cause for another put-down: "You are not yet fifty years old" and here you are saying "you have seen Abraham!" But not only did Jesus see Abraham some 1,800 years earlier, Abraham actually met his Messiah several times, and it made the great patriarch jubilant. Consider these two occurrences:

"The Lord [*Jehovah, the I AM*] appeared to Abraham near the great trees of Mamre...Abraham looked up and saw three men standing nearby. When he saw them, he hurried from the entrance of his tent to meet them and bowed low to the ground. Then the Lord said, 'Shall I hide from Abraham what I am about to do?'" (Genesis 18:1–2, 17).

"The angel of the Lord called to Abraham from heaven a second time and said, 'I swear by myself, declares the Lord [*Jehovah, the I AM*], because you have done this and have not withheld your son, your only son, I will surely bless you...and through your offspring all nations on earth will be blessed, because you have obeyed me'" (Genesis 22:15–18; see also Galatians 3:16).

It is very reasonable Abraham's eyes poured out big tears when his Messiah spoke out of heaven and stopped Isaac's sure death. It was while the hot tears were still in Abraham's eyes that he was rewarded with the promise his seed (the Messiah) would bless "all nations" (Galatians 3:16–19; see also Genesis 12:2–7; 15:18–20; 17:4–8).

This understanding of Jesus as the great I AM was also boldly expressed some three hundred years later in the revelation of God to Moses at the burning bush. The voice Moses heard coming from the bush was his Messiah's (Exodus 3:6, 14; John 8:58; Mark 8:26–27; Acts 7:31–32):

> When the Lord saw [Moses] had gone over to look, God called to him from within the bush, "Moses! Moses...! I am sending you to Pharaoh to bring my people the Israelites out of Egypt."
> Moses said to God, "Suppose I go to the Israelites and say to them, The God of your fathers has sent me to you, and they ask me, What is his name? Then what shall I tell them?"
> 14 God said to Moses, "I AM WHO I AM. This is what you are to say to the Israelites: I AM has sent me to you" (Exodus 3:4, 10, 13, 14).

Jesus Escapes Premature Death

8:59 At this, they picked up stones to stone him, but Jesus hid himself, slipping away from the temple grounds.

Listening to Jesus through the lens of their own righteousness, these elders alleged Jesus was speaking blasphemy and wanted to stone Him on the spot. They understood clearly Jesus was claiming to be the equal of the Old Testament Jehovah, the I AM, and this, their strict monotheism would not allow. But Jesus, again controlling the timing, escaped their grasp, and thwarted premature death.

Yes, Jesus was headed to Calvary, but on His divine timeline, not theirs. His hour was calibrated to the time of the Passover sacrifice. On the Hill called Golgotha, He would triumph over death.

"One Got Out!"

One sleepy Sunday afternoon when my son was five-years-old, we drove together past a cemetery.

Noticing a large pile of dirt beside a newly excavated grave, he pointed and said: "Look, Dad, one got out!"

I laughed, but now, every time I pass a graveyard, I'm reminded of the One who did indeed get out![14]

The revelation of Jesus as the Light of the world, portrayed against this backdrop of dark sinfulness, will continue in Chapter 9 with the story of a very winsome man who was born blind. The Apostle John shows the blind man's miracle created a set of circumstances that motivated the Pharisees to illustrate, albeit unintentionally, the willful and wrathful hardness of heart Jesus encountered in Chapters 8 and 9. John also shows how the man stood up for Jesus at great risk to himself.

Yes, the gospel always advances amid persecution.

John Chapter 9

JESUS
THE LIGHT OF THE WORLD

The Man Born Blind

Chapter 9 continues Jesus' very eventful few days of ministry at the Feast of Tabernacles and further portrays Jesus as the Light of the world. The Apostle John illustrates this with the story of another of Jesus' creative miracles—healing a man born blind. It is the sixth of the seven miracles recorded by John. The drama plays out against the backdrop of some of the fiercest opposition Jesus faced in His ministry and illustrates the wicked hardness of heart Jesus described in Chapter 8.

What Jesus Saw On a Laid-Back Day

9:1 As he went along, he saw a man blind from birth. 2 His disciples asked him, "Rabbi, who sinned, this man or his parents, that he was born blind?"

The phrase, "went along," usually identifies such concepts as "casually and routinely proceeding;" not "rocking the boat." It can suggest a normal day when not much was happening. But a laid-back day quickly was anything but calm when Jesus' eyes fixed on "a man blind from birth."

THINK ABOUT IT: Have you ever been enjoying a relaxed, uneventful day that all of a sudden came alive with unexpected news—information that changed everything?

Has Jesus ever, almost out of nowhere (or so it seemed), stepped into your world?

Jesus brightened the world of a woman caught in the act of adultery in Chapter 8, giving her a new life. In Chapter 9, He opened the eyes of a man born blind. Ah, the power of the Light of the world. Jesus said His Father was always working, and He was too (John 5:17). Hence, even casual days have plenty of need for Jesus' miracle power. Jesus, the Son of Man, saw clearly things others did not see at all. How many people with 20/20 vision had walked by this blind beggar and never looked at him except with casual glances. Others no doubt saw him, but had no perception how much the man truly wanted the help no one could give him.

THINK ABOUT IT: Helen Keller said, "The only thing worse than being blind is having sight but no vision."

On this routine day, Jesus saw the blind man clearly; He truly saw the man. This blind man had never looked at his mother's face, or the beauty of a sunrise, or the grandeur of a rainbow, or the food he ate, or the clothes he wore. He lived in a world of black. He had never been awed by the beauty of snow flakes, or the majesty of the ocean, or the wonder of a snow capped mountain. But for as long as he could remember he had yearned for his eyesight. It is highly probable his dad had taught him Isaiah's prophecies that when Messiah came, He would open the eyes of the blind (Isaiah 29:18; 35:5; 42:7; 61:1).

Jesus perceived this man would quickly become a bold disciple who would stand up fearlessly to the opposition of the religious establishment. Because Jesus "saw" him, the light was about to shine in this unfortunate man's darkness (John 1:5). He was on the cusp of a miracle which would open up a whole new world for him of both sunlight and *Son*light. This *Son*light has also liberated millions in the Lord's church from that time forward;

many of them people who have lived in the darkness of some of the worst guilt to be imagined.

Reincarnation

Someone must be responsible for such a cursed misfortune as an infant born without sight, or so the reasoning went. Even the Lord's disciples thought it, and so, their question: "Rabbi, who sinned—this man or his parents—to cause him to be born blind?" (John 9:2–3 cjb).

This episode raises the question of reincarnation, also identified by the term *transmigration of souls*. How could the disciples have thought "this man" who was born blind, might have sinned prior to his birth, without belief in some form of reincarnation?

While reincarnation takes on a variety of forms, the central idea is when a person dies his soul migrates to a new body and returns in the next life as another person. His new state is routinely viewed as good or bad based on the prior life he has lived. Many reincarnationists also believe a person can be reborn as an animal or a plant. A child being born blind would be viewed as heavy punishment for wrongs done in a prior life. Reincarnation is predominantly a Hindu and Buddhist tenet.

One can only imagine the lifetime of guilt for a child with the birth defect of blindness, if the child is taught he is being punished for his sins in a prior life. The condemnation would also spill over into the low self-estimate the child would carry with him for life.

THINK ABOUT IT: Reincarnation always sets blame while offering no solution to cure the guilt. The gospel establishes responsibility too but also shows how believing Jesus is the Son of God, the one whom God has sent, combined with heartfelt repentance provides the cure.

The cursedness of blame would be even more compounded for a dad and mom who believe their sins in a prior life predetermined their child would live a lifetime of blindness. The guilt associated with reincarnation is astronomical.

Freedom from False Guilt

9:3 "Neither this man nor his parents sinned," said Jesus, "but this happened so that the work of God might be displayed in his life."

What wonderful news! What liberation from guilt! Jesus made no allowance here for the prior life of a soul; therefore, any thought is erased punishment for sins in a prior life can be laid to the account of a new born baby.

With Jesus, neither the sins of this man nor of his parents explained his visual deformity. "You're asking the wrong question," Jesus said. "You're looking for someone to blame. There is no such cause-effect here. Look instead for what God can do" (John 9:3–4 MSG).

This statement from our Lord is the death knell of reincarnation. The notion of the transmigration of souls has never been an orthodox Christian doctrine. Jesus' crucifixion and resurrection establishes this reality regarding reincarnation. Jesus cures guilt and gives His followers eternal life with Him in heaven. We must conclude the gospel does not promise never-ending, eternal transmigration of souls.

THINK ABOUT IT: When bad things happen, it is far better to view them as opportunities for the grace of God to redeem the situation, thereby manifesting the glory of God.

Many forms of blindness exist, such as attitudes that wipe out achievement in life. Jesus as the Light of the world is the great healer of all forms of blindness, including physical and attitudinal blindness.

Inherited Consequences

While the Bible does not teach reincarnation, it certainly does affirm parents' choices can influence for good or ill the lives of their children. The Prophet Jeremiah recorded a proverb many believed: "Parents ate the green apples; their children got the stomach ache." The NIV expresses the fruit this verse identifies as "sour grapes" (Jeremiah 31:29). The Message renders it as "green apples." Either kind of fruit makes the point. Jeremiah added the corrective: "No, each person will pay for his own sin. You eat green apples; you're the one who gets sick" (Jeremiah 31:29–30 MSG).

While Jeremiah was certainly correct, parents can pass on to their children the consequences of their parental choices. When parents sow to the wind, their children regularly reap the whirlwind (Hosea 8:7). To name a few, this dynamic is seen in the tragic births of AIDS babies, and alcoholic parents often rear children with marked tendencies toward alcoholism. The sins of nations, including uncontrolled spending habits, can impact negatively the lifestyle of the next generations. The effect of wars can be extended even to generations born long after the peace treaties are signed. Crimes committed by fathers and the prison sentences that follow can have a powerfully negative effect on their children and even children yet to be born.

But none of these examples suggest reincarnation.

How much better for parents to love the Lord and live by His example and teachings! Their children and grandchildren can then be the beneficiaries of the lavish love of God.

Thank God, the generational curses of the sins of fathers on their children can be overcome. The sons of Korah are a prime example of doing it successfully (Numbers 16:1–50; 21:11). The line of Korah did not die out after Korah's rebellion against Moses (Numbers 26:11). Instead, his descendants went on to become accomplished musicians, who wrote some of the most beloved Psalms in the Psalter (see Psalms 42, 44–49, 84–85, 87–88). In fact, about 3,000 years after Korah's rebellion, the Psalms of the sons of Korah greatly influenced Martin Luther, the father of the Protestant Reformation. Inspired by Psalm 46 (a psalm of the sons of Korah), Luther wrote "A Mighty Fortress Is Our God." It quickly became the "national anthem" of the Protestant Reformation.

Night Is Coming

9:4 As long as it is day, we must do the work of him who sent me. Night is coming, when no one can work. 5 While I am in the world, I am the light of the world."

This claim as the *Son*light from God does not imply Jesus ceased to be the Light of the world after He went back to His Father. Instead, Jesus knew He did not have much longer on earth, and He wanted to redeem the time He had left by radiating His Father's light (Ephesians 5:16; Colossians 4:5). On this Sabbath day in Jerusalem at the Feast of Tabernacles, Jesus felt a strong sense of urgency. "We must quickly carry out the tasks assigned us by the one who sent us," He said. "The night is coming, and then no one can work" (John 9:4 NLT). Adding to the urgency, the Lord repeated, "While I am in the world, I am the light of the world" (John 9:5; see John 8:12).

THINK ABOUT IT: What better way for Jesus to demonstrate Himself as the Light of the world than to give sight to a poor man born blind (Isaiah 29:18; 35:5; 42:7).

After making this claim, Jesus performed a miracle that showed why He carries the title. It also infuriated the Pharisees. Jesus surely reaped their wrath for turning the light on, giving the man his eyesight.

The Mud

9:6 Having said this, he spit on the ground, made some mud with the saliva, and put it on the man's eyes. 7 "Go," he told him, "wash in the Pool of Siloam" (this word means sent). So the man went and washed, and came home seeing.

At the Pool of Bethesda Jesus merely spoke the word, "Get up! Pick up your mat and walk" (John 5:8). This time Jesus stooped down and used His saliva to make mud. It was another *logos* moment; the man who was the authoritative Word from heaven was on the scene. The miracle was tied to obeying a simple order: "Go wash in the Pool of Siloam." As for the man, he surely felt the command communicated highly unusual authority.

To these Pharisees it was illegal work on the Sabbath.

Students of the Scriptures have always wondered about the Lord's intent here. The man at the pool had not walked in thirty-eight years—but he could remember what it was like to walk. This man had been blind from birth and had never seen the noon day sun. Jesus made mud and put it on his eyes. Why mud?

Perhaps the mud symbolized Eden when God made Adam from the dust of the ground, breathed into his nostrils the breath of life, and he became a living soul (Genesis 2:7). John has already said in this book, "All things were made by [Jesus], and without him was not anything made that was made" (John 1:3). Perhaps the mud also symbolized his dark and painful past, and washing it away communicated the beginning of his new life.

This man could have been born without the muscles, nerves, and blood vessels necessary for sight, and possibly without eyeballs in their sockets. Whatever his condition, Jesus created what was missing in his eyes in an instant with His spoken word.

So far in this study, four of the six miracles studied have been creative: turning water into wine, the man at the Pool of Bethesda, feeding the 5,000, and now the man born blind.

Can anyone doubt Jesus' compassion for every hungry, blind, lame and hurting person? His willingness to help is manifest in so many ways, and certainly in the creative power of His spoken word. Yes, Jesus is the *logos*, the Word.

THINK ABOUT IT: How can people of reasonable mind look at Jesus' miracles without giving special attention to John's statement: "Through him all things were made; without him nothing was made that has been made" (John 1:3; Isaiah 44:24; 45:5).

It is also possible the Lord knew making the mud with His spittle would so anger the Jews it would motivate them to reveal the condition of their hearts. They would surely regard mixing a clay paste to go on the man's eyes as unauthorized labor, making Jesus a clear-cut lawbreaker in their minds. As for Jesus, the result of drawing out their wrath would be another gracious opportunity for them to see the depth of their sin and repent, accepting Jesus the Messiah as the Son of God and Lord of the Sabbath (Matthew 12:8; Luke 6:5).

Archeology Confirms the Bible

Workers were digging to repair a sewer pipe in Jerusalem in 2004, and discovered quite by accident the Biblical Pool of Siloam. The sewer pipe had been laid just a few feet above the ruins. The excavations that followed uncovered the four sides of three tiers of steps that went downward into the pool. The excavators also established the water for the pool came from the Gihon Spring. The Pool of Siloam, close as it was to the temple, was most probably used for purification washing rites for pilgrims on their way into the temple. Ancient pottery and coins were also found in the area dated from the time of Christ, further establishing the pool in the time frame of Jesus healing the man born blind.

"There can be no doubt," said William F. Albright, one of the world's most respected archeologists, "that archeology has confirmed the substantial historicity of Old Testament tradition."

Nelson Gluech adds, "It may be stated categorically that no archeological discovery has ever controverted a Biblical reference."[1]

Pure Grace in Action;
Healed by a Stranger

Obviously the healed man did not see Jesus after his miracle. Instead, the man went home without viewing the appearance and features of the kind and gracious stranger who had given him his eyesight. He did, however, remember Jesus' name and the sound of His voice. A dominant trait of blind people is the ability to remember voices.

As he walked home everything he observed was new and fresh; the exhilaration of it all must have pushed him to happy tears, and maybe even to skip, jump and dance. His was joy unspeakable (1 Peter 1:8). One can easily imagine the tearful excitement of his mother and the unbridled happiness of his dad. Their son was actually seeing them for the first time in his life, and with perfect vision.

That called for celebration!

The joy was short lived, however. The healed man was quickly pulled into the middle of the Pharisees anger toward Jesus, whom they despised. The man turned out to be Jesus' sole defender.

Through the centuries of the church, every believer in Jesus Christ has been called on in some setting to defend the Lord with his testimony. Many have paid for their witness with their lives. Their number surely reaches into the millions, with the exact count known only to God.

A Man with a Testimony

9:8 His neighbors and those who had formerly seen him begging asked, "Isn't this the same man who used to sit and beg?"
9 Some claimed that he was. Others said, "No, he only looks like him."
But he himself insisted, "I am the man."
10 "How then were your eyes opened?" they demanded.

The wonder of it all quickly spread to his fellow citizens. The conversations went the whole gamut of disbelief: some said he was indeed the person, others said he only looked like him. This man's eyes had opened for the first time, sparkling with life. It was enough to give him a different look even to his closest friends.

As for the man, "He kept saying, 'I am the one'" (John 9:9–10 NASB).

"How then were your eyes opened?" came the blunt demand.

9:11 He replied, "The man they call Jesus made some mud and put it on my eyes. He told me to go to Siloam and wash. So I went and washed, and then I could see."

Two or three minutes with Jesus was enough; the blind man's life was changed forever in a marvelous act of God. The man no doubt had longed for Messiah to come and give him his eyesight, but had no real sense of Jesus' identity when the Lord came to him (Isaiah 35:5; 42:7). The man surely would have fallen on his knees and begged Jesus for his eyesight if he had known Jesus' identity. But it was not necessary; the Lord already knew his heart, and that was enough. This miracle was all grace—the lavish, God-kind of mercy that always flows from the character of God (Ephesians 1:8; 1 John 3:1).

It is nothing short of amazing how a few seconds with Jesus, the Son of God, can refocus a person's entire life.

Blind Man after Surgery Learns to See

In a book titled, *An Anthropologist on Mars*, neurologist Oliver Sacks tells about Virgil, a man who had been blind from early childhood. When he was 50, Virgil underwent surgery and was given the gift of sight. But as he and Dr. Sacks found out, having the physical capacity for sight is not the same as seeing.

Virgil's first experiences with sight were confusing. He was able to make out colors and movements, but arranging them into a coherent picture was more difficult. Over time he learned to identify various objects, but his habits and behaviors were still those of a blind man.

Dr. Sacks asserts, "One must die as a blind person to be born again as a seeing person. It is the interim, the limbo—that is so terrible."[2]

We certainly rejoice when a surgeon helps a person gain his eyesight, even if the healing process is long and arduous. When Jesus gave this man his vision, however, he instantaneously received both the physical capacity for sight and the ability to use it. It was a gift of perfect vision, including the capability to handle it normally. He did not need time for the muscles of his eyes to learn to operate correctly. Nor did his eyes need to adjust to the light and learn to see. His vision opened up in the seconds of washing the mud off his eyes. This man's walk home had been possible because of memorization of the number of steps and turns; this time he is seeing brand new landmarks for the first time. Wow! (See Luke 18:35–43 for another account of Jesus healing a blind man near Jericho, giving him instantaneous 20/20 vision.)

Where Do You Focus—
The Thimble-Full of Work or the
Ocean of Wonder?

The blind man's testimony is classic, expressed in a few simple and child-like words. "The man they call Jesus" is the first account he gave of the Lord (vs. 11). This description is certainly not a confession of Jesus as the Son of God and Messiah, but it was all he knew, and it was a start.

> 9:12 "Where is this man?" they asked him.
> "I don't know," he said.
> 13 They brought to the Pharisees the man who had been blind.
> 14 Now the day on which Jesus had made the mud and opened the man's eyes was a Sabbath. 15 Therefore the Pharisees also asked him how he had received his sight. "He put mud on my eyes," the man replied, "and I washed, and now I see."
> 16 Some of the Pharisees said, "This man is not from God, for he does not keep the Sabbath." But others asked, "How can a sinner do such miraculous signs?" So they were divided.

Some of the Pharisees immediately picked up on the thimble-full of work it took to make the "mud" on the Sabbath and totally missed the ocean of wonder in the miracle itself (Matthew 23:24). Hence, their retort: "This fellow, Jesus, is not from God because he is working on the Sabbath" (John 9:16 TLB). Others, however, seemed to soften asking, "How could an ordinary sinner do such miracles?" (9:16 TLB).

9:17 Finally they turned again to the blind man, "What have you to say about him? It was your eyes he opened." The man replied, "He is a prophet."

The unbelief of these Jews was blatantly obvious, and the tone with which they spoke to the man communicated he had better be careful how he answered. As for the man, the warning came too late. He had already moved to the next step of faith and was not reluctant to say it: "[Jesus] is a prophet." He was making rapid progress as a disciple!

9:18 The Jews still did not believe he had been blind and had received his sight until they sent for the man's parents. 19 "Is this your son?" they asked. "Is this the one you say was born blind? How is it now he can see?"

This almost humorous unbelief of the Jews was coming from people who had set themselves up as the experts on all things spiritual and godly. But it is obvious they were very nonplussed and caught in a situation not in their control. In their disbelief, as they grasped for straws to get themselves out of their embarrassing circumstances, they called for the man's parents to come and enter into the discussion. These leaders clearly refused to believe the testimony of his father and mother.

The Limits of Testimony

The Jews' next question, addressed to the parents in the form of a curt demand, revealed their hearts: "Why can he see now?" (John 9:19 GW). They were looking for a way to reject the miracle and had no intention to believe in Jesus.

The compelling dynamic working here illustrates the principle in Chapter 8:44–56. The Pharisees *chose* not to believe Jesus. In this case, they refused to accept the blind man's testimony. This meant they would not believe his parents. Neither would they believe Israel's own prophets, or Jesus, or His heavenly Father (see Jeremiah 29:30–32; Matthew 23:37; John 3:11–12; 6:36; 7:28–29; 8:44).

The ministry of Jesus reveals, therefore, the limits of testimony (Luke 10:13–15). These Pharisees had made the choice to develop and then live out their own plan of salvation, which they had anchored in the Law of Moses as they interpreted it. Their blind commitment to "their own way" was so strong no evidence would change their minds, including the presence of their Messiah (Isaiah 53:6; Romans 1:21–25). Jesus said as much regarding the story of Lazarus and the rich man. There is a level of hardness so powerful, "If they do not listen to Moses and the Prophets, they will not be convinced even if someone rises from the dead" (Luke 16:31).

Finding Humor in Tragedy

The matter was indeed serious; yet, it is wrapped in humor. One can easily believe the Lord, though absent from the action, knew what was going on and actually smiled at their dilemma.

THINK ABOUT IT: Jesus had scrambled their world. Amid its seriousness, perhaps He even chuckled about it.

Did not the Psalmist write, "He who sits in the heavens shall laugh. The Lord shall hold them in derision" (Psalm 2:4 NKJV; see 1 Kings 18:27 for another example of the humor of God).

9:20 "We know he is our son," the parents answered, "and we know he was born blind. 21 But how he can see now, or who opened his eyes, we don't know. Ask him. He is of age; he will speak for himself."
22 His parents said this because they were afraid of the Jews, for already the Jews had decided anyone who acknowledged Jesus was the Christ would be put out of the synagogue. 23 That was why his parents said, "He is of age; ask him."

His parents did not see anything humorous in the situation. They were ruled by fear. If they confessed Jesus as their Messiah, excommunication awaited them and they knew it. So they bounced the answer to the question back to their son.

> "We know he is our son, and we know he was born blind. But we don't know how he came to see—haven't a clue about who opened his eyes. Why don't you ask him? He's a grown man and can speak for himself" (John 9:20–22 MSG).

Their statement shows a glaring lack of boldness, and illustrates how Jesus' mighty works can divide families (Luke 12:51–53). The parents were not at all courageous witnesses for Jesus, but their son certainly was.

THINK ABOUT IT: What does this story say to you about this mom and dad's parenting skills?

The story also gives a clue as to the young man's age. A man was considered an adult in Jewish culture at age thirty. This means the man had lived at least for thirty years in the blackness that robbed him of the beauty of any shades of light or color.

The Proof: I Was Blind; Now I See

9:24 A second time they summoned the man who had been blind. "Give glory to God," they said. "We know this man is a sinner."
25 He replied, "Whether he is a sinner or not, I don't know. One thing I do know. I was blind but now I see!"

Talk about trying to intimidate the witness! "Give credit to God. We know this man is an impostor" (John 9:24 MSG). They were actually trying to tell him how to answer, but it did not work. They were holding to a false doctrine, but Jesus had given this man a testimony, and the testimony trumped the doctrine of the Pharisees. If his parents were frightened at the threat of excommunication, their son was not.

The more the story unfolds, the more admiration rises for the man. No, Jesus was not physically present to defend Himself while all this took place, but the man was doing a creditable job (see Isaiah 62:1).

THINK ABOUT IT: It is worthy of repeating: modern religious pluralists assert no religion is the sole source of truth, thereby possessing singular access to God. But to be consistent, pluralists would have been compelled to reject the need for the birth of Christian faith because, in the thinking of religious pluralism, Judaism already held a "valid" path to God.

> In this flawed reasoning, it logically follows Jesus'
> incarnation, crucifixion, resurrection, ascension and the
> birth of the church were unnecessary, turning the Son of
> God into a fool for going to Calvary (1 Corinthians 1:23).

Jesus had the compassion and the power to help the adulterous woman and the man born blind, when no one else could (Luke 4:18). He died on the cross as the final sacrifice to save all who repent. The message of Jesus Christ, therefore, has become the Light of the world and an international force, precisely because Jesus could and did give His life to light up the lives of helpless people. He continues in the 21st century to serve millions more like them. In doing so, the Holy Spirit makes Jesus known to the world (Isaiah 35:5).

Jesus Knows How Sharp Insults Feel

9:26 Then they asked him, "What did he do to you? How did he open your eyes?"
27 He answered, "I have told you already and you did not listen. Why do you want to hear it again? Do you want to become his disciples, too?"
28 Then they hurled insults at him and said, "You are this fellow's disciple! We are disciples of Moses! 29 We know God spoke to Moses, but as for this fellow, we don't even know where he comes from."

This exchange shows the depth of the opposition Jesus faced and expresses what these leaders were saying behind Jesus' back. The more Jesus did good deeds for people, the more loathsome and vile He became in their eyes. This conversation points out how evil self-righteousness can become in its willful unbelief.

Wooden Didn't Trash Knight

John Wooden, former basketball coach at UCLA, seldom left his seat on the Bruins bench during a UCLA game. "I tried to teach players if they lose their temper or get out of control, they will get beat," he says. "Modeling was better than words. I liked the rule we used to have that a coach couldn't leave the bench. I'm sorry they did away with it."

Wooden set records that may never be broken in college basketball. From 1948 to 1975, he had a win-loss record of 885-203—a phenomenal career winning percentage of .813. He had an 88-game winning streak at UCLA. As head coach, he won ten NCAA national championships in a twelve-year period—seven in a row—an unprecedented feat. Players such as Kareem Abdul-Jabbar, Bill Walton, and Walt Hazzard played under him.

Pressed in an interview to be critical of former Indiana University coach Bobby Knight, Wooden would only say, "I think Bob Knight is an outstanding teacher of the game of basketball, but I don't approve of his methods. But I'm not a judge, and I'm not judging Bob Knight. There is so much bad in the best of us and so much good in the worst of us, it hardly behooves me to talk about the rest of us."[3]

If these Pharisees had only understood this principle which guided Coach Wooden's life, they would have treated this highly blessed man very differently. But they were not willing to rejoice with a young man to whom Jesus had given his sight after at least thirty years of total darkness.

They could not deny the miracle happened, but they could deny what it meant. So they tried to tell the man how to answer their questions.

When he would not let them control his answers, they turned to insults. The phrase translated from the Greek in John 9:28 as "hurled insults," communicates the idea of vilifying and reviling. Their words were like spears, cutting yells, piercing words, with the goal to intimidate with the ugliest insults. They would not celebrate the man's miracle because that would have meant acknowledging Jesus. Instead of revering their Messiah, their choice was to silence and eliminate the man's testimony, because he was grateful for Jesus' help and willing to say so. The only weapon they had left was their words, and these Pharisees were very experienced at put-downs. When everything else failed, their strategy was to use the ugliest insults possible.

They accused the man of being "this fellow's disciple,"—another sharp and disrespectful put-down of Jesus. They also claimed to be Moses' disciples. The central problem with the claim is Moses foretold Messiah's coming and would have been the first to celebrate Jesus and His miracles. In fact, Moses did celebrate Jesus at the Transfiguration (Matthew 17:1–5). This fact makes their statement a lie: "We know God spoke to Moses…," because they were rejecting right before their eyes the most important prophecy Moses ever gave (Deuteronomy 18:15; Isaiah 29:13; Matthew 15:8; Mark 7:6).

THINK ABOUT IT: Their system of righteousness celebrated Moses as having been sent by God, but then referred to their Messiah whom Moses foretold as merely "this fellow."

Choices Have Consequences

These Pharisees failed test after test with God by persistently and consistently choosing to reject God's Son, committing the ultimate evil. They did it to the point God turned them over to the consequences of their choices (Matthew 23:37; John 6:29; 8:24). The Apostle Paul's sad description fitted them:

Since they didn't bother to acknowledge God, God quit bothering them and let them run loose. And it's not as if they don't know better. They know perfectly well they're spitting in God's face. And they don't care—worse, they hand out prizes to those who do the worst things best! (Romans 1:28, 32 MSG).

In their rejection of Jesus they actually yelled at the healed man (9:27 GW) who "[would] not keep silent" (Isaiah 62:1).

THINK ABOUT IT: Why would anyone vilify Jesus for performing such a God-revealing and awesome act of mercy? And why vilify the man for feeling grateful?

These leaders refused to admit only God could have given the man his sight, all the while trying to silence the man's testimony by shouting at him with razor-sharp put-downs. Moses was indeed the vessel God used to bring water out of a rock and bread out of heaven, but the Messiah who gave sight to the blind man *was* the Rock, the Bread, the Water, and the Light of the world. They loved Moses (as they interpreted him), but despised their Messiah (Isaiah 53:3; John 6:35, 48; John 8:12–13; 9:5).

Standing Your Ground for Jesus

9:30 The man answered, "Now that is remarkable! You don't know where he comes from, yet he opened my eyes. 31 We know God does not listen to sinners. He listens to the godly man who does his will. 32 Nobody has ever heard of opening the eyes of a man born blind. 33 If this man were not from God, he could do nothing."

The healed man firmly stood up to them and refused to be intimidated by the put-downs, the insults and the yelling. "Why, that's very strange!" he came right back at them. "He can heal blind men, and yet you don't know anything about him!" (John 9:30–31 TLB; Isaiah 35:5).

The healed man spoke a telling indictment and it touched a tender nerve. These Pharisees had set themselves up as the shepherds of the flock of God, yet they were unwilling to act on the facts and honor Jesus as the Son of God.

> "It's well known God isn't at the beck and call of sinners, but listens carefully to anyone who lives in reverence and does his will. That someone opened the eyes of a man born blind has never been heard of—ever. If this man didn't come from God, he wouldn't be able to do anything" (John 9:31–32 MSG; Isaiah 56:11).

The man's understanding was correct in that the Old Testament does not record a miracle of a man being healed who was blind from birth. No one in Israel at the time of this story could say he had ever heard of such a thing either. Some truly great miracles occurred in the Old Covenant, but not on this scale. This is the *logos* in classic form. With this miracle, the Messiah, the Word from heaven who spoke with the authority of God, was in a league all by himself.

The man lacked accuracy, however, in his understanding that God does not hear the prayer of sinners. He certainly does when they call to Him in repentance and cry for mercy. The One with whom we have to do even sends His rain on the just and the unjust (Matthew 5:45; Hebrews 4:13 KJV). In fact, forgiveness is the crown jewel of the gospel. When people repent with Godly sorrow, God always responds with a full pardon—always. Based on his miracle this man drew the conclusion the Pharisees should have easily made: "If this man were not from God, he couldn't do a thing!" (John 9:33 CJB).

When You Are Thrown in the Street for Your Testimony

9:34 To this they replied, "You were steeped in sin at birth; how dare you lecture us!" And they threw him out.

Their words were painfully sharp, but the man was buoyed in His faith because of his glorious experience with Jesus. Meeting Jesus is always life-changing and highly motivating. It routinely emboldens enough to face excommunication and even martyrdom (Acts 4:13).

THINK ABOUT IT: Without question, Jesus selected the right man for the miracle. But then Jesus always finds His man!

How many followers of Jesus through the centuries have taken courage from this man's bold witness!

Do you stand up for and defend the Lord who "redeemed you" and "called you by name?" (Isaiah 43:1–3).

The Pharisees cutting statement, "You were steeped in sin at birth," might have been a reference to transmigration of souls and calculated to heap tons of guilt. When a spiritual authority figure in a person's life bluntly says, you were born blind because of your many sins in your past life, or your parent's sins, it routinely is devastating. But the knife-sharp words did not have the usual effect, because Jesus had given the man a new life with new hope—he had his eyesight and his testimony to go with it. In addition, if they were doing reincarnation thinking, Jesus showed the man was not destined to a lifetime of blindness. Instead, Jesus gave him a creative miracle of sight.

It is hard to win an argument with a man who knows Jesus gave him his sight when he had never seen even the face of his mother.

The man was already changing his loyalty from the Pharisees and their religious system and vesting his trust in Jesus. This very thing is what the Pharisees greatly feared. If Jesus continued to do these mighty works, they would lose control, including their positions of influence. So much in the world's system is based on envy and the desire to rule.

THINK ABOUT IT: The growing rage of the Pharisees meant the cross kept getting nearer.
The Father's plan was working admirably.

Instead of turning to Jesus in humble repentance, the Pharisees set out to silence Jesus at any cost before His message and healing power could silence them. As for Jesus He knew He was the Lamb of God who would take away the sin of the world. The nature of the conflict was becoming ever clearer as the cross came closer and closer.

Their Worst Putdown

"You're nothing but dirt," they retorted to the man. "How dare you take that tone with us?" (John 9:34 MSG). The expression was intended as derision at its worst. They saw no value in the man and treated him like dirt.

If these Pharisees ever knew from the story of creation what God can do with a handful of dirt, they had forgotten it. The result was they expelled the man from the synagogue and threw him into the street. But Jesus saw worth in the man and gave him a miracle. The man would never forget the mud in Jesus' hand he had washed off his eyes at the pool. To the man, the disappearance of the mud into the pool surely meant the washing away of his old life. He was a new man with a new life before him. He surely lived the remainder of his life in the glow of that miracle.

He had his eyesight. The sunshine was very bright!

Even more blessed, his spiritual eyes had opened. He could see the far brighter *Son*shine—the Light of the world. Hence, he boldly stood up to the Pharisees, something he never would have done while he was blind.

THINK ABOUT IT: Meeting Jesus changes our lives forever, including our self-confidence.

"Lord, I Believe"

9:35 Jesus heard they had thrown him out, and when he found him, he said, "Do you believe in the Son of Man?" 36 "Who is he, sir?" the man asked. "Tell me so that I may believe in him." 37 Jesus said, "You have now seen him; in fact, he is the one speaking with you." 38 Then the man said, "Lord, I believe," and he worshiped him.

The Apostle John wrote his book to portray Jesus as the Son of God. At the same time, he recorded events showing Jesus as the Son of Man. This is another example of the latter. Jesus gained information from people. The Messiah "*heard* they had thrown him out." Obviously, someone told Jesus the man had been excommunicated. The statement, "when he found him" indicates the Lord actually searched for the man until He located him. How comforting that Jesus searches us out.

Jesus was also guided by His Father. He practiced a lifestyle of hearing what His Father was saying and saying it, and seeing what His Father was doing, and repeating it (John 5:19–20).

He searched me out—and you too, dear reader!

This character trait makes Jesus stand out as the Good Shepherd and Evangelist sent from God. The Trinity of the Heavenly Father, His Son Jesus, and the Holy Spirit have always been absolutely committed to searching for lost sheep (Luke 15:4–6; Psalm 119:176).

When Jesus "found the man, he asked him, 'Do you believe in the Son of Man?'" (John 9:35 GW). This conversation shows the phrases, Son of Man and Son of God are interchangeable in the gospels. At the Lord's trial, Caiaphas, the High Priest, certainly knew this. Caiaphas actually tore his clothes and accused Jesus of blasphemy when He claimed the title. Caiaphas also concluded no more evidence was needed for a guilty verdict and a death sentence (Matthew 26:65; Mark 14:63; see also Daniel 7:13).

This man to whom Jesus gave his eyesight had a heart of faith like Abraham's. He had also been pondering the great miracle given to him, and knew only God could give sight to a man born blind. He surely knew and believed the prophecies, promising Messiah would arrive one day. His father probably even taught him Isaiah's specific Messianic prophecy: "Your God will come…to save you…Then will the eyes of the blind be opened…" (Isaiah 35:4–5; Luke 4:18). He had possibly prayed many times, over and over again, "Please come in my lifetime and give *me my sight.*"

To Jesus' question, "Do you believe on the Son of Man?" the healed man answered:

> "Point him out to me, sir, so that I can believe in him."
> Jesus said, "You're looking right at him. Don't you recognize my voice?"
> "Master, I believe," the man said, and worshiped him" (John 9:36–38 MSG).

The man had already confessed only God could give sight to a man blind from birth. But he did not see Jesus' face when the Lord healed him. How then would he recognize Jesus? The answer is unveiled in Jesus' statement, "Don't you recognize my voice?" And the man certainly did; all blind people are very good at recognizing voices. Jesus' voice surely stood out as unique. Nobody ever forgets the voice of Jesus after he has heard it once. All His sheep know His voice and will not follow a stranger (John 10:4–5).

A clear progression of faith marks the journey of this man. He started out with:

"The man they call Jesus," then he progressed to
"A prophet." Then he went further to,
"If this man were not from God he could do nothing."
The final step was,
"Master, I believe, and he worshipped [Jesus]" (John 9:11, 17, 33, 38; Isaiah 35:5).

The Lord accepted this very happy man's worship without rebuking him, giving further evidence of Jesus' claim to be the Son of God (Deuteronomy 5:6–10).

THINK ABOUT IT: It is not enough to study and know the facts about the Son of Man and His teachings.

We must meet Jesus for ourselves in the Holy Scriptures, and accept the convincing revelation of the Holy Spirit in our hearts. Only then can we affirm Jesus as truly and in fact the Son of God, the Messiah, the Son of Man, and the Savior of the world (Matthew 16:17).

9:39 Jesus said, "For judgment I have come into this world, so that the blind will see and those who see will become blind."

This is a statement of purpose made by the Lord Jesus in the face of the total rejection He received from His own people. "I came into the world to bring everything into the clear light of day," Jesus said, "making all the distinctions clear, so that those who have never seen will see, and those who have made a great pretense of seeing will be exposed as blind" (John 9:39 MSG).

Many did accept Jesus. But the religious leadership of the nation, with the backing of the large majority of the people, believed they had already figured out the truth. They flatly rejected the evidences and discarded their Messiah. They despised Jesus to the point they would turn their heads when He walked by so that they would not have to look at Him (Isaiah 53:3 LB).

The plan of God from eternity had already factored this abandonment, knowing fully it was coming. These Jews sought God through the prism of a righteousness of their own making, but Jesus weighed their plan in the balances and found it woefully wanting (Daniel 5:27). "You will die in your sins," the Lord announced, "if you do not believe I am the one I claim to be" (John 8:24; Romans 9:30–10:3). This is a classic case of the blind seeing the *Son*light, but those who claimed they could see and had no need of Jesus were judged as blind, and continued to live in soul-destroying blackness. They saw sunlight, but no *Son*light at all.

Very Sincere, But Very Wrong

It should be underscored these Pharisees were sincere in their righteousness; they believed in their system the point of their own ruin. But sincerity provides a shaky foundation for eternal verities.

It is proper, of course, for followers of Jesus to live with basic respect for the values of the faith systems of others. The fault line emerges when this respect concludes all paths lead to God and eternal life for all adherents who sincerely live out the values of their belief system. The person who faces squarely the miracles the Apostle John records and the teaching Jesus presented, without trying to explain any of it away, will find it difficult not to believe Jesus Christ is in a category all by Himself.

THINK ABOUT IT: Based on the love of God revealed at Calvary, we are left with no choice but to assert with a humility that rejects any haughtiness, Jesus is "the one and only Son of God!" (Isaiah 44:6; Revelation 1:17; 2:8).

The Judge's Verdict

The die was cast and the course was set, so Jesus spoke as a judge and His sentence was two-fold:

1. The people who are blind and know they are blind, and know they need help, and are willing to get under Jesus' cross and cry out to God for help, are the people who will experience the Light of the world.

2. Those who claim they see, albeit with sincerity, and pronounce themselves as fully capable of judging a prophet sent from God, even set themselves up as the final judge of who is their Messiah, these are the people who are blind. They do not recognize the miraculous works only God can do, or the desperately sinful condition of their own souls, or fear the frightening reality of spending eternity separated from God (Luke 12:5). "What good is it for a man to gain the whole world, yet forfeit his soul? Or what can a man give in exchange for his soul?" (Mark 8:36–38).

THINK ABOUT IT: The one path to God is the road of Abraham's faith, and it makes its journey through the Old Testament up Mount Moriah and on to the summit of Mount Calvary.

"No there is no other rock; I know not one" (Isaiah 44:7–8).

People in every generation since Cain have tried to develop alternate paths to God (Genesis 4:1–13). The ultimate expression of Cain's kind of unbelief was the rejection Jesus met regarding His diagnosis of the rebellion against God in the hearts of all people. People with hearts like Cain's never accept the antidote Jesus offered—His own blood—poured out on Golgotha to bridge the chasm between God and man (Genesis 4:1–13; John 3:16; Hebrews 11:4; 1 John 3:12; Jude 11).

It should be underscored these elders were not honestly seeking more truth while searching through their doubts. Instead, they were living in raw unbelief, and arrogantly claiming they had already figured out all things holy. They were so self-righteous, in fact, they would not even entertain what Jesus was teaching, although He performed God-sized miracles right under their noses to prove His identity. Self-righteousness by its very nature believes nothing else is its equal; and justifies itself even when it responds to Jesus with murderous denunciation. Self-righteousness "feeds on ashes" (Isaiah 44:20).

This self-righteous rejection culminated in the vicious denial of Messiah by national Israel. The result was the gospel went to the Gentiles; the people who were willing to admit, with all sincerity, they needed help.

Like Abraham, Gentiles through the centuries since Calvary have recognized the voice of their Savior and believed His message. With Abraham's faith in their hearts, they have been willing to plead for mercy and repent at the foot of the old rugged cross (Acts 11:18; 13:46; 14:27).

9:40 Some Pharisees who were with him heard him say this and asked, "What? Are we blind too?"
41 Jesus said, "If you were blind, you would not be guilty of sin; but now that you claim you can see, your guilt remains.

These Pharisees caught enough of the point Jesus was making to realize Jesus was indicting their blindness, although they thought they had it all put together. They were as blind to the Light of the world, as the blind man had been blind to the sunlight. But the blind man knew his condition and no doubt longed for the help he knew only God could give him. The elders in the land, in their rebellion against God, rejected the idea they needed help. Instead, they *chose* to recognize Jesus as "a teacher" but not as their Messiah (John 3:2; 7:28). They did it even while seeing Him doing the mighty works of God among them. This meant, of course, they remained blind to their spiritual condition before God.

The Guilt that Will Not Go Away

Jesus issued a one-sentence indictment against them: "Your guilt remains because you claim to know what you are doing" (John 9:41 TLB; Matthew 23:37–39). This telling verdict meant they were thieves and robbers and not qualified to shepherd God's people, Israel (Isaiah 56:11). Hence, they were on course to lose their influence over the people. This would be followed by losing their homeland, and far worse, their own souls.

The showdown was near and these leaders perceived the implications of the judge's statement: it was either they would turn to Jesus, or get rid of Jesus before Jesus' message took away their power and position. They chose the latter, and determined to eliminate Jesus. They did it thinking they were honoring the God of Abraham and of Moses.

THINK ABOUT IT: The cross of Jesus on Golgotha's hill was looming larger on the horizon with every passing day.

It meant the Father's plan was continuing to succeed, step by step.

Conclusions

Chapter 9 mirrors some very important principles for the maturity of Jesus' followers in the church.

1. It reveals Jesus' powerful gift as the *logos* from heaven to perform miracles with a spoken Word. Jesus fulfilled Isaiah's prophecy, for example, that Messiah would open the eyes of the blind (Isaiah 35:5). The miracle John records includes creating muscles, nerves, and blood vessels that functioned normally at the moment of the Lord's creative word. The man did not have to learn to see, which is a huge miracle all its own for a person who had never seen anything in at least thirty years.

2. John shows the close relationship between Jesus' ability to perform miracles, and His ministry of evangelism. It also anticipates faithful servants in the Lord's church will manifest this same blending in the form of the spiritual gifts of the Holy Spirit.

3. Giving sight to the man born blind was such a profound miracle it has motivated millions since then to affirm Jesus as the Light of the world. The sunlight that spreads its warmth across the earth can also cause momentary blindness if a person looks straight into the noonday sun without protective shades. The one and only way to gaze into the bright *Son*light that is Jesus Christ is with eyes

shielded by the blood of Jesus Christ, God's Son, who cleanses from all sin (1 John 1:7).

4. This chapter illustrates the rejection of Jesus expressed in Chapter 8. It also demonstrates it is people like this blind man who are the true, spiritual sons of Abraham. Chapter 9 contrasts the faith of this man with the attitudes of the leaders in the religious system. They were far afield from their godly roots. They could actually look their Messiah in the eye and claim to have the last word on righteousness and all things godly.

Self-righteousness thrives on arrogant pride. False religion can reach a point, in its Cain-like arrogance, it claims the right to eliminate its opposition, even if it means to kill. The religious leaders, acting in their own volition, would not many days up the road do just that— freely crucify their own Messiah. But there would be consequences that were unintended. In fact, the results were the last thing they wanted. They actually paved the way for Jesus to demonstrate beyond all reasonable doubt that He is the Lamb of God who takes away the sin of the world (John 1:29, 36).

5. Many Jews were too hardened to acknowledge Jesus as the Son of God for fear of excommunication.

6. The man born blind, having his roots in this same environment, was willing to stand up for Jesus boldly, even when it meant being booted out of the synagogue— and he was. He lost his place in Israelite worship but found the worship "the Father seeks" that was springing up right before their eyes (John 4:23; Isaiah 40:28–31; 43:19). The man also represents the millions in the church since then, both Jews and Gentiles, whose transgressions have been blotted out by their Messiah (Isaiah 43:25). So many—their numbers known only to God—have found

encouragement and strength to give their witness for Jesus Christ, all the way through excommunication and even martyrdom.

7. The Apostle John shows in this chapter the Lord routinely did His greatest miracles alongside the tension of raw unbelief. In doing so, John anticipates the same would be true for the Lord's followers, century after century (Luke 11:49; John 15:20; 16:1–4). But amid all of the opposition, the Holy Spirit has performed the miraculous in every generation. Yes, faithful soldiers of the cross, with hearts like the man born blind, have come to Jesus' cross and gone on to represent Him honestly. In doing so, they have "thrust in the sickle" and reaped a great harvest of lost souls among people who have hearts like Abraham's— hearts that recognize and accept Jesus in faith (Luke 10:2; Revelation 14:14–18). Jesus is indeed the Son of God and the great "I AM," who is the Bread of Life, and the Light of the World.

8. This story shows how the religious leaders of Israel struggled to find ways to deny Jesus' miracles happened, but they failed at the effort. Nicodemus was truthful when he confessed to Jesus, "We know you are a teacher who has come from God. For no one could perform the miraculous signs you are doing if God were not with him" (John 3:2). People who reject Jesus' miracles do so because they make a hard-hearted choice not to believe the obvious evidence.

9. The final time in the Book of John that Moses is mentioned is in this chapter, at verse 29. The Apostle John has made the case Jesus is Moses' Messiah too, while showing at the same time Moses is due high honor. Indeed, Jesus has no equal and no close rival. John also shows the religious establishment followed Moses only selectively, as doing so fitted into their self-righteous plan. They certainly did not

have a correct understanding of Moses' prophecies about the coming Messiah.

Jesus Heals the Eyes of the Heart Too

Richard Moore of Derry, Northern Ireland, was just ten years old when blinded by a British soldier who fired a rubber bullet at him at point-blank range. He was on his way home from his local school.

For as long as he could remember, Richard wanted to meet the soldier who shot him. Thirty years after the incident, he finally did. After discovering who the soldier was and where he lived, Richard wrote to him to get permission to visit, and then met with him face-to-face, offering his personal, heartfelt forgiveness.

Here's what Richard later said about the experience:

"After that, something peculiar and wonderful happened. Something inside me changed, something paradoxical. I began to realize the *gift* of forgiveness I thought I was bestowing on the soldier who shot me was actually a gift from God to me.

It didn't even matter whether the soldier wanted or needed forgiveness; the gift freed me, leaving me with a sense of serenity and blessedness.

All through my boyhood my mother had wanted the impossible for me—to be given back my sight. I even woke up one night to find my dear mother on her knees, next to my bed, pleading with God. When I met the soldier and forgave him, I believe my mother's prayers were answered. I was given a new vision, and my real wound, the one that needed healing more than my eyes, was healed."[4]

We celebrate that the miraculous power of God can heal a wounded heart, and that alone can give a person new vision for life. This was Richard Moore's experience. At the same time, we rejoice in our savior who can in seconds give 20/20 vision to a man born blind.

Chapter 10 will complete John's record of Jesus' brief half-week at the Feast of Tabernacles. In doing so, he will present the Lord as the Gate and the Good Shepherd. It will also give insight into the celebration of Hanukkah, known in the first century as the Festival of Lights.

John Chapter 10

JESUS
THE PASTOR

John's account of the ministry of Jesus during the second half of the Feast of Tabernacles begins in John 7:10 and concludes at John 10:21. In this chapter, John presents Jesus, the Son of God, in His pastoral role as the Gate and the Good Shepherd. In doing so John recorded Jesus presenting basic qualities of pastors as "under shepherds" of the Lord's flock. This chapter also introduces the reader to the December Feast of Dedication (also known as the Festival of Lights and Hannukah), and includes Jesus' sixth discourse. It concludes with Jesus visiting Bethabara (Bethany beyond the Jordan) where He wins a harvest of followers.

THE PASTOR/SHEPHERD

10:1 "I tell you the truth, the man who does not enter the sheep pen by the gate, but climbs in by some other way, is a thief and a robber. 2 The man who enters by the gate is the shepherd of his sheep. 3 The watchman opens the gate for him, and the sheep listen to his voice. He calls his own sheep by name and leads them out. 4 When he has brought out all his own, he goes on ahead of them, and his sheep follow him because they know his voice. 5 But they will never follow a stranger; in fact, they will run away from him because they do not recognize a stranger's voice." 6 Jesus used this figure of speech, but they did not understand what he was telling them.

The Authorized Version begins Jesus' teaching with "Verily, verily." The New International Version renders it, "I tell you the truth." Everything Jesus spoke was the truth, of course, but some of His statements, like this one, merit added emphasis and special attention.

What the New International Version describes as a "figure of speech" (vs. 6) can also be thought of as a Biblical parable (KJV)—an earthly story with a heavenly meaning. The word picture Jesus paints contrasts two kinds of shepherds: One is the hireling, who does not love the sheep, and will run away when danger lurks. The other is the Good Shepherd—the Messiah Himself—who loves the sheep enough to die for them. This pastoral story was very common to Jewish life and culture.

THINK ABOUT IT: Jesus' hearers immediately saw in their minds the scene Jesus described.

They stumbled badly, however, over its application.

The prophets predicted when Messiah arrived He would serve as a shepherd. (The Greek word for shepherd in 10:2 is *poimen*, and it is translated in English as pastor.) The tender and caring attitude of Jesus, the Messiah, as the Pastor-Shepherd set the bar high, while at the same time made it easier to identify hireling shepherds.

Jesus' handling of the woman caught in the act of adultery and His compassionate gift of sight to the man born blind, show the Lord as the true shepherd of Israel, His flock (see Psalm 23; Isaiah 40:11; 41:10, 13–14). These false shepherds were His opposite (Isaiah 56:11). They chose their path for reasons other than love for the Lamb of God and His sheep. Among their selfish intentions were the quest for:

Position,
Power,
Love of money,
Ambition,
Comfort, and
Ease.

Jesus spoke boldly in this encounter at Jerusalem against those who try to sneak into the sheepfold to take control of the flock of God (see Acts 20:29–32). They claimed falsely to have the special skill and expertise to care for the sheep of God's pasture (Psalm 100:3). In reality, however, they were charlatan shepherds who "lacked understanding" (Isaiah 56:11).

Ezekiel 34 is a strongly worded prophetic indictment of would-be leaders who care more for their pocketbooks than they do for the sheep, including the values of the Lord of the sheep. In proclaiming these accusations, Ezekiel also recorded in the name of God a wonderful Messianic promise:

> This is what the sovereign Lord says…I will save my sheep; they will no longer be prey…I will set one shepherd over them, and he will feed them—namely, my servant David. He will feed them and will be their shepherd. I, the Lord, will be their God, and my servant David will be prince among them; I, the Lord, have spoken! (Ezekiel 34:20–24, The NET Bible; see also Ezekiel 37:24; Zechariah 13:7; Psalm 23).

These Jewish leaders at the Feast of Tabernacles, however, had already climbed over the wall and commandeered the sheepfold of Israel, God's chosen people. When Jesus arrived on the scene, they absolutely refused to go to the sheep through Jesus, the Messiah-gate. They were like thieves who slip in under cover of darkness and take what is not theirs; and robbers, who grab what they want with force and violence, including murder. These thieves and robbers had usurped control of Israel, God's flock. At the same time the incarnate Shepherd/Messiah was visiting them, the elders of the land treated Jesus with the ultimate insult by rejecting Him. Further, in their quest to keep their own positions secure, they actually executed Jesus because He threatened their domination.

As a result, the Lord spoke a strong warning:

> "Let me set this before you as plainly as I can. If a person climbs over or through the fence of a sheep pen instead of going through the gate, you know he's up to no good—a sheep rustler! The shepherd walks right up to the gate. The gatekeeper opens the gate to him and the sheep recognize his voice. He calls his own sheep by name and leads them out. When he gets them all out, he leads them and they follow because they are familiar with his voice. They won't follow a stranger's voice but will scatter because they aren't used to the sound of it" (John 10:1–6 MSG).

Like these religious leaders, many people today carry the title, pastor, in the Lord's church but are actually hirelings. They do not walk up to the Jesus-gate and bow their hearts at Messiah's cross. In fact, hirelings never want to pass through the gate that is the cross. In the case of the elders of Israel and in the spirit of Cain, they actually looked for ways to reject and bypass their Messiah (Genesis 4:1–16). Jesus' response was to label these fence climbers as thieves and robbers.

A Pastor's Role

The function of a shepherd is to care for the sheep (Isaiah 40:11). This includes confronting their enemies from outside and the grievous sins of "hireling shepherds" inside the church.

Jesus' ministry at the Feast of Tabernacles shows this to be a huge challenge. In every generation the Lord has had enemies, meaning His church has always faced major opposition (John

15:20). Chapter 8 specifically spells out the rebellion and hard hearted hostility Jesus faced, and Chapter 9 illustrates it with the story of the man born blind. Chapter 10 identifies the role of the Lord's under-shepherds, who must care for His sheep, although facing the same kinds of hostility (John 15:20; Matthew 24:9).

In this exchange with the Pharisees (10:1–6), the Apostle John portrays the basic qualities shepherds in the Lord's church are to manifest. Please note these are all qualities of character, not qualities of administration. Among them are:

- Jesus is the Chief Shepherd and pastors are His under-shepherds (1 Peter 5:4).

- Their love for Jesus, the Good Shepherd, is characterized by faithfulness to His values and vision;

- The Gatekeeper (the Holy Spirit) opens the Jesus-gate to these pastors.

- They win the loyalty of their sheep with loving kindness and faithful provision.

- The sheep quickly come to recognize the voice of their under-shepherd.

- These pastors know the names of their sheep, and the sheep recognize the voice of their pastor calling their names.

- The shepherd leads his sheep out, going ahead of them to point the way and protect them.

When sheep have this kind of pastor who consistently leads them to green pastures and cool streams (Psalm 23:2), they will reject all other voices and refuse to follow them. It is true hirelings have always been in the Lord's church. However, tens of thousands of God-fearing shepherds every day walk boldly "right up to the gate" that is Jesus Christ and faithfully tend the Lord's sheep (Hebrews 4:16), willingly risking their own lives to do it.

"Head Toward My Voice!"

When the infamous September 11 passenger jet barreled into the Pentagon, Officer Isaac Hoopii was nearby but outside the building. Immediately he began helping people straggle out of the building—in some cases, carrying them out.

But Hoopii wanted to do more. Wearing only his short-sleeved blue police uniform—no mask, no protective coat, not even a handkerchief—he ran into the inky blackness of the Pentagon. Someone yelled at him to stop. "We gotta get people," he shouted back.

Suffocating on smoke, Hoopii heard the building cracking. He called out, "Is anybody in here? Anybody here?"

Wayne Sinclair and five coworkers were crawling through rubble and had lost all sense of direction when they heard Hoopii's voice. They cried out, and Hoopii responded. "Head toward my voice. Head toward my voice."

They did follow Hoopi's voice, and this brave firefighter was able to lead them out of a building already beginning to crumble.

Jesus saves us in the same way. He says, "Head toward my voice."[1]

Jesus, the Gate

10:7 Therefore Jesus said again, "I tell you the truth, I am the gate for the sheep. 8 All who ever came before me were thieves and robbers, but the sheep did not listen to them. 9 I am the gate; whoever enters through me will be saved. He will come in and go out, and find pasture. 10 The thief comes only to steal and kill and destroy; I have come that they may have life, and have it to the full."

Verses 7–10 present the third of the seven "I AM" statements in the book of John. Jesus is Himself the Gate, the passageway to peace with God that births eternal life.

The Pharisees claimed they were the shepherds of God's people, Israel, and controlled the gate to righteousness. It was absolutely clear, however, they were not motivated by the same love guiding the life of Jesus. This stands out in the story of the woman caught in the act of adultery, whom they dragged into court. It is also demonstrated by their attitude toward the man born blind to whom Jesus gave his sight. Obviously, Jesus never appointed them. Because God's Son is the one and only true gate for the sheep, He has the right to reject all frauds as imposters— as well as "thieves and robbers." The litmus test is this: does the shepherd love the sheep enough to give his life for them?

A closed gate is a barrier; an open gate is a passageway. The death and resurrection of Jesus is its own form of an open gate (Matthew 27:31). All who come to God through the way of the cross, the Messiah-gate, will inherit eternal life.

Shaq Rejected at Gate to White House

Some doors, like the front gate of the White House, are tough to walk through. The White House has one phalanx of security after another, and you simply don't get in unless you are wanted, unless you have clearance, unless you have an appointment.

Some people do get into the White House based on who they are. Some get in based on who they know.

One of the biggest and most famous men in the world—NBA star Shaquille O'Neil—tried to get into the White House without an appointment on Sunday July 26, 2009. At 7-1 and 325 pounds, with a winning smile, and NBA championship rings on his fingers from years of playing for the Los Angeles Lakers, Shaq has what it takes to walk into most places he wants to go. Doors open for Shaq.

Shaq decided to put his celebrity, and President Obama's love of basketball, to the test. He was on a D.C. sports radio show on Friday July 24th, and he put this question to the listeners: "Check this out, I got on a nice suit, I'm in D.C. paying a visit, I jump out of a cab in front of the White House, I don't use none of my political or law enforcement connections. If I go to the gate and say, 'Hey, I'm in town, I would like to see the President,' do I get in, or do I not get in?"

Two days later, Shaq gave it a try, and just as Shaq has rejected those who would drive past him to the hoop, so the security guards at the White House gate rejected him.

Later that day, Shaq tweeted, "The White House wouldn't let me in, whyyy?"[2]

The theme of Jesus as the Gate was addressed by the Apostle Paul to the Christians in Corinth:

> "We preach Christ crucified, unto the Jews a stumbling block, and unto the Greeks foolishness; But unto them which are called, both Jews and Greeks, Christ the power of God, and the wisdom of God" (1 Corinthians 1:23–24 KJV).

THINK ABOUT IT: Sheep require shepherds. Only the pastors who walk through the Jesus Gate will be able to lead their people to the rich pasture known as eternal life.

Great leaders have the ability to make profound distinctions with a few words. Jesus paints in simple language the whole picture of the gospel in John 10:10: "The thief comes only to steal and kill and destroy; I have come that they may have life, and have it to the full."

A thief's purpose is to eliminate all who would oppose him and then take their possessions. Jesus came to die on the cross, so that this thief is stopped in his tracks and all of God's children can have life "more abundantly" (KJV).

Jesus, the Good Shepherd

10:11 "I am the good shepherd. The good shepherd lays down his life for the sheep. 12 The hired hand is not the shepherd who owns the sheep. So when he sees the wolf coming, he abandons the sheep and runs away. Then the wolf attacks the flock and scatters it. 13 The man runs away because he is a hired hand and cares nothing for the sheep."

Jesus said twice that He is the gate to righteousness (vs. 7 and 9; see Romans 10:4). Then in verses 11 and 14 He identified Himself as the good shepherd. This is the fourth of the seven "I Am" statements, and it is recorded only in John's Gospel. These affirmations associate Jesus directly with the Jehovah name of God in the Old Testament, and describe His true essence: "I am who I am" (Exodus 3:14). They also assert Jesus' claim as the only path to God.

> I am the bread of life—John 6:35
> I am the light of the world—John 8:12
> I am the gate—John 10:7, 9
> I am the good shepherd—John 10:11, 14

THINK ABOUT IT: Jesus taught the most important character trait of a good shepherd is He loves His sheep enough to die for them.
Then He modeled it on His cross.

The horror ahead for Jesus the Chief Shepherd included being surrounded by angry people who would be like "strong bulls." They would gape at Him with their mouths open like "roaring lions" (Psalm 22:12–13). Jesus did not break and run from the bulls or the lions that wanted to gobble Him up and His sheep— and neither will His true under-shepherds (1 Samuel 17:34–37). In fact, Jesus did not even shrink from crucifixion (Hebrews 10:39).

A hired hand lacks ownership of the sheep, however, and will abandon his flock. He will run away when trouble arises. He allows "the sheep to be ravaged and scattered, and is "only in it for the money. The sheep don't matter to him" (John 10:12–13 MSG).

Taking the Wrong Gate

In **Life on the Edge,** Dr. James Dobson writes:

"What are the characteristics of sheep that remind the Lord of you and me? What is He really saying when He refers to us in this way? Well, shepherds and ranchers tell us these animals are virtually defenseless against predators, not very resourceful, inclined to follow one another into danger, and they are absolutely dependent on their human masters for safety. Thus, when David wrote, "We all, like sheep, have gone astray," he was referring to our tendency to move as an unthinking herd away from the watchful care of the shepherd.

"I observed this herd instinct a few years ago in a documentary on television. It was filmed in a packing house where sheep were being slaughtered for the meat market. Huddled in pens outside were hundreds of nervous animals. They seemed to sense danger in their unfamiliar surroundings.

"Then a gate opened that led up a ramp and through a door to the right. In order to get the sheep to walk up this ramp, the handlers used what is known as a "Judas goat." This is a goat trained to lead the sheep into the slaughterhouse.

258

"The goat did his job very efficiently. He confidently walked to the bottom of the ramp and looked back. Then he took a few more steps and stopped again. The sheep looked at each other skittishly and then began moving toward the ramp. Eventually, they followed the confident goat to the top, where he went through a little gate to the left, but they were forced to turn to the right, and went to their deaths."[3]

When Jesus went to the cross, He died in our place as our substitute. Instead of being a Judas Goat, Jesus leads us, not to the death we deserve, but to eternal life, life to the full, abundant life in the here and now, and eternal life in the world to come.

10:14 "I am the good shepherd; I know my sheep and my sheep know me—15 just as the Father knows me and I know the Father—and I lay down my life for the sheep."

Jesus reaffirms here in this fourth "I am" statement that He is the ideal shepherd and no one else can compete with Him in this role. It was a Messianic claim, supporting His identity as the Son of God. Jesus goes on to explain His relationship with His Father makes Him the good shepherd. He expressed it: "the Father knows me and I know the Father." It also follows Jesus knows His sheep and His sheep know Him. Yes, the word picture Jesus paints in these verses portrays two kinds of shepherds—the hireling shepherds and the Good Shepherd (and His under shepherds). The line of demarcation between them is clear. The sheep are Jesus' first priority. He was willing to sacrifice Himself so that His sheep could live (John 10:15–16; see 1 Samuel 17:34–37; 19:1–6; 2 Samuel 23:20; 1 Chronicles 11:22).

"You're Narrow-Minded!"

Religious pluralists often accuse Jesus' followers of being narrow-minded for maintaining Jesus is the Son of God and the only path to eternal life with God. So how can the charge be handled? Here's one possibility.

First, ask the challenger, "Would you please give me your reason for the charge?"

He will usually give a reply akin to this: "You believe you are right and all others are wrong."

Then respond with a question, "May I please ask you, 'Do you believe you are right?'"

The typical answer will be "Yes," or "of course."

Then follow up with another question, "Am I correct that your answer assumes you believe I am wrong?"

This question too will usually get an affirming nod.

Then follow up with the clincher. "If you believe you are right and I am wrong, then doesn't your own reasoning say you are narrow-minded too?"

The conclusion: followers of Jesus Christ are not narrow-minded if the evidence for the life, death and resurrection of Jesus is based on solid information; and it is!

10:16 "I have other sheep that are not of this sheep pen. I must bring them also. They too will listen to my voice, and there shall be one flock and one shepherd."

The Lord's "other sheep" would be the entire Gentile world. Anyone, in fact, with Abraham's heart to take God at His Word can come to Jesus by way of His cross. The Apostle Paul addressed this theme in his letter to the Galatians:

> "There is neither Jew nor Greek, there is neither bond nor free, there is neither male nor female: for ye are all one in Christ Jesus. And if ye be Christ's, then are ye Abraham's seed, and heirs according to the promise" (Galatians 3:28–29 KJV).

These two "I am" statements: "I am the gate," and "I am the good shepherd," are strong assertions Jesus has no peer and no close rival. The gospel of Jesus Christ, anchored in the love of God, is the way to peace with God. Followers of Jesus must never compromise here.

Religious pluralists also say Jesus' claims are dogmatic, and we answer that indeed they are! But they are not made with a loaded gun or a terrorist's knife or even with the brow beating that compels people against their will. Indeed! Jesus has never owned a sword. His claims are backed up with the great love He showed on His cross and proved by His resurrection, with both being historical events.

THINK ABOUT IT: His "lavish" love is beyond comprehension! (1 John 3:1). The love of God makes it easy to believe and accept Jesus as the *only gate* and the singular definition of the *good shepherd*.

Why the Heavenly Father Loves His Son

10:17 "The reason my Father loves me is that I lay down my life—only to take it up again. 18 No one takes it from me, but I lay it down of my own accord. I have authority to lay it down and authority to take it up again. This command I received from my Father."

The term, a*gape,* characterizes the relationships in the Trinity between the Father, the Son and the Holy Spirit. Each person in the Tri-Unity of the Godhead always acts in the best interests of the others. "Self-interest" is not even a concept in the interactions of the Trinity.

The love of God always acts in our best interests too, as only God knows our needs. Jesus, the incarnate Messiah, lived out this love to the extent He was willing to "lay down His life" in our place (John 15:13). Jesus' death on the cross as our substitute, therefore, is the very heart of the gospel and the holy magnet that draws people to bow at His feet in repentance.

The Lord makes another strong claim to Deity in these verses, asserting He held in His own person resurrection power: "I have the authority," He said. Jesus' death was His personal decision; He voluntarily *gave* His life. In fact, in the long-ago eternal councils of the Godhead, Jesus said the heavenly Father issued a command, giving Him "authority to lay [His life] down and authority to take it up again." Jesus is the "Lamb slain from the foundation of the world" who went to Calvary solely "because of His great love wherewith He loved us" (Ephesians 2:4; Revelation 13:8; I Peter 1:20).

In this setting at the Feast of Tabernacles and as the cross of Jesus loomed ever larger, Jesus said His Father had granted Him a free choice to offer His life and to take it up again. This alone rules out the idea Jesus was only a mere man, or died as a martyr, or that His heavenly Father was cruel in sending Jesus to the earth in the incarnation.

In fact, Jesus said boldly, "No one can kill me without my consent." He also said, "I lay down my life voluntarily. For I have the right and power to lay it down when I want to and the right and power to take it again" (John 10:18 TLB). Both the Sanhedrin and the Roman soldiers thought they were killing Jesus—and they did voluntarily participate.

Said another way, only one explanation for the death of Jesus is possible:

> The Father loves me because I give my life in order to take it back again. No one takes my life from me. I give my life of my own free will. I have the authority to give my life, and I have the authority to take my life back again. This is what my Father ordered me to do" (John 10:17 GW).

THINK ABOUT IT: The heavenly Father accepted Jesus as the fully adequate sacrifice (Hebrews 10:10–12). But the combined power of the Sanhedrin and the Roman army was not adequate to take Jesus' life.

The writer of Hebrews also focuses this great truth. Jesus was committed from eternity to doing the will of God (Hebrews 10:7; Psalm 40:7–10). To this end, "a body was prepared for [Him]," a prophecy fulfilled in His incarnation (Psalm 40:6 Septuagint version; 1 Timothy 3:16; Hebrews 10:5). The religious leaders by their own choice, albeit unintentionally, helped to fulfill this prophecy and make Jesus the Lamb of God. And by His own choice Jesus let them. He loved the sons of Adam enough to die as the final sacrifice for the sins of all humanity.

Through the millennia from Adam to Christ, offering the blood of bulls and goats proved time and time again animal sacrifices were not sufficient ransom for man's salvation. The sheer volume of the ongoing repetition meant only one thing: the price could never be fully paid with Moses' system of worship.

Jesus was the God-man. As the Son of Man, His sacrificial death represented all mankind. As the Son of God, He satisfied the requirements of the Holy Trinity in the Godhead (Isaiah 53:11). Jesus' blood was sinless (John 8:46) and this meant "the Lamb of God" was the first-ever perfect sacrifice (John 1:29, 36; Hebrews 4:14–16; 5:9–10; 6:19–20).

Jesus did on His cross what a million lambs had not been able to do—make the one sacrifice that would be so adequate worldwide there would never be need for another (Isaiah 53:11–12). Jesus' blood continues today to be sufficient to redeem all who accept responsibility for their sins, repent, and believe the good news of the gospel that Jesus is the Son of God.

THINK ABOUT IT: The trail of blood that flowed from Eden to Golgotha ended at the old, ragged cross (Hebrews 7:24–28; 9:11–15; 26–28). The result is we are sanctified through the offering of the body of Jesus Christ once for all. Yes, "this priest [Jesus] offered for all time one sacrifice for sins" (see Hebrews 10:7–18; 13:10–15; 1 Peter 3:18; Psalm 110:1; Acts 2:34).

It remains in this discussion to address the statement, "The Father loves me because I give my life in order to take it back again." The *agape* love of God, as expressed in the plan of redemption, has two powerful dimensions. The first is Jesus had the sole choice to "give [His] life," and He made the choice. *Agape* love always acts in the best interests of others. So the question becomes, since Jesus was willing to die on the cross for our salvation, acting in our best interests, what would be in *His best interests* when He "bowed his head and gave up his spirit?" (John 19:30). The answer is the second dimension of the plan of redemption, to which *agape* love thundered only one response: resurrection!

THINK ABOUT IT: The *agape* love in the heart of the Triune Godhead continues to challenge every generation: "To whom will you compare me or count me equal?" (Isaiah 40:18, 25; 46:5).

The answer will keep on echoing through all eternity: Jesus has no equal or close rival. He is "the one and only" and the "Lamb of God who takes away the sin of the world!" (John 1:18, 29, 35).

Jesus "gave His life in order to take it back again." The love of the Father would not have been love at all if resurrection had not been on the other side of the cross.

> "Praise be to the God and Father of our Lord Jesus Christ! In his great mercy he has given us new birth into a living hope through the resurrection of Jesus Christ from the dead, and into an inheritance that can never perish, spoil or fade—kept in heaven for you, who through faith are shielded by God's power until the coming of the salvation ready to be revealed in the last time. In this you greatly rejoice…" (1 Peter 1:3–6).

Yes, the death of Jesus was God's most loving act of the ages, intended to benefit fallen man. Right beside it is the ultimate expression of the love of the Father toward His Son, vesting Him with the authority and power to empty His tomb on the other side of His crucifixion.

This was Jesus' ultimate weapon in the war to "*take away* the sin of the world" (John 1:29; Genesis 22:8). The Pharisees thought they could kill Jesus and do away with Him. They totally missed the messianic prophecy of Isaiah in the fourth of the Songs of the Servant foretelling Jesus' death and resurrection. Yes, Jesus came out of the tomb, seeing again "the light of life" and feeling "satisfied" that the price was worth it.

Agape Love Compels a Choice

10:19 At these words the Jews were again divided. 20 Many of them said, "He is demon-possessed and raving mad. Why listen to him?"
21 But others said, "These are not the sayings of a man possessed by a demon. Can a demon open the eyes of the blind?"

Agape love expressed in Jesus Christ has the capacity to hem people in. It does so without overriding free will or coercing godly decision making (Psalm 139:5). But *agape* love does have the power to compel *making a choice*—and we must then live with the consequences (2 Corinthians 5:14–15).

The background of this teaching is the court case releasing the woman caught in the act of adultery from her inner prison, and the creative miracle given to the man born blind (John 8 and 9). Both were deeds of *agape* love. This is the love of God that acts in the best interests of people as only God knows their best interests, doing it unconditionally. These acts of love brought great deliverances to these two people, but also served to box in the religious leadership and the Jews following them.

Jesus miracles, in their own way, were actually deeds done in the best interests of these leaders too. At a minimum they were given another opportunity to make their choice about the Nazarene. Jesus, in fact, left them no wiggle room—they had to make a "yes" or "no" decision, and they made it. "Many" said Jesus was "demon-possessed and raving mad," and not worthy of a listening ear. But "others" were not so sure. "No one talks like this if he's possessed by a demon," they said. "Can a demon give sight to the blind?" (John 10:21 GW). But none of them were willing to step forward and publicly affirm Jesus, as did the man born blind (in John 9). They would not take the risk of faith and confess Jesus as the Son of God and their Messiah. Hence, the love of God did not coerce the right decision, but it did compel a choice. They gave their Messiah a resounding "NO!"

THINK ABOUT IT: Jesus' example works for us too. One of the greatest lessons to be learned from Jesus' visit to the Feast of Tabernacles is the gospel always advances amid unbelief, even when the opposition becomes violent. All shepherds of the Lord's sheep must understand this.

To be accused of being "demon possessed" and "raving mad" no doubt hurt Jesus, but it did not prod Him to make a solo decision, independent of His Father and the Holy Spirit who guided His life. Quite the opposite; Jesus was marching to a different drum beat. The more the tempers of His enemies flared, and as the name calling intensified, the better the Lord knew His strategy was working. They made their choices to rebuff Him, but in doing so, they also paved the way for His march to Calvary.

The negative response to Jesus was cruel beyond imagination. But Jesus' demeanor did not demonstrate He was a depressed man with crushed expectations and broken dreams. Instead, the Lord remained confident and self-assured. His manner exuded optimism about His tomorrows. Jesus was driven by a God-sized vision—a huge job description worthy of Messiah (Isaiah 49:6). He was the Lamb of God, the Bread of Life, the Light of the world, the Gate, and the Good Shepherd. His mission was to save the world. The amazing thing about Him was the uglier things became, and the tougher the persecution, the closer He came to "mission accomplished."

Yes, the plan framed in eternity for Jesus to go to the cross was working splendidly!

On this ugly note of deliberate rejection the half-week long story of Jesus' September visit to Jerusalem for the Feast of Tabernacles came to an end.

What miracles!

What teaching!

What lost opportunity!

THINK ABOUT IT: The silhouette of the cross was hanging on the horizon. In fact, it was right up the road, a short six months away.

JESUS' MINISTRY
AT THE FEAST OF DEDICATION

10:22 Then came the Feast of Dedication at Jerusalem.

The Feast of Dedication was a festival of the Jews starting on the 25th day of Kislev, which usually occurs in December. The festival was birthed out of a Jewish rebellion against the rule of the Selucid Empire centered in Syria some 165 years before the Lord's incarnation. While it remains important to the Jewish people in the modern era, it is obviously not one of the seven annual feasts of Israel instituted by God as part of the Mosaic Covenant. The Feast of Dedication was added to celebrate the Jewish people who were willing to fight to the death to preserve their freedom of worship; in this case, in a historic triumph over the Seleucid Empire.

Seleucus, one of Alexander the Great's generals, gained control of a large portion of Alexander's empire after Alexander's untimely death (323 BC). [Daniel gave a specific and accurate prophecy about this development almost two centuries before it happened (Daniel 11:1–4).] Seleucus' son, Antiochus, succeeded his father as ruler of an empire that stretched from Syria to Persia. The result was the Selucid dynasty.

About a century after Seleucus' death (ca. 281), Antiochus IV Epiphanes successfully invaded Judea (ca. 167). He massacred thousands of Jewish men, women, and children and spoiled the temple. Daily sacrifices stopped for forty-two months. He ordered an altar for the pagan god, Zeus [king of the Greek gods] to be erected in the temple. He also added the ultimate insult to the Jewish people by ordering pigs to be sacrificed on it. In addition, he banned circumcision.

Antiochus invasion marked a fulfillment of the abomination of desolation spoken by Daniel the prophet (Daniel 9:27).

A primary goal of his assault was to force Greek customs and idolatrous practices on the Jewish people.

In Biblical prophecy, Antiochus is a type of the antichrist to come, who will ravage not only Israel but the whole earth (Daniel 12:9–11; Matthew 24:25; Mark 13:14; 2 Thessalonians 2).

Antiochus' actions provoked a large-scale revolt led by Mattathias, a Jewish priest, and his five sons. After Mattathias' untimely death amid the struggle, his son Judas succeeded his father in the war. Judas and his forces drove the Selucids out of Israel in 164 BC, and liberated the temple.

Judas ordered the temple cleansed of all Greek symbols and a new altar built. To celebrate this event, he decreed an eight-day feast to celebrate the re-dedication of the temple. As part of the dedication, Judas ordered that the temple menorah burn for eight successive days. But enough processed olive oil was available to burn for only one day. Miraculously, the menorah continued to burn for the eight days.

To celebrate the success of the revolt and the miracle of the menorah, an eight day festival, *Hanukkah*, emerged in Jewish history. [The Hebrew word, Hanukkah, means dedication.] It is also remembered as the Feast of Lights, commemorating the miracle of the menorah. In the time of the Lord, the celebration was known as the Feast of Dedication. The festival has continued into the 21st century as a secondary festival in Judaism. It is celebrated for eight days annually in December, running somewhat parallel with the Christian celebration of Christmas.[4]

The Apostle John's account marks the sixth of the Lord's seven discourses leading to Passion Week, the last week of the Lord's life.

10:22 It was winter, 23 and Jesus was in the temple area walking in Solomon's Colonnade.

The time between the Lord's visit in Jerusalem for the September Feast of Tabernacles and the December celebration of *Hanukkah* was about three months. The Apostle John is silent regarding Jesus' work for these weeks, but Luke the physician recorded His ministry, and it was very active (see Luke 10–13). The crucifixion was less than four months away.

John records "it was winter," the rainy season in Israel. If it was raining at the time of this event, staying out of the rain could explain why Jesus was walking in King Solomon's colonnade, first erected almost a millennium earlier. Like the other parts of the temple, the colonnade did not survive the wrath of the Roman legions in 70 AD.

Recognizing Fake Enthusiasm

10:24 The Jews gathered around him, saying, "How long will you keep us in suspense? If you are the Christ, tell us plainly."

The Jews circled Jesus with their strategy carefully crafted. "Are you going to keep us guessing? If you're the Messiah, tell us straight out" (John 10:23–24 MSG). The sense of the fabrication was, "You're killing us with suspense!" But it was all a sinister lie. Their goal was to prod Jesus into admitting He was God's Son and a king, so they could report Him to Pilate, the Roman governor.

THINK ABOUT IT: To Jesus, their deceitful question came through like a personal slap in the face as He discerned their motive. But Jesus responded honestly, and not with the anger that wants to even a score.

They were admitting they did not believe any of His prior teaching about His identity or the testimony of His miracles.

The Witness of Jesus' Miracles

10:25 Jesus answered, "I did tell you, but you do not believe. The miracles I do in my Father's name speak for me, 26 but you do not believe because you are not my sheep."

So far in this study of the book of John, we have noted six of the seven God-proving miracles John records. They certainly make the point: Jesus is the Son of God and the Messiah foretold by Moses and the prophets. Jesus performed these miracles in His Father's name and gave the honor to His Father. *Only God* could do these things:

1. At Cana in Galilee Jesus affirmed the institution of marriage and the family. He also gave the young couple a wedding gift they could never forget, turning water into wine. In this creative miracle, Jesus demonstrated He is Lord over the seasons of growth and the cycles of nature that mature and ripen all the blessings of the food chain, such as fresh fruits and vegetables (John 2:1ff). *Only God* can create wine from water in an instant, without the benefit of sunshine, soil and rain, time and seasons.

2. While at Cana for a second visit, Jesus healed with a spoken word the nobleman's son who was dying in Capernaum. The Lord showed He is sovereign over space and distance (John 4:43ff). *Only God* can speak the word and heal a dying child in the precise moment of speaking the word, with the youngster about 20 miles away. This is all the more significant, considering He had never met the boy. But the

truth is Jesus' word would have healed the child from a thousand miles away, no matter the illness. Jesus is the Lord of the spoken Word, and distance is no barrier to Him.

3. Jesus performed another creative miracle when He restored the poor man who lay for thirty-eight long years at the Pool of Bethesda (John 5:2ff). His leg muscles had atrophied years earlier. Helping this hapless man required creative power. In the seconds of speaking just a few words, "Get up! Pick up your mat and walk" (John 5:8–9), strong bones, muscles, nerves and blood vessels appeared on his legs and feet.

THINK ABOUT IT: *Only God* can instantaneously make dead limbs brand new and send a man on his way, carrying his mat as he walked. Jesus did it for this man without physical therapy or any need to relearn to balance himself.

---

4. Jesus fed 5,000 men to the full, in addition to the women and children, and did it by multiplying a lad's lunch of five barley loaves and two fish (John 6:1ff). It was His third creative miracle, and *only God* could do it. This miracle proved Jesus is the Bread of Life. The miracle was so sufficient the disciples picked up twelve baskets of leftovers! Yes, Jesus is interested in saving leftovers, including people who feel like leftovers.

5. After feeding the 5,000, that same night Jesus walked on water for at least three miles in a storm. In the darkness He found the proverbial "needle in a haystack" by locating His very frightened disciples in their little boat on the Sea of Galilee (John 6:16ff). *Only God* has the control over nature to turn rough seas into a strong sidewalk; indeed, no mere man does! This miracle demonstrated Jesus'

mastery over the forces of nature, and shows such control over the power of gravity a person should feel strongly encouraged to affirm Jesus as the Creator of all things, including the natural order. This miracle also shows Jesus' keen interest in His followers when they are frightened and caught in life-threatening situations.

6. At the Feast of Tabernacles in Jerusalem, Jesus healed a man born blind (John 9:1ff). It too was a creative miracle. This was a man who had never seen anything, not even his mother's face. *Only God* could give the man the full and perfect capability to see, 20/20 vision, without any need for therapy, and do it in an instant of time. The man quickly became a strong defender and spokesman for Jesus.

Why Miracles?

Miracles were not new in the history of Israel; they are certainly recorded in the Old Testament. The miraculous crossing of the Red Sea stands out as arguably the greatest demonstration of divine power in the Old Covenant.

Jesus' miracles were new, however, in their sheer volume, as well as their broad scope. Jesus loved all people, people of every race and ethnicity, and showed it with His miracles. He performed them to meet graciously the pressing needs in their lives.

Jesus miracles also had an additional purpose. The Lord's critics on one occasion charged Him with casting out demons in the power of Beelzebub. Jesus answered, "If it's God's finger I'm pointing that sends the demons on their way, then God's kingdom is here for sure" (Luke 11:20 Msg). Jesus' miracles revealed Himself as the Son of God and signaled the dawn of a new day. "Thy kingdom come" was being unveiled right before their eyes (Mark 6:10; Luke 11:2). As Jesus made the great paradigm switch from the Jewish temple to the fleshly temple-of-the-heart, so the Lord made the kingdom of God spiritual, saying, "The kingdom of God is within you" (Luke 17:21). Jesus is Himself the reigning monarch of this worldwide domain.

Helping people who had no hope by merely pointing "the finger of God" opened the hearts of people with Abraham's faith to confess Jesus as the Son of God. Jesus demonstrated His Lordship over sickness, disease, demons, oppression, and even death itself. He also showed Himself supreme over the awesome forces of nature. His miracles spoke loud and clear that God was on the scene, intervening in His creation to redeem all who will believe Him and confess His Lordship.

Jesus' own resurrection was the greatest miracle of them all, showing loud and clear the kingdom of God was at hand.

Yes, history was being re-written and the world would never be the same.

My Sheep Listen to Me

Amazingly, however, none of these astounding miracles the Apostle John recorded, nor the combined weight of all of them, softened the hard hearts of Israel's religious leaders. To the contrary, they actually hardened. Despising Jesus all the more, they plotted to kill Him.

While surrounded by death threats, Jesus continued to help people and to teach. Consider:

10:27 "My sheep listen to my voice; I know them, and they follow me. 28 I give them eternal life, and they shall never perish; no one can snatch them out of my hand. 29 My Father, who has given them to me, is greater than all; no one can snatch them out of my Father's hand. 30 I and the Father are one."

Only one conclusion was possible. These leaders were not His sheep, and had no intention to become His sheep. They were Abraham's blood descendants who knew nothing about

Abraham's dominant character trait: his faith in God. They were also unwilling to learn. While looking at His miracles and hearing His teaching, they rejected their own Messiah. They thought they had already figured out everything about God and righteousness.

But the man born blind heard Jesus' voice and believed it was the sound of his Messiah. The story ends with the man worshipping Jesus. The Lord accepted his worship, giving him no rebuke.

THINK ABOUT IT: Jesus tried repeatedly to reach these national leaders. He really did try.

Jesus knew well they did not trust Him. Yet, He continued to assert His Lordship over all things, and especially everything related to redemption and life everlasting.

Jesus also knew those who did listen to His voice. The woman at the well and the man born blind are examples of people who trusted and followed Him. No outsider can break the bond between Jesus and His sheep. Unbelievers can be used by Satan to entice, but only the individual can make the choice to walk away. Anyone who decides not to follow Jesus does so because he chooses to depart.

Jesus alone can give His followers eternal life. Only He holds eternity in His hands. He is the:

Bread of life (John 6:35),
Light of the world (John 8:12),
Gate (John 10:9), and the
Good Shepherd (John 10:11).

Satan, the Destroyer

Jesus also knew the devil was a demolisher of peoples' lives, and these leaders had chosen this thief and liar as their father. He was deeply saddened by their decision, but not intimidated, because He knew His Father was incomparably greater than the destroyer.

It has already been noted in this study people can make the choice to pull away from the truth of the gospel, and give their loyalty step by step over time to Satan (see the discussion on John 8:44). Unchecked, this downward spiral ends in an addiction-like bondage to Satan. The result is Satan's "children" will do what their "father" orders, even when they know what they are doing is wrong.

People can give their loyalty to Jesus Christ too, doing so to the point they truly become Jesus' servants. The Apostle Paul, for example, understood himself as a slave of Jesus Christ (Romans 1:1). The people who make this big decision, and follow it up with many smaller decisions, come to the place they belong to Jesus for life. These people are secure in Jesus Christ, trusting Him unto death, and believing His promise of eternal life. It is in this sense the Lord's statement is understandable: "no one can snatch them out of my Father's hand."

THINK ABOUT IT: Religious pluralism, which holds all world religions are valid paths to God, falls far short before this kind of evidence. Isaiah recorded God's own affirmation about His would-be competition: "I am God [Elohim, the supreme God] and there is no other. I am God and there is none like me. I make known the end from the beginning...My purpose will stand and I will do all I please" (Isaiah 46:5, 9–10).

Less than four months down the road—after Jesus' crucifixion and resurrection—He would begin to have a great harvest of sheep who would know His voice. They would be faithful unto death. Indeed! The destroyer's "men" were not able to steal these sheep out of Jesus' hand. They would mature in faithfulness as disciples to the point they remained faithful at the price of their lives (see John 10:29 TLB, and the story of Stephen in Acts 6–8).

THINK ABOUT IT: The blood of more martyrs for Christ has soaked the twentieth century than all of the other nineteen centuries combined. Of all Christian martyrs since Jesus launched His church at the Feast of Pentecost fifty days after His resurrection, 65 percent have been in the twentieth century. The two leading forces that fuel the persecution of Christians today are the varied forms of Muslim fundamentalism and Communism. The twenty-first century started out in the bloody tracks of the twentieth as the blood-red river of Christian martyrdom continues to hallow the earth.[5]

Jesus' Claim to Deity

Jesus spoke in verses 27–30 with the confidence of the Son of God. In doing so, He asserted the prerogatives of a sovereign, although they were actively refusing Him as their Messiah. Jesus was not at all cowed by their brutal denials. And to make this crystal clear, Jesus added the claim to Deity that was sure to upset them even more: "I and my Father are one" (John 10:30 KJV).

In John's record Jesus asserted His Deity to the woman at the well and to the man born blind, for examples. But here He fully revealed His identity to His sworn enemies, and did it only weeks away from the cross.

THINK ABOUT IT: Jesus' claim is not that He and the Father are one and the same identical Person, but rather *one in essence or substance.* The mystery of the Trinity is that Jesus, His Father and the Holy Spirit are truly one in nature or essence, while at the same time they are indivisibly three distinct Persons. It is in this sense that Jesus is the great I AM.

This admission is a classic example showing Jesus as a strategic thinker. He knew the time had come to make His identify known clearly.

In the exercise of their free will, these leaders had only two choices: they could accept Jesus or reject Him. Jesus foreknew their free choice would be the latter. This also meant they would ratchet up their efforts to eliminate Him. Yes, Jesus' plan was progressing splendidly. He knew He came to this earth to die. But He, and not them, would control the timing.

If we could have been on the scene and watched their body language when Jesus expressed His claim to Deity, no doubt we would have seen their heads snap and jaws drop; perhaps like they had been slapped. The blood rushed to their faces, reddening their cheeks, as their anger quickly came to a boil. Murder was in their hearts, justified in their thinking by the charge of blasphemy.

THINK ABOUT IT: Does Jesus' claim to Deity shake you up too? Yes, Jesus is the only founder of a major world religion who claimed to be God.

More Death Threats

10:31 Again the Jews picked up stones to stone him, 32 but Jesus said to them, "I have shown you many great

miracles from the Father. For which of these do you stone me?"

Jesus showed again His sovereignty over time, and would not allow His death to occur before His appointed hour. The rocks were in their hands, yet Jesus deflected their anger by appealing to the great improvements in people's lives, produced by His miracles. "At God's direction I have done many a miracle to help the people," Jesus said. "For which one are you killing me?" (John 10:32 TLB).

10:33 "We are not stoning you for any of these," replied the Jews, "but for blasphemy, because you, a mere man, claim to be God."
34 Jesus answered them, "Is it not written in your Law, 'I have said you are gods'? 35 If he called them 'gods,' to whom the word of God came—and the Scripture cannot be broken—36 what about the one whom the Father set apart as his very own and sent into the world? Why then do you accuse me of blasphemy because I said, 'I am God's Son'?"

Please note again they did not try to deny His miracles. This is implicit in the statement and says it all: "We are not stoning you for any of these."

Their indictment, of course, was Jesus claim of Deity. In their spiritual blindness, they knew for certain He was a mere man and absolutely not God's Son. Yes, the incarnation of Jesus, God becoming flesh, was a master stroke of genius in the Messiah's march to the Hill of the Skull.

Jesus further deflected their rage by showing His superior knowledge of the Law and the Psalms. He quoted Asaph, King David's choir director who made the assertion: "You are gods; you are all sons of the Most High" (Psalm 82:6). One is left to wonder if the Holy Spirit, who knows the end from the beginning (Isaiah 46:10), had dropped this prophecy into Asaph's heart almost a thousand years earlier so that Israel's Messiah would be able to use it to defuse these Jews' boiling fury. It certainly did help prevent His premature death.

Jesus also asserted here the great authority of the Old Testament: "the Scripture cannot be broken." This is a strong affirmation the Bible is the divinely-inspired and revealed Word of God.

Asaph's statement in its historical setting referred to Israelite judges who represented God in making judgments about the lives of people; rendering the judges god-like. The point here was if Asaph could use the term about Israel's own judges, how much more was it appropriate for Jesus to use the term about Himself. Jesus is the judge of the hearts of all men, and, as the equal of the Father, makes decisions about the eternal destiny of people.

Asaph's prophecy in Psalm 82 sat on the shelf of salvation history for a millennium, awaiting its moment in the life of Jesus.

THINK ABOUT IT: Mormon doctrine, a very works based belief system, uses passages like Psalm 82 and John 10:34–35 to teach the false doctrine of deification—the notion men can progress through a series of steps to the level of Deity. Hinduism and New Ageism include it as well. Jehovah Himself, in Mormonism, started as a man and progressed to become God. The Bible refers to the redeemed as "sons of God," but not as deified little gods (Matthew 5:9; 1 John 3:1–2).[5]

10:37 Do not believe me unless I do what my Father does. 38 But if I do it, even though you do not believe me, believe the miracles that you may know and understand the Father is in me, and I in the Father."

Jesus' logic was clear: since I am doing things only God can do, why do you not believe me when I say I am God's Son?

> "I'm only quoting your inspired Scriptures, where God said, 'I tell you—you are gods.' If God called your ancestors 'gods'—and Scripture doesn't lie—why do you yell, 'Blasphemer! Blasphemer!' at the unique One the Father consecrated and sent into the world, just because I said, 'I am the Son of God'? If I don't do the things my Father does, well and good; don't believe me. But if I am doing them, put aside for a moment what you hear me say about myself and just take the evidence of the actions that are right before your eyes. Then perhaps things will come together for you, and you'll see not only are we doing the same thing, we are the same—Father and Son. He is in me; I am in him" (John 10:34–38 MSG).

The miracles were not denied because they could not be denied. The rulers in the Sanhedrin even admitted them (John 3:2; 11:46). A man at least thirty years old, who was born blind, for example, all of a sudden had perfect vision, because Jesus spoke the word. The miracle was a divine act and beyond dispute to the people who knew the blind man. They had watched him grow up with the many traumas of blindness. How many times they had seen him walk into a building or stumble over a rock. In addition, in the Gospel of Mark, Jesus used His miracles that had an undeniable divine origin to prove He had authority to forgive sin (Mark 2:5).

In the twenty-first century, the strategy all too often is refusal to believe the claims of Jesus by asserting the miracles never happened.

These rulers made the choice to reject Jesus as the Son of God while admitting His miracles. Each of these conclusions is based on their decision not to believe the obvious about Jesus Christ. The choice is born out of a self-righteousness that is simply unwilling to admit it is wrong and bow in repentance at the feet of the Son of Man.

10:39 Again they tried to seize him, but he escaped their grasp.

Jesus was fully capable of preventing a premature arrest. He was also determined to honor His Father's timeline. Hence, He escaped and withdrew from Jerusalem.

REVIVAL BEYOND THE JORDAN

40 Then Jesus went back across the Jordan to the place where John had been baptizing in the early days. Here he stayed and many people came to him. They said, "Though John never performed a miraculous sign, all John said about this man was true." And in that place many believed in Jesus.

It must have been refreshing for Jesus to get out of Jerusalem and minister across the Jordan at Bethabara ("Bethany on the other side of the Jordan").

This is one of the sites where John the Baptist had blazed the trail (John 1:28 KJV). [John also baptized at Aenon (John 3:23)]. The site is located in modern Jordan. It is thought to be about three miles north of the northern mouth of the Dead Sea and about three miles east of Jericho. "Many people came to [Jesus]" at Bethabara and received Him warmly. Jesus had spoken the truth at the Feast of Dedication—He would have a following, and Jesus saw its seeds on this visit. The actual time He stayed there John did not disclose. What we do know is the people flocked to Him. Their attitude was so very different from what had confronted Him in Jerusalem. They began to recognize "the king in His beauty" (Isaiah 33:17).

THINK ABOUT IT: In Chapter 10 the Son of God makes three persuasive announcements about Himself. What has been your response to each of them?

1. Jesus is the Gate. Have you walked through this door and experienced the new birth through Jesus Christ that saves the soul and gives eternal life?
2. Jesus is the Good Shepherd. Have you recognized His voice and made the choice to trust your very life to Him for time and eternity? He gave His life for you.
3. Jesus is the Son of God. "I and my Father are One," He said.

Has Jesus convinced you of His true identity, based on His teaching and His miracles thus far? Has this been enough evidence to satisfy you?

Progress Amid Persecution

A clear theme of John's Gospel is Jesus' greatest miracles occurred surrounded by the greatest harassment. It included ugly name calling, raw and willful unbelief, and death threats. This was certainly true at Jerusalem when Jesus concluded His ministry at the Feast of Hanukkah by asserting He was God's Son.

It is a fact the gospel's progress in every century has been shrouded by pain (John 1:29, 36). Every foot of ground Satan surrendered has come with a fight. Jesus expected the struggle and was not surprised by it. Neither did the Lord ever become fearful that His one weapon, *agape* love, might not be adequate to destroy the works of the devil (1 John 3:8). Jesus never even considered the sword as a backup weapon (Matthew 26:52; John 18:11). Nor did He ever lose sight of His all-encompassing, international vision (John 3:16; Matthew 28:16–20; Isaiah 49:6). In fact, the tougher the fight, the more assured Jesus was about His ultimate success. The brilliance of the plan was when Jesus' enemies thought they were winning it meant they were actually losing.

Why, do you ask, is this true?

THINK ABOUT IT: The ultimate weapon in the hands of Israel's leaders was *crucifixion*. The ultimate weapon in the hands of Jesus—the Son of God, Son of Man, and the Messiah—is *resurrection*!

John clearly linked Jesus' testimony at Hanukkah, "I and the Father are one," to His warm welcome across the Jordan, where the people accepted His identity.

In the twenty-first century, the clash of religions and cultures pivots around the same issue: who is Jesus Christ? Islam, for one example, will join Nicodemus and accept Jesus as a prophet and teacher, but not as the Messiah and Son of God. The implications are far reaching.

Ravi Zacharias Speaks to a Leader of Hamas

Do you know why the Middle East is in the cauldron of hate? Because it's living with the logic of unforgiveness.

I was talking to one of the founders of Hamas, Sheikh Talal. I was part of a group who had gone to the Middle East to try and bring the people together to a peace table. Sheikh Talal gave us a great meal, told us of eighteen years he'd served in prison, and how some of his children had been lost in suicide bombings.

When my turn came to ask a question, I said, "Sheik, forgive me if I'm asking you the wrong question. Please tell me, what do you think of suicide bombing and sending your children out like that?"

After he finished his answer, I said, "Sheik, you and I may never see each other again, so I want you to hear me. A little distance from here is a mountain upon which Abraham went 5,000 years ago to offer his son. And as the axe was about to fall, God said, 'Stop.'"

I said, "Do you know what God said after that?"

He shook his head.

I said, "God said, 'I myself will provide.'" He nodded his head.

I said, "Very close to where you and I are sitting, Sheik, is a hill. Two thousand years ago, God kept that promise and brought His own Son, and the ax did not stop this time. He sacrificed His own Son."

He just stared at me. The room was full of smoke with all of his security people.

I said, "I may never see you again, Sheikh, but I want to leave this with you: Until you and I receive the Son God has provided, we will be offering our own sons and daughters on the battlefields of this world for land and power and pride."

I could see the man's lips beginning to quiver; he was sitting right next to me. Nobody said anything after that…

As we were walking out…Sheikh Talal went quickly and shook hands with everyone, and then he came over to me and grabbed me by the shoulders, kissed me on both sides of the face, patted my face, and he said, "You're a good man, I hope I see you again someday."

When you understand [Christ's grace], it is an unparalleled message. In Hinduism, you pay with karma. In Islam you never know if your good deeds will outweigh your bad deeds. But the grace of Christ comes to you and says, "If any man comes unto me I will in no wise cast him out."[6]

The Apostle John gave considerable attention in his book to the rejection Jesus received in Jerusalem as the Son of God, particularly at the Feast of Tabernacles. Then he recorded the story of Jesus' warm reception at Bethabara.

In setting up this contrast, John prepared his readers to witness the capstone; one more miracle. It will be the most outstanding of the seven Deity proving miracles John records.

Surely if you have any lingering doubts that Jesus is the Son of God, this next miracle will put them to rest!

We now turn our attention to Chapter 11, the grand story of just that miracle, the resurrection of Lazarus.

JESUS
THE PRINCE OF LIFE

When the reader arrives at chapter 11, he is ready to climb the remaining steps to the summit, the peak of Jesus' seven miracles and seven discourses that prove Jesus is the Son of God. This chapter is full of human pain and disappointment; it unveils high drama fed by the rawest of human emotions. Many of the great stress issues families' face surface in this chapter. In John 11, the Apostle John looks death squarely in the eye as he describes the human condition. In doing so, he tells the story of the undeniable manifestation of Jesus' awesome resurrection power that foreshadowed Jesus' own resurrection. This authority proves He is the Son of God, the resurrection and the life. The first eleven verses of chapter 12 are also included in this study to wrap up John's account of Jesus' ministry leading up to Passion Week, the last week of the Lord's life before His crucifixion, and resurrection.

THE RESURRECTION OF LAZARUS

11:1 Now a man named Lazarus was sick. He was from Bethany, the village of Mary and her sister Martha.

The primary players in this drama are:

- Jesus Christ, in the relationship He enjoyed with His Father and the Holy Spirit, His co-equals in the Tri-Unity of the God who is One.

- Jesus' friends: two sisters and their brother—Martha, Mary and Lazarus.

- Jesus' disciples.
- The mourners who cried with Mary and Martha.
- The national Jewish leaders who hated Jesus.
- The common people from Bethany and from Jerusalem, who came out just to see Jesus and Lazarus.

Bethany was about two miles from Jerusalem, on the southeastern slope of the Mount of Olives. The town was far enough from the Holy City to enjoy suburban living and close enough to have a good grasp of events transpiring there. This village's place is forever established in salvation history as the home of Lazarus and his sisters, Mary and Martha. The setting was perfect for the miracle in the ministry of Jesus that is second only to the resurrection of the Lord Himself.

In choosing Bethany for this most important miracle, Jesus knew exactly what He was doing, and it reveals the Lord as a masterful strategic thinker. With Bethany so close by, one can be certain what Jesus did in Bethany quickly became news in Jerusalem; the reports, in fact, would sprout wings and fly straight into the halls of the Sanhedrin. Raising Lazarus would also push Caiaphas over the edge, and he would sign the order for Jesus' arrest (John 11:57).

When this story began to unfold, it is probable Jesus was still at Bethabara, a very hard, all day, and uphill journey by foot from Lazarus' home in Bethany. A person would have to be in excellent physical condition to do it in a day.

The timeline of the drama fits into the ministry of Jesus in His last winter before Calvary. The events played out sometime between the Feast of Hanukkah and the annual celebration of Passover. Jesus' crucifixion was, at most, only a few weeks away.

Without any effort to be exhaustive, the drama unfurls around ten interrelated benefits of suffering.

1. Suffering helps us see what we are like on the inside—our inner heart.

2. Suffering helps us discover agape love.

3. Suffering shows the need for a well thought out "but if not" doctrine.

4. Suffering gives opportunity to think about the sovereignty of God.

5. Jesus is the ultimate solution to suffering.

6. Suffering spotlights the bruises and grief that sometimes come from the hand of God.

7. Suffering teaches the wisdom of obedience.

8. Suffering shows the high price the sin curse demands.

9. Suffering liberates by aiding the discovery of new meaning.

10. The "after" to suffering.

Lazarus' Tomb

Ancient Bethany today is populated largely by Palestinians and Arabs, and the name of the town is *el-Azariyeh*. The term means "the place of Lazarus."

A particular tomb in Bethany has been recognized since the second century AD as the place where Lazarus' broken hearted sisters laid their brother to rest, and where Jesus raised him from the dead.

This site witnesses to the historical integrity of the New Testament, because this tomb has been largely undisputed for almost two millennia as the site of the greatest of Jesus' seven miracles.

The Cry for Help

11:2 This Mary, whose brother Lazarus now lay sick, was the same one who poured perfume on the Lord and wiped his feet with her hair.

The Apostle John's account of Mary emptying the jar of perfume on Jesus' feet and drying His feet with her hair is recorded in John 12, and had not yet occurred. John cited it here to help identify the family whose story he told.

3 So the sisters sent word to Jesus, "Lord, the one you love is sick."

1. Suffering Helps Us See Inside Ourselves

Suffering can indeed have benefits. One of them is it can show what is inside us, with the goal to bring us to healing in some meaningful way (Deuteronomy 8:2). Too often we do not know ourselves, but keen disappointment, crushed expectations, or major illness will bring to the surface our secret heart, and force us to face ourselves. This is not only true of the person who is suffering, but also his relatives, friends, and acquaintances who witness the process. Sickness makes us all face our mortality.

When the sisters sent word to tell Jesus Lazarus was sick, they used the phrase, "Lord, the one whom you love..." The Greek word for love here is *phileo* (friendship love), and it describes their perception of Jesus' relationship with Lazarus.

A number of people in the Old Testament are identified as having enjoyed closeness with the pre-incarnate Messiah. Two who stand out are Abraham and Moses. Some eighteen hundred years before the ministry of Jesus, Abraham and Jehovah had warm fellowship and talked with each other often (e.g., Genesis 12; 15; 17; 18–22). Moses too had a special relationship with Jehovah that opened the door for them to converse regularly.

> Whenever Moses went out to the tent, all the people rose and stood at the entrances to their tents, watching Moses until he entered the tent. As Moses went into the tent, the pillar of cloud would come down and stay at the entrance, while the Lord spoke with Moses. Whenever the people saw the pillar of cloud standing at the entrance to the tent, they all stood and worshiped each at the entrance to his tent. The Lord would speak to Moses face to face, as a man speaks with his friend (Exodus 33:8–11; Genesis 22:11 ff).

As had been true with Abraham and Moses, the bond between Jesus and Lazarus was obviously strong. Hence, the message to Jesus from Lazarus' two sisters was urgent.

THINK ABOUT IT: "Sir, your good friend is very, very sick" (John 11:3 TLB). And the unstated request was *"We need you, now! Please come and heal him."*

Jesus' Purpose in the Illness

11:4 When he heard this, Jesus said, "This sickness will not end in death. No, it is for God's glory so that God's Son may be glorified through it."

The phrase, "When he heard this," shows Jesus learned about Lazarus' illness for the first time from the messenger. This statement is another of the Apostle John's indications demonstrating how the Son of Man and the Son of God functioned as the God-man in the incarnation of Jesus Christ. Jesus learned from a messenger about Lazarus' serious illness. How He handled the situation came from His Father, as guided by the Holy Spirit.

At the outset of this story, Jesus gave a prophecy about what the end result of Lazarus' situation would be: "This illness is not to end in death, but is to promote the glory of God, in order that the Son of God may be glorified by it" (John 11:4 Weymouth).

Jesus had stated some months earlier at the unnamed feast in Jerusalem how He received guidance from His Father. It came in His discourse after healing the man at the Pool of Bethesda: "Very truly I tell you, the Son can do nothing by himself; he can do only what he sees his Father doing, because whatever the Father does the Son also does. For the Father loves the Son and shows him all he does" (John 5:19–20). Jesus also gave a prophecy affirming how this would apply to raising the dead (John 5:21). This prediction was about two days away from finding a grand fulfillment in the resurrection of Lazarus.

"Chariots of Fire"

"Chariots of Fire" is the true story of two British runners competing in the 1924 Olympics. Eric Liddell was a devout Christian and one of the finest runners in the world. Eric's sister, Jennie, wanted him to leave competitive running to join the family on the mission field in China. Jennie feels Eric was putting running ahead of serving God, and she questioned his commitment.

In one scene, Eric attempts to help his sister see his point of view. Eric announces with a smile, "I've decided I'm going back to China. The missionary service has accepted—"

Jennie interrupts him. "Oh, Eric, I'm so pleased."

Eric continues, "But I've got a lot of running to do first. Jennie, you've got to understand. I believe God made me for a purpose, for China. He also made me fast, and when

I run, I feel His pleasure. To give it up would be to hold Him in contempt. You were right; it's not just fun. To win is to honor Him."[1]

Eric Liddell made the choice to compete, because he understood his running gave delight to his Lord. But the sovereign purposes of God are not always understood up front. In the case of Lazarus' terminal illness, he did not even get to make a choice. Yet, when Lazarus was restored to life, Jesus' purpose became fully understandable as they witnessed the glory it brought to the Lord as the Son of God.

Lazarus and his sisters had to discover what Fannie Crosby (1820–1915) expressed in poetry centuries later. Learning it can be a painful journey.

> All the way my Savior leads me;
> What have I to ask beside?
> Can I doubt His tender mercy,
> Who through life has been my Guide?
> Heav'nly peace, divinest comfort,
> Here by faith in Him to dwell!
> For I know, whate'er befall me,
> Jesus doeth all things well.

2. Suffering Helps Us Discover Agape Love

11:5 Jesus loved [*agape*] Martha and her sister and Lazarus. 6 Yet when he heard Lazarus was sick, he stayed where he was two more days.

The sovereign authority of God often comes into focus in the tension between two kinds of love, *phileo* and *agape*. The Apostle John used the word, *agape (God's love)*, to describe Jesus' love for Lazarus and his sisters. The sisters interpreted Jesus' love for Lazarus with the word, *phileo* (friendship love—John 11:3).

They had not yet come to appreciate the height and depth of the heavenly Father's love for them *[agape]*.

God's love is always unconditional and in our best interests, in the perfect way only He knows our best interests. Friendship love always comes with attached obligations, including the expectation of returned favors and kindnesses. A friend (*phileo*) is much more likely to act out of duty, doing what his buddy wants him to do. A person guided by God's love, *agape*, will do what will benefit another the most.

Jesus was indeed their friend (*phileo*) but He was much more than their friend. He was also their Messiah and the greatest benefit He could give them was His unconditional march of love to Calvary. He would sacrifice Himself there as the atoning substitute for the sins of all people worldwide, including His three friends in Bethany.

THINK ABOUT IT: The word *agape* expresses Jesus' love for *you*, too, dear reader (Psalm 13:5–6 MSG). A loving father and mother will give their child what is best, even though it is often not what he wants. So it is with the heavenly Father. The term, *agape*, means God will do what is right or best in the situation, based on His perfect knowledge of what is the ultimate good. And when Jesus acts in the best interests of His kingdom, for example, He is always acting in our best interests too, even though we might not comprehend it at the time.

Parents routinely do the same thing. They give to a child according to a balance of what is good for the child and in the best interests of the family.

This understanding explains John's use of the expression, "yet when he heard..." in verse 6, or, "in view of what He heard." Knowing Lazarus was seriously ill, Jesus made a conscious decision not to go immediately to him. In the sisters' expectations, the greatest blessing Jesus could give Lazarus was to heal his terminal illness. Besides, they were friends (*phileo*), and this is what friends do. If at all possible, a friend will give the help requested. In Martha's and Mary's expectations, Jesus owed it to them. They had welcomed Him, fed Him, given Him a place to sleep, and Mary had sat as a learner at His feet.

Jesus, on the other hand, understood the greatest act of love (*agape*) He could show Lazarus and his sisters was not to heal him but to raise Lazarus from the dead. As this unfolds, the story reveals the painful process by which the sisters' moved from *phileo* to *agape*, and aligned their expectations with the purposes of God.

Yes, suffering requires us to examine ourselves while at the same time it compels us to think about God and His ways. Jesus' love for Martha, Mary, and Lazarus stands out in this story. It also shows how Jesus acted in their best interests, knowing what was best for them (*agape* love). Jesus also knew their expectations of Him, based on friendship love (*phileo*), would make them misunderstand His motives. In fact, it is not at all unusual for friendship love to misinterpret the choices of *agape* love.

THINK ABOUT IT: For all of God's children, adjusting expectations so that we discover and accept the richness of *agape* love, often seems to be a painful process.

Dear reader, have you ever walked in Martha's and Mary's shoes?

Jesus had already affirmed to His disciples what His objective was in Lazarus' terminal illness: "It is for God's glory so that God's Son may be glorified through it" (vs. 4). But these two sisters did not know this yet.

One can only imagine the trauma Mary and Martha suffered as they watched their brother's life ebb away, all the while hoping by the moment Jesus would show up and heal him. One is left to wonder how many times these very distraught women, who felt friendship love for Jesus (*phileo*), stared out their window, yearning to see Jesus walking up the street. Jesus was their only hope, but He did not come to their brother's aid. They had no choice but to surrender Lazarus to the Grim Reaper. As that process unfolded, they surely began to ponder what went wrong in their relationship with Jesus.

These sisters had looked death in the eye before, having most probably surrendered their mother and their father. Now, the only man left in their lives was gone.

With loving hands and devastated hearts, they wrapped their brother's face and body in burial cloths, and poured the burial ointments over him. Then, with the help of friends, they carefully walked his cold body down the roughly chiseled steps and placed it at the bottom of the tomb that earlier might have claimed their father and mother. After each of the girls gave their brother's chilled body a hug and a kiss that always marks the final goodbye, a stone was placed over the mouth of the burial chamber. As they began walking away albeit with a few glances back, these two heartbroken sisters slowly departed the cave to face a bleak future together. They had once been a happy family of at least five, secure and safe. Now they had only each other, and were loaded with all the emotions of insecurity.

"If Jesus had only come to help us! Why didn't He rescue our brother?"

Mary and Martha loved Jesus with the love that is between close friends. But these two sisters did not know God's purposes yet. Nor would they have been able upfront to understand, even if Jesus had told them, how Lazarus' death and resurrection would bring great honor to the Lord, and to them as a family. They had not yet comprehended they had the most powerful Person in the universe on their side, and that Jesus is always bigger than any crisis. In fact, Jesus is good all the time (Psalm 34:8; 73:5; 100:5; 1 Chronicles 16:34; Mark 10:18; John 10:11). But in their overwhelming grief these very lonely sisters could not even entertain the thought Jesus' two-day wait might be an act of *agape* love.

They were staring death in the face, while Jesus was looking at resurrection, so they did not perceive how Jesus' delay would ultimately align their best interests and their brother's with the purposes of God. The deliberate interval did, however, begin the process of showing the sisters their own hearts, even as it required them to think seriously, at a whole new level, about the plans of God.

THINK ABOUT IT: Tears have a way of washing out the soul. But until this cleansing is complete, tears can also blind us to the new possibilities ahead.

The story of Lazarus and his sisters puts on the front burner three of the most profound statements people in crisis make about Jesus. Martha and Mary expressed them, and people through the centuries have thought them too:

- "We earnestly prayed, but Jesus did not answer our prayers," and
- "He could have prevented this if He had wanted too."
- Hence, "can Jesus be trusted to do good in the crises of life? Is He truly good, all the time?"

3. Suffering Shows the Need for a
"But If Not" Doctrine

Thoughts like these show each child of God needs balance, including a well thought understanding of *but if not*. The story of the three Hebrew young men in Babylon makes the point. On the plain of Dura they refused to bow before Nebuchadnezzar's image of gold. The infuriated king gave them one final chance to obey the order. Instead, they responded:

> "Your threat means nothing to us. If you throw us in the fire, the God we serve can rescue us from your roaring furnace and anything else you might cook up, O king. *But even if he doesn't*, it wouldn't make a bit of difference, O king. We still wouldn't serve your gods or worship the gold statue you set up" (Daniel 3:16–18 MSG).

God did not prevent their going into the furnace, saving them *from the fire* (Daniel 3:21–30; Isaiah 43:2; Ephesians 2:1–10). Instead, He took the route of the greater miracle, saving them *in the fire*. It happened in the split second the fourth man, the Son of Man, the Messiah, stepped into the furnace even as "they fell into the fire." When God's Son walked into the furnace hot enough in a second to take their breath away, the nature of the fire changed. It was no longer a furnace to destroy them, but to usher them into new liberty.

The great symbol of this deliverance was the rope on the three Hebrew boys' hands and feet. Their *bonds* went up in smoke, but not them; nor did the "seven times hotter" fire turn them to cremated ashes (Daniel 3:19). Instead, they walked around in the furnace as free men with their Messiah (Daniel 3:25). And when they stepped out of the fire, it "had not harmed their bodies, nor was a hair of their heads singed. Their robes were not scorched, and there was no smell of fire on them" (Daniel 3:27).

To his credit, Nebuchadnezzar had the good sense to promote these survivors to the highest levels of Babylonian government!

Nebuchadnezzar later lost his throne for about seven years resulting from God's judgment of his colossal pride. After being restored to power, he made a prophetic exclamation about the greatness of God: "Now I, Nebuchadnezzar, praise and exalt and glorify the King of heaven, because everything he does is right and all his ways are just" (Daniel 4:37).

THINK ABOUT IT: The king of Babylon's great conclusion has helped many children of God walk through life's crises with their faith in God intact.

May the grace of our Lord help each of you, dear readers, to accept this admonition: purpose in your heart if God does not answer your prayer the way you pray it, you will still praise and exalt and glorify the King of heaven, because everything he does is right and all his ways are just.

Suffering Revealed the Hearts of the Disciples Too

11:7 Then he said to his disciples, "Let us go back to Judea."
8 "But Rabbi," they said, "a short while ago the Jews tried to stone you, and yet you are going back there?"
9 Jesus answered, "Are there not twelve hours of daylight? A man who walks by day will not stumble, for he sees by this world's light. 10 It is when he walks by night that he stumbles, for he has no light."

The disciples did not grasp what was ahead any more than did Mary and Martha. For sure, they did not want to go back to the suburbs of Jerusalem. "Rabbi," they said, "you can't do that. The Jews are out to kill you, and you're going back?" (John 11:7–8 MSG). It had only been a few weeks since the Jews had picked up stones to kill Jesus at the Feast of Dedication, and the very unnerving experience was still raw in their memories (John 10:31).

The disciples had not yet connected their situation to the miracle of the nobleman's son (John 4:46–50). They could have encouraged Jesus merely to speak the word of healing for Lazarus. Nor had they fully assimilated the hand of God in Jesus' many "escapes" from the death-traps to which they had been eyewitnesses (e.g., John 10:39).

THINK ABOUT IT: Do you link your present crises to how well you have absorbed God's delivering hand in your yesterdays?

Jesus demonstrated (in Chapter 7) He was master of *kairos* time which includes the events of our lives, the minutes and hours, and even the seconds. In this setting, Jesus again asserted confidence in His control of time, reminding the disciples a summer day has twelve hours of daylight. It was Jesus' way of saying His work was not finished. Jesus' sacrifice on the Hill of the Skull could not be made while there was still daylight left on the timeline of His ministry.

We can believe Jesus had not felt fear earlier at the sight of His very livid enemies who despised Him and showed it with the rocks in their hands. But His disciples certainly did. To them, daylight for Jesus had already ended in Judea, and Bethany was much too close to Jerusalem for them to feel any motivation to return. They simply did not want to make the trip and tried their best to discourage Jesus from returning to Bethany.

THINK ABOUT IT: Sometimes the people closest to you will try their best to stop you from obeying God and witnessing His miracle power. What about your children? Your spouse? (Job 2:9).

Have you ever tried to stop someone, only to realize later they were acting in the will of God?

11:11 After he had said this, he went on to tell them, "Our friend Lazarus has fallen asleep; but I am going there to wake him up."
12 His disciples replied, "Lord, if he sleeps, he will get better."
13 Jesus had been speaking of his death, but his disciples thought he meant natural sleep.

Jesus' statement to His disciples, "our friend Lazarus," uses the word *filos* (friend or friendship love), to describe the relationship of the group as a whole to Lazarus. The disciples' relationship with Lazarus was on a friendship level too. As this story unfolds, they too learned new lessons about agape love.

The word picture, "fallen asleep" is used elsewhere in Scripture to describe death. The Apostle Paul, for example, chose the phrase four times in his first letter to the Corinthian believers and twice to the church at Thessalonica (I Corinthians 11:30; 15:6, 18, 20; I Thessalonians 4:14, 15). Paul also used it in his sermon in the synagogue at Pisidian Antioch (Acts 13:36).

Jesus the Prophet Announces Lazarus' Death

The messenger sent by Mary and Martha reported only Lazarus was sick, and not that he had died. Consequently, Jesus' statement to His disciples, "our friend Lazarus has fallen asleep," expressed a bold and easily measurable prophecy. When the disciples reached Bethany, they discovered Lazarus was indeed dead, just as Jesus had foretold. Jesus could have known this only in the unique way the Holy Spirit guided His life (John 5:19–21). If Jesus had been wrong in making so clear and specific a prophecy, it would have been a heavy blow to the disciples' growing faith in Him as the Son of God.

Two Biblical prophets are credited with one hundred percent accuracy. The Lord was with Samuel and "let none of his words fall to the ground" (1 Samuel 3:19). This accuracy helps to explain why people so feared Samuel (e.g., 1 Samuel 3:20; 16:4). Jesus was one hundred percent accurate too. He was the ultimate prophet, and the significance of His predictions far exceeded Samuel's. In fact, the spirit of prophecy was on everything Jesus said, motivating John to write, "The testimony of Jesus is the spirit of prophecy" (Revelation 19:10).

Prophecy in the church is one of the gifts of the Spirit (Ephesians 4:9–13; I Corinthians 12:10; 14:1). As a result, many of the Lord's followers know what it feels like for the spirit of prophecy to come on them, anointing what they speak. With Jesus, the spirit of prophecy never left Him. The Revelator went on to quote an angel who told him this ability alone is cause to "worship God" (19:10).

The Apostle John surely never forgot this display of Jesus' prophetic accuracy regarding Lazarus. How could he not remember his emotions when he realized Lazarus was indeed dead and Jesus was again accurate to perfection?

THINK ABOUT IT: This understanding of Jesus as the perfect prophet sets the Lord apart from the founders of all other world religions.

The Lord fulfilled each of the Old Testament prophecies about himself and spoke new ones, always with total accuracy. Fulfilled prophecy is a very strong witness to Jesus as the Son of God.

How important to listen to what Jesus says. He is "the one and only," so believe Him and obey Him!

Jesus' statement, "I am going there to wake him up" was a prophecy too. Jesus knew in the Spirit what He was going to do before He began the journey to Bethany: He intended to raise Lazarus from the dead. The disciples' responded, "Master, if he's gone to sleep, he'll get a good rest and wake up feeling fine." But "Jesus was talking about death, while his disciples thought he was talking about taking a nap" (John 11:12–13 MSG).

11:14 So then he told them plainly, "Lazarus is dead, 15 and for your sake I am glad I was not there, so that you may believe. But let us go to him."
16 Then Thomas (called Didymus) said to the rest of the disciples, "Let us also go, that we may die with him."

The agape love of God stirs different emotions than friendship love. Mary and Martha actually took offense and felt anger at Jesus because He did not measure up to their expectations as a friend. Jesus actually felt gladness for the disciples' sakes that He was not there. This was true because Jesus knew what was ahead for them, and in the best interests of Mary, Martha, and Lazarus. [The term, *chairo* (glad), communicates cheerfulness, calm happiness, and joyfulness.]

THINK ABOUT IT: Jesus could be calm because He knew the end from the beginning; He saw the whole picture.

Dear reader, He can step into your crisis as the calm and collected Great Physician, not only because He knows the end but because He is the solution!

Jesus said Lazarus had "fallen asleep" (vs. 16), and then interpreted what the phrase meant by saying, "Lazarus is dead."

Jesus' prophetic response to His disciples was both factual and full of hope and promise. Jesus pulled back the curtain further here to permit His disciples to see God's purpose in action. "I am glad for your sakes I wasn't there. You're about to be given new grounds for believing" (John 11:15 MSG). The miracle ahead would give great glory to God and immeasurably expand Mary's and Martha's trust in Him. It would also make for another quantum leap in maturing the faith of Jesus' disciples, preparing them for His own resurrection.

The disciples missed the Lord's message, however. They did not make the connection (verses 11 and 14). If they had absorbed the prophecy, the anticipation and excitement would surely have made the long walk uphill to Bethany far easier. At the moment they were bound by tunnel vision, focused on their traumatic memory of the Jews with the rocks in their hands. Knowing Jesus would not change His mind, Thomas' statement of resignation, said it all: "Come along. We might as well die with him" (John 11:16 MSG).

With that attitude, it was a long walk to Bethany!

Thomas' tone of voice and attitude, however, communicated he had no intention to die with Jesus if he could help it; instead, he would have run as fast as he could! Thomas joined the other disciples and did just that when the Lord was arrested (Matthew 26:45). At this point in the maturity of Thomas' faith, he was not close to the level of confident trust in Jesus as the Son of God that would motivate him to give his life for his Messiah. But neither were any of the other disciples.

This kind of faith, however, did come after Jesus' resurrection. Thomas, for example, took the gospel outside the Roman Empire, going into India. Good evidence supports he died as a martyr in the ancient Indian city of Mylapur (ca. 72 AD). Many believers in India today trace their spiritual roots back to the Apostle Thomas.

What Jesus "Found" at Bethany

11:17 On his arrival, Jesus found Lazarus had already been in the tomb for four days.

Jesus knew in the Spirit and prophesied before He left Bethabara that Lazarus had died, but the disciples missed it. The Lord was going to Bethany to bring him back to life. Yet, Jesus "found" or pinpointed from the townsfolk the exact amount of time he had been dead! This is another situation showing how the Father and the Holy Spirit gave the Son of God guidance, and how the Son of Man sought information from people.

11:18 Bethany was less than two miles from Jerusalem, 19 and many Jews had come to Martha and Mary to comfort them in the loss of their brother.

This passage gives insight into the social status of Lazarus, Martha, and Mary. Lazarus' family obviously had some wealth and many friends.

The Jewish comforters who came to console Mary and Martha also show an important aspect of Jewish funeral customs. Mourning typically lasted for seven days; the role of friends was to participate in the weeping and grieving. It was normal for a person not to wash his body during the early days of mourning or wear any perfumes or ointments. Men were also known not to trim their beards for the full seven days.

4. Suffering Gives Opportunity to Ponder the Sovereignty of God.

The term, sovereignty, embraces the idea God has independent and supreme authority over all He created, and acts according to His will (Psalm 115:3; Daniel 4:35–37; Matthew 28:16–20; Romans 9:20). In doing so, He *manifests* His Lordship over people and the natural order according to His character, based on the essence of who He is. The Apostle John described the inner core of the Godhead with the statement, "God is love" (1 John 4:8, 16).

Suffering powerfully motivates people to ponder both God's love and His sovereign authority. In fact, to the extent pain encourages people to think about how God's sovereignty and His love actually blend, it can be man's friend. It is certain God has never performed a sovereign act that was not grounded in His love. This merging of these divine character traits undeniably took place in the story of Lazarus.

Jesus could have healed Lazarus' terminal illness. He did not, and this fact lets us glimpse into the thinking and the soul of the Son of God. The Lord saw a greater necessity amid the death threats on His own life than a decision to intercept Lazarus' sickness. Jesus intended instead to:

1. Bless Lazarus and his sisters with the far greater miracle of resurrection. Lazarus' resurrection would be glorious. In fact, it would redeem fully all of Lazarus' pain and suffering, and all of the grief of his sisters. In doing so, it would take their friendship with Jesus to the far higher level of *agape* love.

2. Deepen the faith of His disciples.

3. Give great glory to the heavenly Father.

4. Maintain sovereign control of the many circumstances regarding His life. For example, the same miracle that would give such great glory to God, would also push the Sanhedrin "over the cliff" to a decision to kill Jesus. This miracle meant Jesus was more than they could handle. The success of His ministry was luring too many of their followers.

The miracle reaffirmed to Jesus that in just a few short weeks, resurrection awaited Him too on the other side of a wicked cross. Lazarus was the prototype, albeit glorious. Jesus' death and resurrection would be immeasurably more wonderful than His great miracle restoring Lazarus to life. Jesus' empty tomb would stand-out as the singular achievement of His incarnate life which brought such glory to God. Its afterglow has continued to light up every generation since then. Little wonder: Lazarus was raised in mortality, but Jesus came out of the grave immortal and incorruptible, never to die again. With His own crucifixion and resurrection Jesus conquered death itself, a monumental accomplishment indeed (Revelation 1:18).

THINK ABOUT IT: The Apostle Paul capsuled Jesus' success at Golgotha with the phrase, "The last enemy to be destroyed is death" (1 Corinthians 15:26). Death should never be portrayed, for example, as a deliverer that "releases people from their suffering." Instead, death must always be understood as an enemy; a killer. Death is a curse and has no good in it. Only the triumph at Calvary of Jesus' resurrection power continues to defeat death in every generation. In doing so, it anchors the soul of every believer with the hope of everlasting life.

Paul went on to explain the significance of the triumph. He said it meant the fulfillment of King David's prophecy: the God who is both *Adonai* and Jehovah "has put everything under [the Son of Man's] feet" (Psalm 8:6; see also Ephesians 1:22; Hebrews 2:8; 6:19–20). The conquest at Calvary was immediate and total: "It is finished" (John 19:30). The centuries to follow in salvation history have continued to demonstrate the eternal meaning of the altogether glorious sacrifice the Son of God made on the Hill of the Skull.

This triumph is so expansive and comprehensive Paul said it actually takes us into the inner workings of the Trinity:

> The end will come, when [Jesus] hands over the kingdom to God the Father after he has destroyed all dominion, authority and power. For he must reign until he has put all his enemies under his feet. The last enemy to be destroyed is death. For he "has put everything under his feet." Now when it says "everything" has been put under him, it is clear this does not include God himself, who put everything under Christ. When he has done this, then the Son himself will be made subject to him who put everything under him, so that God may be all in all (1 Corinthians 15:24–28).

When Sovereignty Embraces Silence

The interval between Martha and Mary's sending their message to Jesus, and the Lord's arrival in Bethany included many long hours of waiting and hoping. As far as these very hurting sisters were concerned, they received only painful silence from Jesus.

Satan, the archenemy of our souls has indeed turned the silence of God so many times into mistrust of God. His goal has always been to drive a wedge of doubt that soaks faith out of a person's heart.

THINK ABOUT IT: The silence of God is always purposeful. It can be very humbling when it helps us see how much more growing in Christ we still need to do. This was certainly true with Martha and Mary as they watched their brother die while waiting in vain for Jesus to show up.

Isaiah proclaimed in a nutshell the best response to the silence of God: "I will wait for the Lord," he said, even when it feels like He "is hiding his face... I will put my trust in him" (Isaiah 8:17).

Walking with God does indeed have its seasons when God's answers do not come quickly. The interaction of God with us in those periods is intended to draw us into deeper trust, dependence and obedience. Then, when it's all over, and we realize we have passed the test and learned the lesson, the new discoveries often radically transcend for the better anything we had been hoping to gain.

- We are introduced to the sin we needed to confront, and

- Recognize patterns of behavior that beg to be broken.

- We gain insights into who we are that we did not know before, and

- Realize a depth of relationship with God we have never experienced.

Such revelation makes the journey into the silence of God worth it.

Job's Experience with the Silence of God

Satan the accuser stood before God and alleged Job was faithful out of self-interest because of God's many blessings that had so enriched Job's life:

> "Does Job fear God for nothing? Have you not put a hedge around him and his household and everything he has? You have blessed the work of his hands, so that his flocks and herds are spread throughout the land. But stretch out your hand and strike everything he has, and he will surely curse you to your face" (Job 1:9–11).

Satan did strike Job with multiple, painful losses, including his servants, as well as his oxen, donkeys, sheep, and camels. Since his wealth was measured by his possessions, he went from prosperity to poverty overnight. But worse was to come. A fierce desert wind storm blew the house down on top of his children, killing each of them on the spot. It was a blow so very heavy anyone lacking Job's depth of trust in God would have broken faith and accused God. The indictment against God routinely is that He is responsible because He permitted it to happen. Hence, the charge asserts human suffering challenges the fairness of God's justice. But that was not Job's experience. Instead, when he heard the news, Job got up and tore his robe and shaved his head. Then he fell to the ground in worship and said:

> "Naked I came from my mother's womb, and naked I will depart.
> The Lord gave and the Lord has taken away; may the name of the Lord be praised."
> In all this, Job did not sin by charging God with wrongdoing (Job 1:20–22).

Another blow soon followed for Job. Satan alleged before God, "Skin for skin... A man will give all he has for his own life" (Job 2:4). Job had apparently enjoyed good health, but soon he was covered "from the soles of his feet to the top of his head" with highly painful welts and sores. The result was "Job took a piece of broken pottery and scraped himself with it as he sat in the ashes" (Job 2:7–8).

For Job and his wife, the grief over their many losses in such a short amount of time had to be overwhelming. As for Job's wife, she had given birth to their five children; now she had to bury them all. She was left with only a very sick husband, and had gone from riches to rags. In her crisis she could not bear to look at her husband in his sickness, so she responded to Job, chiding him: "Are you still holding on to your integrity? Curse God and die!" Job's answer back to his wife, however, remained full of robust faith: "'You are talking like a foolish woman. Shall we accept good from God, and not trouble?' In all this, Job did not sin in what he said" (Job 2:10).

Arguably the greatest challenge to Job's trust in God still lay ahead. It came as he tried to process the silence of God. This conclusion comes through in the lonely wail of his broken heart crushed by the loss of his children, his health and his fortune.

It is one thing to "walk through the valley of the shadow of death" when God is with us, holding our hearts in His compassionate hands (Psalm 23:4). But will your faith hold when the windows and doors of heaven are closed to your prayers even as you are fighting the battle of your life? When all you get from God is silence right at the time you think you need Him the most? Here's how Job expressed it:

2 "Even today my complaint is bitter; his hand is heavy in spite of my groaning.
3 If only I knew where to find him; if only I could go to his dwelling!

4 I would state my case before him and fill my mouth with arguments.

5 I would find out what he would answer me, and consider what he would say.

6 Would he oppose me with great power? No, he would not press charges against me.

7 There an upright man could present his case before him, and I would be delivered forever from my judge.

8 "But if I go to the east, he is not there; if I go to the west, I do not find him.

9 When he is at work in the north, I do not see him; when he turns to the south, I catch no glimpse of him" (Job 23:2–9).

Out of this depth of Job's pain, loss, and loneliness, Job felt like God was not speaking. But even in the deepest silence, deep calls to deep. Said another way, the deepest silence can be the birthplace of the deepest and richest, life-changing revelation (Psalm 42:1–7).

Yet again Job climbed up on the wings of faith to express his trust in the God who was silent, without even telling Job "the why" of his dilemma. It is a heartwarming affirmation of Job's confidence in the goodness of God: "He knows the way that I take; when he has tested me, I will come forth as gold" (Job 23:10).

Daniel and the Silence of God

Sometimes what looks like the silence of God might be a result of Satan's efforts to block the sovereign purposes of God. Daniel prayed for twenty-one days before the breakthrough came in the spiritual warfare between Michael and the Prince of Persia. In Daniel's case, he recognized the source of the opposition was actually Satanic.

It is very comforting to realize, however, God was with Daniel all of that time: "Since the first day...your words were heard," although Daniel did not realize it until after the spiritual victory was won in prayer and fasting (Daniel 10:12–14).

THINK ABOUT IT: It is important to recognize the silence of God does not presuppose the absence of God.

Jesus' Experience with Forsakenness

The classic example of the silence of God occurred on Mt. Calvary. The heavenly Father's only Son was hanging on three crude nails between two thieves. Jesus was already weak from loss of blood and His body was beginning to shut down. The Grim Reaper was standing in the shadows, patiently hoping, albeit vainly, to claim his prey. Dehydration was already doing its work, and Jesus' headache must have been pounding.

Matthew and Mark record what happened. In His weakened condition, the Lord cried out in the specific, prophetic words of Psalm 22: "My God, my God, why have you forsaken me?" Jesus might have also expressed what else David prophetically wrote: "Why do you refuse to help me or even to listen to my groans?" (Matthew 27:46; Mark 15:34; Psalm 22:1–3 TLB; Psalm 83:1 KJV).

What is the worst thing that can happen to a person? The supreme tragedy is for God to pull back His hand of grace and turn us over to the consequences of our evil choices. Is anything more scary than separation from God?

Why did the heavenly Father forsake Jesus on His cross?

Of all places on His cross?

The prophet Habakkuk offers an insight. "Thou art of purer eyes than to behold evil, and canst not look upon iniquity"

(Habakkuk 1:13 KJV). The Apostle Paul wrote, "He hath made him to be sin, who knew no sin" (2 Corinthians 5:21 KJV). Jesus took into His holy body the full essence of everything sin is, and became the sacrifice to forgive and elevate to sonship all who take responsibility for their choices and call on Jesus in repentance.

Dear reader, please ponder Paul's insight and assimilate it into your lifestyle: "He hath made him to be sin…" The verb, to be, describes a state of being, not an action or a deed. The sense here is that Jesus pulled into His bosom everything the curse of sin had blighted and profaned, beginning with Eden.

Jesus drank the biter dregs of the cup to the last drop, becoming sin for us, so that we can become the righteousness of God through Him (Isaiah 51:22; 2 Corinthians 5:21; Matthew 20:22; John 18:11).

But must we conclude the heavenly Father deserted His Son amid the agony of the cross, as some have believed? Daniel learned God heard his prayer on day one (Daniel 10:12–14). As regards Jesus, is it not true He walked into His agony with full knowledge of the Father's plan from eternity? (Hebrews 13:20; Revelation 13:8).

THINK ABOUT IT: Jesus' very human, heart-wrenching cry of "Why…?" is not the end of the story. Instead, His final words on the cross were said in the loudest voice His remaining ounces of energy could muster: "Father, into your hands I commit my spirit.' When He had said this, He breathed his last" (Luke 23:46).

Like Daniel discovered, Jesus died knowing His Father was there all the time. This is true even though in Jesus' true humanity, the pain and horror of the cross shrouded him from His Father's intimate presence.

- What was God doing while His Son was dying? Just what the Trinity planned from eternity: "God [was so loving] the world that he [was giving] his only begotten Son..." (John 3:16 KJV; Titus 1:2).

- What was Jesus doing, dying on the cross? Just what the Trinity planned from eternity: "Greater love has no man than this, that a man lay down his life for his friends" (John 15:13 KJV; 1 Peter 1:18–23).

Then, knowing everything was finished exactly according to the eternal plan (John 19:30), Jesus and His Father were reunited on the other side of the river called Death; in fact, His Father was eagerly waiting for His Son over there across the divide.

Three days later, exactly according to the eternal plan, Jesus' triumphant resurrection made sense of everything.

THINK ABOUT IT: For you, dear reader, what is God doing in your season of His silence? In the vivid imagery of the Apostle Paul, God is still writing a beautiful poem with your life, and it will be another of His masterpieces (Ephesians 2:10).

Jesus' sovereign silence did come to an end. He did arrive in Bethany but on His schedule. Yes, the silence of God is always purposeful and has a time line on it.

Martha's Faith and Mary's Deep Grief

11:20 When Martha heard Jesus was coming, she went out to meet him, but Mary stayed at home.

Luke records a story about Jesus paying a visit to a home owned by a woman named Martha, in a village Luke did not name. She had a sister named Mary living with her. No mention is made of a brother. The women prepared a meal for Jesus and His disciples that evening. Martha was caught up with getting the meal ready, while Mary wanted to sit at the feet of Jesus and drink in what He was saying. Martha became upset and asked Jesus to "tell her to come and help me" (Luke 10:40 TLB). Jesus responded:

> "Martha, dear Martha, You're fussing far too much and getting yourself worked up over nothing. One thing only is essential, and Mary has chosen it—it's the main course, and won't be taken from her" (Luke 10:41–42 MSG).

Over the centuries of church history this Martha has come to symbolize people in the church who are *doers*, while Mary is the model for *worshipers*, "the main course."

If this Martha and Mary of Luke's account are the same women presented in John 11, Martha obviously absorbed the lesson because the roles reversed. For example, when Martha learned Jesus was coming into town, she went out to meet Him. "But Mary stayed at home."

Grief is an emotion that strikes everyone sooner or later. However, it can become inappropriately controlling and paralyzing. Grief can actually walk a person down the lonely valley of the mind into the deep well of depression. In this state, a person can easily believe prayer is useless. A person might not even get up and go to the house of God to meet Jesus. This reality often embraces the very painful thought *Jesus has failed me*. It is routinely expressed like this: "*I know He does not care about me, so why go to the Lord's house?*"

Yes, suffering will show what is in our hearts.

THINK ABOUT IT: Were Mary's expectations of Jesus—*come heal my brother*—too crushed for her to go to Him with her sister?

Has Jesus ever offended *you* when He did not answer your prayers by giving you what you were sure was a right and proper request?

"Whatever You Ask!"

11:21 "Lord," Martha said to Jesus, "if you had been here, my brother would not have died. 22 But I know even now God will give you whatever you ask."

This is the sad language of disappointed faith colored by deep grief and wrapped with a sliver of hope. Martha's statement, which Mary would also repeat in her own way a short while later (vs. 32), was obviously a faith statement, although enclosed in a cocoon of disillusionment.

The sisters were no doubt correct: if Jesus had been there, He surely would have healed Lazarus. Even if Martha did speak in faith both sisters missed that Jesus could have spoken the word of healing from Bethabara, as soon as Jesus heard about Lazarus' illness (John 4:46–53).

So many people in the extremities of life have asked similar questions, some in faith and some in unbelief.

I prayed earnestly; so why did Jesus not hear me?

Jesus had the power to intervene; why didn't He?

Can I depend on God to be good in the crises of my life?

Those who express these thoughts in faith do so out of the struggle of their own hearts, and in time almost invariably they draw closer to the Lord. Those who ask them in unbelief usually use the questions to challenge the love of God, "the great love wherewith he loved us" (Ephesians 2:4). These people are often hardened further in their doubt and unbelief.

"I Miss Him"

In the late 1940s, Charles Templeton was a close friend and preaching associate of Billy Graham. He effectively preached the gospel to large crowds in major arenas. However, intellectual doubts began to nag at him. He questioned the truth of Scripture and other core Christian beliefs. He finally abandoned his faith and made an unsuccessful attempt to persuade Billy to do the same. He felt sorry for Billy and commented, "He committed intellectual suicide by closing his mind."

Templeton resigned from the ministry and became a novelist and news commentator. He also wrote a critique of the Christian faith, *Farewell to God: My Reasons for Rejecting the Christian Faith*.

Journalist Lee Strobel interviewed Templeton for his book, *The Case for Faith*. Templeton was 83 and suffering from Alzheimer's disease. He revealed some of the reasons he left the faith:

> "I started considering the plagues that sweep across parts of the planet and indiscriminately kill—more often than not, painfully—all kinds of people, the ordinary, the decent, and the rotten. And it just became crystal clear to me it is not possible for an intelligent person to believe there is a deity who loves."

Lee Strobel then asked him about Jesus and was surprised at the response.

Templeton believed Jesus lived but never considered Him to be God:

> "He was the greatest human being who has ever lived. He was a moral genius. His ethical sense was unique. He was the intrinsically wisest person I've ever encountered in my life

or in my readings. He's the most important thing in my life. I know it may sound strange, but I have to say I *adore* him! Everything good I know, everything decent I know, everything pure I know, I learned from Jesus. He is the most important human being who has ever existed. And if I may put it this way, *I miss Him.*"

Templeton's eyes filled with tears and he wept freely. He refused to say more."[2]

It is also possible Martha did not take Jesus' absence and the loss of her brother as hard as did Mary. After all, Mary had sat at Jesus' feet. Did she not have the right to expect her friend Jesus (*phileo*), to come heal her brother? Suffering really does show us what is inside us, even as it requires us to face the sovereign ways of God's love (*agape*). Yes, moving from friendship love to *agape* love is almost always a journey wrapped with the black ribbons of disappointment and hurt.

THINK ABOUT IT: "God whispers to us in our pleasures, speaks to us in our conscience, but shouts in our pain," said C. S. Lewis. "It is His megaphone to rouse a deaf world."[3]

Suffering and the love of God, as expressed by Jesus, the Great Physician, are compatible in the same way medical doctors often inflict excruciating agony to save life. A doctor's scalpel is a painful cut of love, intended to heal. A murderer's blade is sharpened on the stones of revenge and hate, and cuts to kill.

As for Martha, faith flashed in her at a new level when she met Jesus on the outskirts of town. She perceived Jesus' sovereignty and believed He could give Lazarus a miracle, right there on the spot. Amid her painful grief she had blossomed into a new faith in Jesus: "Even now it's not too late, for I know God will bring my brother back to life again, if you will only ask him to" (John 11:22 TLB). This statement suggests before Jesus arrived, it is possible Martha had thought the whole situation through to the point she had already perceived Jesus could raise Lazarus from the dead. In addition, she could have known about the two prior restorations in the Lord's ministry: Jairus' daughter and the widow's son at Nain. Those stories would surely have encouraged her to believe Jesus could do it again (Matthew 9:18–25; Luke 7:11–15).

THINK ABOUT IT: Mary is most often thought of as the more spiritual of the two sisters.

Does this conclusion need to be re-thought?

---

5. Jesus, the Ultimate Solution to Suffering

11:23 Jesus said to her, "Your brother will rise again."

This is all the answer needed, when fully assimilated, to heal a wounded heart with broken expectations. Yes, the Lord who experienced unimaginable pain on His cross sometimes uses pain to heal. In doing so, His followers routinely are motivated to climb to a new level of trust.

Indeed! Jesus' conquest of the cross, including His own death by crucifixion, meant He had taken on the worst suffering devils and men had ever devised, and had soundly defeated it. In doing so, He sealed the guarantee of eternal life for all His followers.

The student of the scriptures should not miss the Apostle John quotes Jesus using the phrase, "eternal life," fifteen times in his Gospel, more than the other three gospel writers combined.

The point is obvious. What is ahead for the people of God, their eternal reward, is far better than anything in their past. Both the Apostle Paul and the Apostle Peter later spoke to this great truth:

> "I reckon the sufferings of this present time are not worthy to be compared with the glory which shall be revealed in us" (Romans 8:18 KJV).

> "Concerning this salvation, the prophets, who spoke of the grace that was to come to you, searched intently and with the greatest care, trying to find out the time and circumstances to which the Spirit of Christ in them was pointing when he predicted the sufferings of Christ and the glories that would follow" (1 Peter 1:10–11; see also 5:1).

THINK ABOUT IT: In the absence of their pain, would Mary and Martha have been able to comprehend Jesus as the resurrection and the life?

Experiencing the resurrected Messiah is all the explanation needed to handle even the greatest pain and suffering. Job too learned this same great truth. The reader of the book of Job knows up front, in chapter 1, why Job suffered. But Job was never given that information. Job discovered his solution to his suffering when he said, "I have heard of you by the listening of the ear, but now I see you. Therefore, I abhor myself, and repent in dust and ashes" (Job 42:5–6). Just beholding the grandeur of Jesus, triumphant and exalted, does indeed answer all questions and resolve all hurts and disappointments.

Esther Kerr Rusthoi (1909–1962), poet, song writer, and evangelist is remembered for her service as associate pastor of Angeles Temple in Los Angeles. She captured this great truth in her most famous hymn, "When We See Christ" (1941):

Chorus: "It will be worth it all when we see Jesus,
Life's trials will seem so small when we see Christ;
One glimpse of His dear face all sorrow will erase,
So bravely run the race till we see Christ."

11:24 Martha answered, "I know he will rise again in the resurrection at the last day."

It is possible Martha made this faith statement to the Lord with an implied but unspoken tag on the end of it: "I know he will rise again in the resurrection at the last day," *but I also believe you can do it now!*

"I Am Life Itself"

11:25 Jesus said to her, "I am the resurrection and the life. He who believes in me will live, even though he dies; 26 and whoever lives and believes in me will never die. Do you believe this?"
27 "Yes, Lord," she told him, "I believe you are the Christ, the Son of God, who was to come into the world."

Jesus, the "I Am" who is "life itself" (verse 25, GW) had a marvelous ability to express His identity in a few words. He certainly did it here in His testimony to Martha. This teaching applies to the resurrection of the dead at the last day, and there on the spot in Bethany—*all* resurrection power belongs to Jesus.

Jesus' claim to Martha was that He personified resurrection power and life itself, a powerful assertion that He is the Son of God. He, in fact, holds full authority over death. Jesus restores life, snatching a person out of the teeth of the Grim Reaper. He also gives life back when death has gobbled it up, breaking the death squeeze of the evil python.

He in His own person is the "I Am," the source of existence and the purest essence of being. This means He and He alone can give life, including eternal life to whomever He chooses. Wonder of wonders! His choice is to do so freely and lovinglyfor every person who repents and believes the gospel (John 3:16; 8:21, 24).

Jesus was about half an hour away from demonstrating this awesome authority. In twenty-first century terms, it would show Him more powerful that the most deadly nuclear weapon (Matthew 10:28). The reason is obvious: bombs kill, but Jesus resurrects.

Perchance thirty minutes away!

THINK ABOUT IT: When we have absorbed Jesus as the origin of all life, including resurrection life, how can the body of Christ ever endorse abortion on demand, for example, that legally ends life in the womb? It is unthinkable that Jesus Christ, who is "the resurrection and the life" would affirm such a choice.

Embracing Jesus as the source of life places Him in a category all by Himself, making Him "the one and only." Yes, miracles like this one prove Jesus is far more than one among many equals. No other world religion has an equal footing with God's Son, nor is even a close rival.

To her credit, Martha drank in Jesus' testimony and absorbed the grand revelation: Jesus *is* the resurrection and is Himself the fountain of all life. Eternal life in His hands. Jesus is the solution. Martha responded to this revelation with the faith of Abraham. She believed what Jesus said and confessed Him as her Messiah and the Son of God (vs. 27). It was a bold and categorical statement that surely delighted Jesus.

THINK ABOUT IT: *Dear reader,* "Do *you* believe this?" (John 10:25–26). *This* is the heart of the message of salvation, and it makes the gospel such "good news."

Jesus gave the great revelation of the new birth to Nicodemus, one person. The Lord shared the blessed message *He* is resurrection and life to one person as well. Neither was spoken for the first time to the masses. Certainly an important lesson here is we should never despise our opportunities to share the gospel with a single individual.

Soul Sleep

The Lord's statement to Martha (vs. 25–27) drives the final nail in the coffin of the doctrine of "soul sleep." This teaching says when a person dies, his soul actually "sleeps," having no conscious awareness, until the time of the future resurrection. Seventh–day Adventists hold to this doctrine, as do Jehovah's Witnesses in a related form. But Jesus here shows when a believer dies, he continues to live and will never cease to exist. Death to a child of God does not mean the end of existence, but rather the discovery of a new spiritual form of reality (Matthew 17:2–8).

The transfiguration of Jesus shows the best Biblical insight into that world. Moses had been "dead" some fifteen hundred years and Elijah some eight hundred years. Yet, both met Jesus on the mountain and discussed intelligently with the Lord His pending sacrifice on Calvary and the exodus He would lead from this world into the arms of God (Matthew 17:2–8; 22:31–32; Acts 24:15; 1 Corinthians 15:42).

Martha as an Evangelist

11:28 And after she had said this, she went back and called her sister Mary aside. "The Teacher is here," she said, "and is asking for you."
29 When Mary heard this, she got up quickly and went to him.
30 Now Jesus had not yet entered the village, but was still at the place where Martha had met him.
31 When the Jews who had been with Mary in the house, comforting her, noticed how quickly she got up and went out, they followed her, supposing she was going to the tomb to mourn there.

After making her grand confession of faith in Jesus, Martha became a witness to her sister. She called Mary aside and her message began to pull her sister out of her deep grief. Martha explained to Mary by telling her secretly, "The Teacher is here," and He told me to ask you to come to Him.

This statement is evangelism in its purest form. Martha had been with Jesus herself and was a faithful witness of her experience with Him. In this setting—sister to sister—it is reasonable Martha went further into her testimony, possibly relating that their friend, Jesus, is the Prince of Life who…

- Holds resurrection in His hands.

- Is the source of all life.

- Gives eternal life, so that those who believe in Him will never die.

- Is her Messiah and the Son of God, and

- At that very time was asking to talk with Mary.

6. Suffering Sometimes Includes
Bruises and Grief from God

Many people hold to a doctrine that the God who is good in His very essence would never bruise anyone ["crush" is the word in the NIV], or be the cause of a person's grief (see Isaiah 53:10, also 53:10 in the KJV).

Jesus is indeed good in His essence, and yes there are times when God the Father is the cause behind suffering. The sense in which this is true can be illustrated by the same word picture, noted earlier from the medical profession. We give a surgeon freedom to cut into our bodies and cause us great pain and suffering to achieve a higher good. Why then, would we deny the Great Physician the same prerogative?

The prophet Isaiah opens up this truth in the values of the heavenly Father. He foretold the Messiah would:

> "Make his grave with the wicked and with the rich in his death, because he had done no violence, neither was any deceit in his mouth. Yet it pleased the Lord to bruise him; He hath put him to grief. When thou shalt make his soul an offering for sin, he shall see his seed, he shall prolong his days, and the pleasure of the Lord will prosper in his hand. After the suffering of his soul he will see the light of life and be satisfied (Isaiah 53:9–11 KJV).

Please consider that Jesus never sinned. Hence, In His true innocence He did not deserve the rigors of Calvary. People widely understand the sinless Savior was not given to violence. But few have assimilated Jesus was so completely sinless He never deceived anyone—not even once. Yet:

- "It was [the Father's] will to crush Him" (NIV).

- God "caused Him to suffer" (NIV).

- The Lord made "his life an offering for sin" (Isaiah 53:10 KJV; see also 2 Corinthians 12:7–10).

A very short list of what he endured included disrespect, name calling, scorn, greed for position, racial epithets, shame, threats against His life, back stabbing, and the plots of religious leaders—and they all hurt. So how did the Lord handle them?

The writer of Hebrews said Jesus "endured the cross, despising its shame" (Hebrews 12:2). Yes, the Lord felt the humiliation deeply. But thank God, He persevered, and did not come down from His cross.

This crushing of Jesus had a wonderful result for the spiritual sons of Abraham: Jesus became the sin offering who made atonement for all sin. The writer of Hebrews said "it was by the grace of God" that "Jesus tasted death for every man" (Hebrews 2:9, KJV; see also Exodus 19:14, 36; Leviticus 4–7; Hebrews 3:17–18; 13:11–13). The Son of God, who was perfect in His own moral character so that He never sinned, walked through the valley of suffering to complete the plan of salvation. He was literally "made perfect [or complete] through suffering" (Hebrews 2:10, KJV).

What was the redeeming thread in all of that suffering for Jesus? It was the joy of His triumph at His empty tomb – His resurrection made it all worth it. In fact, the reward was nothing short of heavenly: He "sat down at the right hand of the throne of God" (Hebrews 12:2).

> When his soul has been made an offering for sin, then he shall have a multitude of children, many heirs. He shall live again, and God's program shall prosper in his hands. And when he sees all that is accomplished by the anguish of his soul, he shall be satisfied; and because of what he has experienced, my righteous Servant shall make many to be counted righteous before God, for he shall bear all their sins. Therefore, I will give him the honors of one who is mighty and great because he has poured out his soul unto

death. He was counted as a sinner, and he bore the sins of many, and he pled with God for sinners (Isaiah 53:10–12, TLB).

THINK ABOUT IT: One kind of suffering in life is God-caused grief – albeit always with a higher and redemptive purpose in mind.

Recognizing this form of suffering calls for spiritual discernment (Genesis 32:24–31; 50:20; John 11:4; Acts 3:14–15; 2 Corinthians 12:7–10).

It took a number of years after Joseph's brothers sold him into Egyptian slavery for Joseph to be able to understand and express who was the real source of his suffering in Egypt. But he did finally figure it out. Then, when his brothers went down to Egypt the second time to buy bread, Joseph revealed himself to them. In the midst of their speechless shock, Joseph offered this explanation:

> "Come close to me," he said to them. When they had done so, he said, "I am your brother Joseph, the one you sold into Egypt! And now, do not be distressed and do not be angry with yourselves for selling me here, because it was to save lives that God sent me ahead of you.... God sent me ahead of you to preserve for you a remnant on earth and to save your lives by a great deliverance. So then, it was not you who sent me here, but God."

If you, dear reader, have not embraced this understanding yet, would you please reconsider?

Ask yourself, do you remember an experience of painful suffering in your yesterdays that seems now to have come directly from the hand of God? And do you recognize today the good that has come from your suffering?

7. Suffering Teaches the Wisdom of Obedience

As Mary plunged into her despair, is it not reasonable she had the thought, "When I do see Jesus again, I fully intend to give Him a piece of my mind. I'll tell Him plainly, 'Jesus, my brother did not have to die; and if you had come, he would be alive and happy now! We lost him because you did not come.'"

THINK ABOUT IT: Have you, dear reader, ever been angry enough with Jesus to tell him in no uncertain terms why you are angry with Him?

Please remember, it's OK to tell Jesus how you feel. He can handle your anger. Go ahead; pour it all out to Him; He won't stop loving you!

After Martha left to meet Jesus on the outskirts of town, it is entirely possible that Mary, left sitting at home, wished she had gone with Martha. In any case, when Martha returned, the witness from her sister was enough to shake Mary, even though what she perceived as Jesus' inaction had so deeply offended her. This time she stood up quickly and obediently headed to the Lord. Her quickness to respond to Jesus' personal invitation is another example of the immediacy that was such a striking trait in the faith of Mary's forefather, Abraham (Genesis 19:27).

The writer of Hebrews said although Jesus "was a son, he learned obedience from what he suffered" (Hebrews 5:8–9 NIV). The sense of this verse does not suggest Jesus had a moral flaw of disobedience in His character (John 8:46). Instead, "He learned" the wisdom of "obedience from what He suffered."

This included learning "from experience what it was like to obey when obeying meant suffering. It was after He had proved Himself perfect in this experience that Jesus became the giver of eternal salvation to all those who obey him" (Hebrews 5:8–9 TLB.)

Yes, Jesus made the perfect sacrifice and there would never be a need for it to be repeated, because "that which is perfect has come" (1 Corinthians 13:10; see Hebrews 9:11; 10:10–14; 11:40; 12:23; 13:21).

Since Jesus learned the wisdom of obedience through suffering, how much more does suffering teach us "to obey is better than to sacrifice" (1 Samuel 15:22).

Life Can Start Over Again

Yellow is not my favorite color. But now that I know the story of Vincent van Gogh (1853–1890), I have come to value yellow differently. This famous Dutch painter, sadly, tossed away the truth imparted to him in his Christian home and sank into depression and destruction. By the grace of God, as he later began to embrace the truth again, his life took on hope, and he gave that hope color.

The best-kept secret of van Gogh's life is the truth he was discovering, seen in the gradual increase of the presence of the color yellow in his paintings. Yellow evoked (for him) the hope and warmth of the truth of God's love.

In one of his depressive periods, seen in his famous *The Starry Night*, one finds a yellow sun and yellow swirling stars, because van Gogh thought truth was present only in nature. Tragically, the church, which stands tall in this painting and should be the house of truth, is about the only item in the painting showing no traces of yellow. But by the time he painted *The Raising of Lazarus*, his life was on the mend as he began to face the truth about himself.

The entire picture is (blindingly) bathed in yellow. In fact, van Gogh put his own face on Lazarus to express his own hope in the resurrection.

The color, yellow, tells the whole story: life can start over again because of the truth of God's love. Each of us, whether with actual yellows or metaphorical yellows, can begin to paint our lives with the fresh hope of a new tomorrow.[4]

Escaping the Mourners

For Mary to get to Jesus, however, she first had to get past the mourners. They thought she was going to the tomb to weep, and did not have a clue who had just walked into town.

Anyone who comes to Jesus, in fact, must have the courage "in the obedience of faith" to bypass the "mourners," the detractors in life who see it as their mission solely to help you live with your pain (Romans 16:26). But evangelism is all about enabling a person, amid his hurts, to get to the Teacher who can actually cure a person even if he is painfully bruised and bleeding—soul, mind or body. As a result, a new disciple discovers a fresh start in Christ.

The Heroes of Faith

The writer of Hebrews, in his catalog of the faithful, underscored how suffering encourages obedience by helping us gaze into the sovereignty of God (Hebrews 10:19–11:40). This particularly comes into focus with the many champions of faith who did receive answers to their prayers; some even had their children restored to life. But others "died in faith" (Hebrews 11:13).

> They did not receive the things promised; they only saw them and welcomed them from a distance. And they admitted they were aliens and strangers on earth. People

who say such things show they are looking for a country of their own. If they had been thinking of the country they had left, they would have had opportunity to return. Instead, they were longing for a better country—a heavenly one. Therefore God is not ashamed to be called their God, for he has prepared a city for them (Hebrews 11:13–16; see also vs. 10).

The fact that "they saw [the things promised] and welcomed them from a distance" says they peered into the sovereignty of God and found it worthy of their obedience. Their faith said if they did not get their answer in their lifetime, they would believe in the inherent goodness of God's sovereignty to their last breath. Their longing for a "better country—a heavenly one" would be worth the wait, even if they stepped into eternity while waiting.

THINK ABOUT IT: These heroes of faith believed the promises of God and were obedient in trust, even when they did not see the answer in their lifetime. They were certain future generations would enjoy it, so they lived and died in the obedience of faith (Romans 16:29).

The heavenly Father has special feelings and plans for such people. "That is why God is not ashamed to be called their God." And, in fact, "He has prepared a city for them" (Hebrews 11:16 GW; see also vs. 10).

Mary, Disheveled and Shattered

11:32 When Mary reached the place where Jesus was and saw him, she fell at his feet and said, "Lord, if you had been here, my brother would not have died." 33 When Jesus saw her weeping, and the Jews who had come along

with her also weeping, he was deeply moved in spirit and troubled. 34 "Where have you laid him?" he asked. "Come and see, Lord," they replied.

It must have been very stirring for Jesus to see Mary coming to Him:

- She brought her grief with her, and
- Her deeply disappointed expectations, and
- Her disheveled appearance.
- She went as she was, a very fragile and broken woman. But she did the right thing.
- She obeyed the Lord's invitation and went to Jesus!

In better times Mary might have sat at Jesus' feet, drinking in His teaching. This time her demeanor said her heart had been shattered. She thought her world had come to an end, and she would never be happy again.

THINK ABOUT IT: Jesus can put back together a thousand broken pieces so that the latter heart is stronger than the former! (Haggai 2:9; Joel 2:23; Psalm 34:18).

Mary had no comprehension at this point she and Martha, because of the loving grace in the heart of her Lord, were on the threshold of blossoming into a new life (Isaiah 43:19). What was ahead for them was wonderful beyond their present comprehension. It would also enshrine their names forever in salvation history.

THINK ABOUT IT: What Mary thought was the end of the world was actually the beginning of a new and far better world. With God every ending has within it the seeds of a new beginning! Every ending—until we reach our heavenly home where there will be no more endings!

When Mary saw Jesus "she fell at his feet." What was inside her flooded from the well of her disappointed hopes. She blurted out what was in her soul, "Lord, if you had been here, my brother would still be alive" (John 11:32 TLB). Mary's statement, spoken with such great passion, would put lesser men than Jesus on heavy guilt trips: *Lord, You could have prevented this had You wanted to.*

8. Suffering Shows the High Price the Sin Curse Demands

"Deeply moved in spirit and troubled" is an apt description of the Lord's emotions. The Greek term for "deeply moved" conveys a variety of feelings such as anger, indignation, groaning with sorrow, and the stern voice that starts giving orders. The word translated "troubled" communicates the word picture of the highly disturbed, churning waves on the ocean; roiling waves, stirred and agitated.

It was a stern Jesus who faced what the curse of sin had done to Lazarus and his sisters. Jesus knew bad things happen to good people too. It is true that the best of us is a son of Adam, fallen and very much in need of God's grace. "No one does anything good; not even one person" can ever claim he has earned the benefits of Jesus' death on the cross (Romans 3:12; Psalm 14:3 GW). Suffering, therefore, often motivates us to surrender to God in repentance and send down deeper roots in His loving grace. Who can deny, even while this painful process is happening, suffering is yielding good fruit in our lives?

"In Adam all die" is the ultimate toll of the curse of sin on all people. Death always demands a high price of the survivors left behind too; grieving family members are a major part of the toll. But resurrection hope shines brightest at the point where the sin curse has done its worst: "in Christ all will be made alive" (1 Corinthians 15:22 KJV).

Jesus' emotions were churning, akin to the roiling waves of the sea. How many times in Jesus' ministry had He listened to the cries of brokenhearted people. In addition to their wails, Jesus suffered routinely the attitudes of ugly disdain on the faces of His critics, day-after-day-after day. Yes, time and again Jesus drank the sour dregs of grief and knew its pain well. In fact, Isaiah prophesied He would live as "a man of sorrows" who was "acquainted with bitterest grief." Isaiah continued to describe the typical response of His own people: "We turned our backs on him and looked the other way when he walked by. He was despised, and we didn't care" (Isaiah 53:3 TLB; see Luke 13:34; consider also the death of His step-father, Joseph, and the many funerals He no doubt had attended growing up).

In a few words, Mary had poured her heart out to Jesus. But in His sovereignty Jesus did not try to answer her, or explain to her, as He did to Martha that He was the resurrection who held eternal life in His hands. At this point even Jesus' words might not have stopped Mary's weeping, as she was inconsolable in her grief. So were the tears of her relatives and friends. Instead of trying to reason with Mary, the Great Physician simply moved forward to achieve the purpose of His pure goodness revealed in His sovereign purpose. But the sadness of the situation did stir the heart of God.

Jesus' Emotions

11:35 Jesus wept.

While in Bethabara, Jesus had showed gladness to His disciples that they were not in Bethany when they learned of Lazarus' illness (John 11:15). Jesus felt that way because of the benefit that would come to the disciples' faith from Lazarus' death and resurrection. Here in 11:35 Jesus feels the heavy emotions of grief caused by the penalty of the sin curse that had so bruised this precious couple and their brother (Genesis 3:14–24). These two words say it all. It is the shortest verse in the Bible, but common sense and human nature understand and explain it easily. Out of the inner earthquake of Jesus' churning emotions, a fountain of hot tears sprang up from the Messiah's holy heart and began pouring out of His pure eyes (see Genesis 6:6). Jesus as the Son of Man had sinless motives. He felt deeply the heart-breaking pain the sin curse demanded of His friends. And Lazarus was a special friend whom Jesus cared for with the love of God (*agape*).

THINK ABOUT IT: To this day the Lord who is "acquainted with grief" has special feelings for people suffering loss. This includes you too, dear reader.

Surely one of the greatest achievements in the ministry of Jesus was His ability to stay focused in the midst of the tsunami of satanic opposition He routinely faced. Fury has tripped so many people through the centuries. In anger, even Moses disobeyed and smote the rock the second time instead of speaking to it as God told him to do (Numbers 20:8–12). Without doubt, Satan's strategy was to make the pressure so hot Jesus would blow up and do something solo—acting independently of His Father and the

Holy Spirit (Matthew 27:39; Mark 15:32; 1 Corinthians 4:12; 1 Peter 2:23–25).

We recognize Jesus today as our ultimate champion because He never did break and snap-back in kind. Instead, He kept doing the mighty works only God can do as He continued His march to Calvary.

Yes, a benefit of suffering is it helps people see clearly what the curse of sin has done since the fall of Adam and Eve in Eden, and explains why bad things happen to good people. Sin is the great terminator. It kills opportunity; it destroys vision and hope; it squanders wealth; it ultimately enslaves a person's free will; it sends every person's body back to dust, and eternally destroys the soul of all who do not come to Jesus in repentance.

The curse of sin has also corrupted nature. This explains the aberrations of the elements—tornadoes, earthquakes, tsunamis, hurricanes, mudslides, wild fires, and the list goes on. All viruses and bacteria, even the stinging prick of a mosquito, spring from the curse of sin.

Little wonder Jesus' salty tears at Bethany mingled with those of Mary and her friends, and were quickly absorbed by the thirsty, dust-covered rocks in front of the sepulcher.

Mother Nature Needs a Redeemer Too

The largest tornado that had ever been recorded was 2.6 miles wide, an EF-5. It tore across Oklahoma on May 31, 2013. The storm packed killer winds reaching 295 MPH+. The super cell producing this deadly monster actually spawned many tornadoes in central Oklahoma on this tragic Friday evening. The multi-vortex storm also included several rain-wrapped tornadoes.

All of this anger in the skies that long night terrorized metropolitan Oklahoma City with deadly fury.

My wife and I (your author), with guests Jonathan Hill and his family were glued to our TV. We witnessed the mortal danger swirling just a few miles from us.

The storm tracked north from El Reno, Oklahoma, and for almost 15 minutes ran parallel with a country road. Then it took an unexpected and sharp 45 degree turn toward I-40 catching the interstate traffic off guard. A few people in their fright actually tried to escape the storm by driving 70 MPH into oncoming traffic!

This predator in the atmosphere had been preceded on May 20 by another fatal EF-5; the two storms were only 11 days apart. The first one left a large slice of the city of Moore, Oklahoma, looking like a war zone. The total of lives lost in the two storms climbed to over 40, including three veteran tornado storm chasers. Some 12,000+ homes were damaged or totally destroyed. The estimates of the property loss soared upward toward $800 million. The 24 MPH forward speed of the May 20 storm meant it did its destruction in a matter of a few short minutes, maybe three or four, and then lumbered on to gobble up its next victims.

We know Mother Nature can be peaceful and tranquil, as perfect as paradise. She can also produce angry assassins in the skies that slaughter indiscriminately, showing no respect for people or property—not even grade school children trying to hide for their lives in their school buildings.

The Bible gives one explanation for the cruelties of the elements: nature is under the curse of sin (Genesis 3:17; Romans 8:19–22). All people too are sons of Adam with corrupted hearts in rebellion against God. We are fallen people living in a fallen world.

To find peace with God, each of us needs the redemptive new birth provided by Jesus our Savior. One day, the whole of the natural order will be redeemed too (Romans 3:23; 8:23).

The scene at Lazarus' tomb in Bethany two millennia ago no doubt motivated Jesus to think again about His mission. For Him to redeem mankind and ultimately the natural order in which we all live, He had to destroy this last enemy, death itself (1 Corinthians 15:26).

How many millions of people since Adam had faced the Grim Reaper and lost. In the whole Old Testament era, only Elijah and Enoch defeated death's grip (Genesis 5:24; 2 Kings 2:11–12). But they were enough to show the sovereign power of God could stop death in its tracks.

THINK ABOUT IT: The time had indeed come for Death to be thoroughly humiliated.

Indeed! "In Christ, all will be made alive" (1 Corinthians 15:22).

Mourners—Friends or Foes?

11:36 Then the Jews said, "See how he loved him!"
37 But some of them said, "Could not he who opened the eyes of the blind man have kept this man from dying?"

Now the scene shifts from Jesus and Mary and their hot tears to the Jewish relatives and friends who were mourning with the sisters. Grief motivated them to show their inner selves too, their way of thinking. These observers quickly understood Jesus loved Lazarus. But they too were consumed with what they thought was the big question: Why did Jesus not heal Lazarus and prevent his death? After all, they remembered He had opened the eyes of the man born blind. Millions have asked the same question since then. It is such a human response to cry out, "Why God?" amid our brokenness and confusion. These mourners appear to have had no perception, however, of what might have been God's sovereign purposes in the situation.

Said another way, Mary was so far down in the well of grief, talking to her about God's plans would have been useless. So would offering the explanation of the effects of the sin curse on all people, including nature. Nor did Mary perceive how transparently she was revealing the condition of her own heart. She was not ready to think it all through. Mary just knew she hurt all over. She was also convinced Jesus had arrived too late to help her, and neither could her friends.

THINK ABOUT IT: Have you ever felt Mary's despair—a sense that it is absolutely too late? But "too late" is not in Jesus' vocabulary!

Mary and the mourners were minutes away from witnessing the miracle of miracles, second only to the Lord's resurrection. But their eyes were much too red from crying to perceive it. Grief can easily turn into a dangerous, even a monstrous emotion, if it prevents our recognizing Jesus standing with us in our crisis.

Jesus knew there is a depth of mourning capable of seeing only the present moment of a broken heart and trampled dreams. This level of grief blocks gazing on the big picture of God's pending plans. Jesus showed His great compassion by not rebuking them for a lack of faith; instead, He was content to cry with them.

We can be eternally grateful, thank God, that Jesus' tears did not blur His vision or His thinking. Instead of talking, Jesus acted. He simply proceeded to do something about Lazarus' death.

Something only God could do.

Move the Stone!

11:38 Jesus, once more deeply moved, came to the tomb. It was a cave with a stone laid across the entrance. 39 "Take away the stone," he said.

This is the second time the Apostle John used the phrase, "deeply moved" to describe Jesus' emotions (see vs. 33). Jesus felt anger as He approached the tomb; He was indignant. The Apostle Paul put into words thirty years later the essence of Jesus' emotions: "Be ye angry, and sin not... Neither give place to the devil" (Ephesians 4:26–27, KJV).

For so long—millennia, in fact—death had reigned as a cruel, virtually absolute despot over the sons of Adam. People have always lived their entire lives in fear of the Grim Reaper (Hebrews 2:13–15; Romans 5:15, 21).

It would be in keeping with the emotions of "deeply moved" to read the statement, "Jesus sternly commanded, 'Take away the stone'!"

The Lord ordered them to do what they could do, thereby involving them in the miracle. Then He did what only He could do.

11:39 "But, Lord," said Martha, the sister of the dead man, "by this time there is a bad odor, for he has been there four days."

Martha on the outskirts of Bethany had implied Jesus could raise her brother on the spot. Her "even now" expression (11:22) had evidenced this great confidence. She had received Jesus testimony affirming He was the resurrection and the life, and confessed Him as the Son of God and her Messiah. She also gave a strong witness to her sister, telling Mary Jesus had come and was asking for *her*. But at the tomb, her response was, "By now the smell will be terrible, for he has been dead four days" (John 11:39 TLB). Consumed by what appeared to be the sovereign finality of death, she had moved from "Even now…" to, *Jesus, you're too late!*

So the real question was who was sovereign at Lazarus' tomb? Yes, death can be very intimidating, but this story shows the grave is not supreme.

THINK ABOUT IT: It is worth considering that raising Lazarus from the dead anticipates what would truly be the big event, the game changer of game changers. Jesus' own resurrection was just a short few days up the road.

The devil would be given no place that day either.

11:40 Then Jesus said, "Did I not tell you if you believed, you would see the glory of God?"

This is clearly a rebuke, spoken with a kind tone but said firmly: *"Martha, it is never too late for God. You are focused on what has always been and it is motivating you to accept death as the victor— but I am not. I am anticipating the new order. I have come to turn the impossible into the new reality. You are about to see the Grim Reaper thoroughly shamed and soundly defeated. And the glory of God, in the new tomorrow of victory over death, will be so wonderful as to make the pain of these recent days only a faint memory."*

9. Suffering Liberates by
Aiding the Discovery of New Meaning

This resurrection scene shows suffering helps people find fresh freedom as they discover higher, redemptive reasons for the ups and downs of life. Suffering enables us to think through what is most important, as we awaken to our true priorities.

In this ultimate sense of what is truly important, Jesus is the only priority that matters. C. T. Studd (1860–1931), a British missionary to China and founder of the Worldwide Evangelization Crusade International, expressed it:

> "Only one life, 'twill soon be past,
> Only what's done for Christ will last.
> And when I'm dying, how happy I'll be
> If the lamp of my life has been burned out for thee."

This understanding makes suffering a friend. It liberates us to live in the freedom of eternal hope, no matter the toll the sin curse demands in suffering. The writer of Hebrews asked his readers to look back:

> "Remember those early days after you first saw the light? Those were the hard times! Kicked around in public, targets of every kind of abuse—some days it was you, other days your friends. If some friends went to prison, you stuck by them. If some enemies broke in and seized your goods, you let them go with a smile, knowing they couldn't touch your real treasure. Nothing they did bothered you, nothing set you back.
>
> So don't throw it all away now. You were sure of yourselves then. It's still a sure thing! But you need to stick it out, staying with God's plan so you'll be there for the promised completion…But anyone who is right with me thrives on loyal trust; if he cuts and runs, I won't be very happy.
>
> But we're not quitters who lose out. Oh, no! We'll stay with it and survive, trusting all the way" (Hebrews 10:32–39 MSG).

This new meaning always bears special fruit: the ability to help others. The Apostle Paul was exuberant when he penned:

"Praise be to the God and Father of our Lord Jesus Christ, the Father of compassion and the God of all comfort, 4 who comforts us in all our troubles, so that we can comfort those in any trouble with the comfort we ourselves receive from God" (2 Corinthians 1:3–4).

Andrea Crouch, (1942–2015), an American gospel singer, songwriter and pastor, captured this liberating role of suffering and the higher meaning it gives to life:

"Through it all,
Through it all,
I've learned to trust in Jesus,
I've learned to trust in God.
Through it all,
Through it all,
I've learned to depend upon His word."

Suffering Brings Baseball Pitcher to Faith

Barry Zito was once known as one of the most dominating pitchers in Major League baseball. But in 2010, Zito reached his lowest point. He was removed from his team's starting roster. The next season he was plagued by injuries and poor performances. By the end of 2012 he had returned to his peak performance, winning his last 14 starts and playing a pivotal role in the San Francisco Giant's World Series victory.

In a 2012 interview Zito explained how God used suffering to get his attention and lead him to commit "his life to Jesus Christ as Lord and Savior." Zito said:

> Sometimes you have to go through difficulty and physical trials to really get broken down. In 2011, I got broken down physically as well as mentally. In August of that year, I had this very odd injury... I came off the field that day after never being hurt in

eleven years, and I said, "All right, something bigger is going on here. A message is being sent, and I've got to listen." A few months later, I realized I'd been doing it alone.

My best friend told me an old story I really love. A shepherd will be leading his sheep, and one of the sheep keeps walking astray from the pack. The shepherd will take his rod and break the sheep's leg, and the sheep will have to rely on the shepherd to get better. But once that leg is completely healed, that sheep never leaves the side of the shepherd ever again.[5]

10. The "After" to Suffering

11:41 So they took away the stone.

Getting past our suffering always embraces removing ours too, even if it is cherished and polished granite!

Luke wrote that the Lord showed himself alive with many infallible proofs *"after* his suffering," (Acts 1:3 KJV). A great principle of life is unveiled here. We conclude, because Jesus was raised from the dead, there is always an *after* to suffering. Yes, all suffering has a time line on it. Although we do not always know the duration, one day we will leave our suffering behind. The ultimate expression of this principle occurs when we part this life for our eternal home, when there will be no more "after's."

Nobody should conclude death is a deliverer. The Grim Reaper, "the last enemy to be destroyed," is a curse and a killer (1 Corinthians 15:26). The liberation occurs because of the death and resurrection of Jesus. "To be absent from the body" is "to be present with the Lord" (2 Corinthians 5:8, KJV).

THINK ABOUT IT: What is the "rock" keeping you in a "tomb?" You must remove it for your faith to blossom into your full potential in God.

The grand result about to happen in Bethany foreshadowed another and far greater miracle. Mt. Everest in the Asian Himalayas, at 29,029 feet is the world's tallest mountain and the "roof of the world." Jesus Himself in a few more days would die on a cross, and then rise from the grave on the third day. This world changing event in Jerusalem has lived in history as the supreme miracle of all time, the "Mt. Everest of miracles," and the utmost ceiling of the miraculous. Yes, there is an after to suffering.

Dead beyond Dispute

The Apostle John included seven miracles in his book, and each of them in its own way has made one and the same point: only the Son of God could do such things! But the seventh is the pinnacle. Lazarus had been in the tomb for four days, not merely twenty minutes, or perhaps an hour. His body had already begun to decompose. Everyone in the village knew Lazarus had died four days earlier and had been buried. Two miles away, many in Jerusalem also knew it. And the mourners—especially the mourners—had been crying profusely with Mary and Martha; they certainly knew the facts. Lazarus' death and burial had many first-hand witnesses; it was beyond dispute.

11:41 Then Jesus looked up and said, "Father, I thank you that you have heard me. 42 I knew you always hear me, but I said this for the benefit of the people standing here, so that they may believe you sent me."

Here Mary and Martha, and their friends, began the shift into a new and higher dimension of life. They were stepping into the sphere of resurrection. The power of the Holy Spirit around Lazarus' tomb must have been nuclear.

Jesus' prayer is eye opening: "I thank you that you have heard me"—indicating again the close bond between Jesus and His Father. Their communication in this situation had started in Bethabara beyond the Jordan, and continued while Jesus walked to Bethany. Jesus implicitly trusted His Father. He expected His Father and the Holy Spirit to give Him the guidance in His humanity to meet the need perfectly in Bethany. The bond between the incarnate Son of Man and His heavenly Father was so firm Jesus added, "I knew you always hear me."

A few days later, while hanging on His cross, Jesus, in His humanity, asked the "Why" question. "My God, my God, why have you forsaken me?" But His last prayer on the cross before He gulped His final breath began with, "Father, into your hands I commit my spirit." The bond of trust held.

Jesus' prayer is a model of trust. He was certain His Father was "always" with Him and could be depended on to guide His words and actions. This prayer is also a portrait of the Lord's tender care for the very raw emotions of Mary and Martha, their friends, the mourners and the townsfolk. "I said it because of all these people standing here, so that they will believe you sent me" (John 1:42 TLB). Jesus wanted each of them to discover a whole new level of meaning by experiencing the faith capable to lead them to inherit eternal life.

Jesus went to great lengths to raise Lazarus from the dead with this premier miracle; His greatest before Calvary. His efforts included the wisdom of the two-day delay in Bethabara, and the bone-tiring fatigue of the day-long trek from Bethabara to Bethany. It was an up-hill, winding climb of 3,300 feet over a walk of some fifteen miles, essentially uphill all the way.

Jesus had brought Martha to her affirmation of faith and sent her back to get her sister. He then poured out His own tears with theirs at Lazarus' tomb as He prayed with thanksgiving to His Father.

THINK ABOUT IT: Since Jesus went to this kind of effort to restore these three precious sheep, what should a pastor, or an evangelist, or a church member do to raise a soul dead in trespasses and sins, and then to care for the sheep?

11:43 When he had said this, Jesus called in a loud voice, "Lazarus, come out!"

This command represents par excellence the power of Jesus over death. Jesus expressed it in a simple, three-word command showing He was the divine *logos*. Jesus is indeed the Word, the final Word, the authoritative Word, the resurrection Word.

The Overwhelming Extent of the Miracle

The insight here into the sphere of life after death is illuminating. Lazarus had been alive in the world of the spirit for four days. Jesus called Lazarus by name, and although Lazarus had died physically, he was very much alive in spirit and answered to his name. Lazarus heard and obeyed the voice of Jesus, his *agape* friend. Jesus is your *agape* friend too, dear reader.

At Jesus' command, Lazarus' spirit returned to his already decaying body. The magnitude of this miracle, with all of its elements happening simultaneously, defies all rational comprehension.

1. Lazarus' brain, indeed! the whole electrical system of his body had to be miraculously restored in seconds, so that it started sending again all of the proper messages to every part of his body, including full reinstatement of his memory.

2. In those same seconds Lazarus' entire nervous system with its billions of neurons had to come back to life, every nerve in his body.

3. A body has thousands of blood vessels, but in Lazarus' case they all were full of coagulated blood. In addition, coagulation was already at work in the tens of thousands of cell-thin and blood clogged capillaries, especially in his lungs but also throughout his body. Lazarus' entire blood system had to be miraculously purified and brought back to life in seconds of time. The process was done to perfection; there was no risk of a single blood clot later.

4. Lazarus' lungs had to be washed clean and oxygen miraculously supplied to his lungs. Normal breathing was not yet possible because his mouth and nose were covered in grave clothes.

5. His heart had to be rinsed and restarted with a perfect electrical rhythm. The Franklin Institute in Philadelphia claims there are more than 60,000 miles of veins, arteries, and capillaries in an adult's body. Lazarus' restored-to-normal heartbeat began to pump his miraculously purified blood through all 60,000 miles of them [a distance almost three times around the earth]. Not even one was missed on the journey to every part of his body, even the microscopic parts—and did it all—all of those miles in those same seconds.

6. The billions and billions of cells in his body, each of them dead, had to each come back to life at the same time and

start welcoming again the clean blood stream of oxygen and nutrients flowing from Lazarus' heart and lungs.

7. Lazarus' eyes had to open and start seeing again, although he was blindfolded by the grave clothes wrapped around his head.

8. His kidneys had to receive instantaneous dialysis.

9. Lazarus' stomach and digestive tract had to be cleansed and made operational, without any stomach ache!

10. His liver had to resume normal function.

11. So did all of the other glands, organs and nerves in his body.

12. Four days had elapsed since Lazarus' death. His flesh was already in decay. His skin, flesh, muscles and bone structure all had to be restored in seconds.

13. People who have visited the ancient tomb of Lazarus in Bethany know it is necessary to descend into the actual tomb area by a series of stairs. This also means Lazarus' legs, including their blood vessels, nerves and muscles had to function properly for him, with fully restored balance and strength to walk up those same stone stairs at Jesus' command, without a support rail. Doing this bound in grave clothes is a huge miracle all its own. This climb would have surely taken a few minutes. Those moments of waiting, to the bystanders, must have been some of history's longest minutes!

All of this and so much more was restored inside Lazarus' body in the seconds of Jesus' command.

Was there a skeptic in the crowd who muttered, "I don't see anything happening!"

Then, did someone shout out, "Oh my God! Look! Wow! Oh my God! Look! I don't believe what I'm seeing. He's walking out!"

DNA Comes Alive

"Three millennia ago King David wrote that every human being is "fearfully and wonderfully made" (Psalm 139:14). Now modern science unveils the psalmist's teaching.

"Consider this example. The human body is made up of about one hundred million, million cells. Each of these cells has a complete set of instructions about how to make your cells and your cells' components. This set of instructions is called the human genome.

Your genome is packed with at least four million gene switches residing in bits of DNA.

"For years, scientists thought many of these bits of DNA were useless. In the 1970s, Francis Crick, the co-discoverer of DNA's structure, suspected it was all "little better than junk." The phrase "junk DNA" has haunted human genetics ever since. In the early 2000s, scientists still believed perhaps 97 percent of what is called "the sequence of bases" in human DNA had no apparent function.

"But in September 2012, a team of 440 scientists from 32 labs around the world made a startling discovery. Your "junk DNA" really isn't junky after all. As these scientists delved further into "the junk," they discovered a complex system controlling genes. Apparently, so far these scientists have determined 80 percent of this DNA is active and needed. It turns out what was called "junk" is now called a "hidden treasure"—a treasure playing a critical role in controlling how cells, organs, and other tissues behave."[6]

And to think all of this DNA structure had to come alive with four million gene switches turned back on in the blink of an eye. Yes, the countless trillions of cells in Lazarus' body also obeyed Jesus' loudly shouted, three-word command, "Lazarus, come out!" (11:43 GW). The miracle of the resurrection of Lazarus, therefore, is actually a combination of multiple millions of smaller miracles.

It goes without saying if Lazarus' dad and mom had been buried in the same cave, they too would have been raised if Jesus had not named only Lazarus.

11:44 The dead man came out, his hands and feet wrapped with strips of linen, and a cloth around his face. Jesus said to them, "Take off the grave clothes and let him go."

Turn Him Loose!

We can only wish we had been standing there to see the stunned looks on the faces of the people milling around the tomb when Lazarus walked out, bound in his grave clothes. The wonder of it all would have been evident in their bulging eyes, their dropped jaws, in their stunned faces, and for a few, their fleeing feet!

Would you have gone into shock too? Would you have run from the scene?

When you collected your senses enough to begin to absorb what was happening, would you have started applauding Lazarus?

What about freely worshipping Jesus?

THINK ABOUT IT: Even in the face of this kind of evidence, religious pluralists keep repeating their mantra, "All roads lead to God."

No, Jesus is the road!

The final command in the miracle was "take off his grave clothes and let him go." Again, Jesus was not willing to do for them what they could do. They put the grave clothes on Lazarus' dead body, and they needed to take them off. It was part of their accepting the magnitude of the miracle.

With only a little imagination we can see Mary's eyes as they begin to brighten and her countenance start taking on a new look. She had walked with Jesus to the tomb depressed and carrying lots of emotional baggage. How quickly the cold grip of her depression began to loosen in the face of Lazarus' obedience to Jesus' sovereign word!

Talk about discovering new meaning! Perhaps Martha and Mary ran first to help remove the grave clothes from Lazarus, and then to embrace him. Next, they ran to Jesus and fell at His feet, weeping this time for joy (Psalm 30:11–12).

In those moments Lazarus' tomb had all the atmosphere of the Most Holy Place in the temple. Jesus remains even today the epitome of the Shekinah, the Presence. He was the essence of the Spirit of God at the tabernacle in the wilderness (Leviticus 9:23–24; Numbers 7:89). This same Spirit moved in at Solomon's dedication and settled down, claiming the house (1 Kings 8:11; 2 Chronicles 5:14; 7:2).

At Lazarus' tomb, the Presence, who is the *logos* Word that is the source of life was standing among them. He had faced down a challenge so great as to befit the word impossible, but for the Presence of the *logos* word. Everybody there knew death was final; everyone that is, except Jesus.

The horrendous emotional pain of Lazarus' death fled from the sisters' minds as quickly as the realization dawned on them their brother was indeed alive.

Archeology Defends John's Description of
First Century Jewish Funeral Customs

For years scholars puzzled over a curious detail mentioned in the Gospel of John concerning Jewish burial practices in the first century. In describing the entombments of Jesus and His friend Lazarus (John 11:44; 20:7), John writes both men had their bodies wrapped with a linen cloth for burial, but with a separate, smaller cloth wrapped around their heads.

While archaeology has confirmed many details of the Gospels, ancient fabrics are very fragile and decay completely within a few decades unless preserved under extraordinary circumstances. However, in the spring of 2000, a set of highly unusual circumstances led to a once-in-a lifetime discovery.

That morning Israeli archaeologist Shimon Gibson and Professor James Tabor of the University of North Carolina-Charlotte, with some of Dr. Tabor's archaeology students, happened on a first-century Jewish tomb in Jerusalem's Hinnom Valley.

Their most important find that day had remained undisturbed for almost two millenia in one of the tomb's small chambers. In the third level of the tomb, which is the lowest level, they found the skeleton of a person with a burial shroud still over his shoulders. But even more remarkable, the man's body had been wrapped with two pieces of fabric—one around the body and a separate, smaller piece around the head, just as described in John's Gospel.

Small samples of the fabric were radiocarbon dated to the first century—the time during which Jesus lived. Clearly John had faithfully and accurately recorded this detail of Jewish burial practices from the first century.

How had the fabric been preserved all those centuries? Through a geological fluke, a crack in the limestone from which the tomb had been carved had drained ground moisture away from that one particular chamber, leaving it dry and protected—and giving additional evidence the Gospels are an accurate historical record of real first-century customs and events.[7]

It is very worthy of reaffirmation: the answer to suffering ultimately rests in a person, the Lord Jesus Christ himself.

- Jesus went to great effort to step into the troubled world of the woman at the well and offer her living water (John 4).

- Jesus was on the temple grounds as daylight began to dawn, waiting for the Pharisees to drag to him the woman taken in the act of adultery. He became the answer to the embarrassment and anguish of her trapped soul when He accepted her case as her attorney (John 8).

- Mary and Martha overcame the loss of their brother precisely because Jesus stepped into their world. He makes all the difference.

THINK ABOUT IT: Jesus in His own person is the answer to our pain and suffering. Everything changes when He steps into our world.

The deeper we go in an intimate relationship with Him, the better we handle our own throbbing discomforts. The answer to the problem of pain is not to be found in a doctrine, or a treatise, or a philosophy, but in the lowly Nazarene who proved He is the resurrection and the life. To know the Son of God who endured the penalty of our sin is to perceive Jesus is the answer to our sorrows. The Lord demonstrated it at Lazarus' tomb and proved it on His own resurrection morning.

Our Lord suffered, and His example teaches us how to handle our sorrows with an attitude of hope in this life as we await the great Resurrection. That day that will wipe all tears from our eyes (Revelation 7:17; 21:4, KJV).

Yes, life is unfair, and bad things happen to good people, and evil often goes unpunished. But the grand hope of resurrection unto eternal life resolves all inequities, gives life meaning, and makes life worth living.

Jesus Himself, in His own Person, is the very essence of resurrection. Hence, He gives purpose to life and assures by His own resurrection that all who commit sin, as well as sickness, famine, disease, disasters, and accidents—all that hurts or destroys—will bite the dust of history forever and meet it's just due at the bar of eternal justice (Revelation 20:11–15).

Good will indeed triumph over all evil. The proof is revealed when we pull into our embrace the cross of Jesus with one arm and the Lord's empty tomb with the other, holding tightly to Jesus as the Son of God. Ah, to stand with one foot at Calvary and the other at the Lord's empty tomb!

Edward Mote (1797–1840) expressed it in his enduring hymn:

> "On Christ the solid rock I stand;
>   All other ground is sinking sand.
>   All other ground is sinking sand."

Yes, Jesus Christ is himself the answer to the problem of pain and of evil.

THINK ABOUT IT: The miracle helped Martha and Mary start assimilating higher meaning. When the light turned on inside the sisters, revealing Jesus in fact as the resurrection, they also began to comprehend the sovereign purposes of God. It was surely a "WOW" moment for them.

Comprehending this truth is a "WOW" experience for us too: "I consider the sufferings of this present time are not worthy to be compared with the glory which shall be revealed in us" (Romans 8:18–19 NKJV).

Early in this chapter three questions were presented that people typically ask in their crises.

- "We earnestly prayed, but Jesus did not answer our prayers," and

- "He could have prevented this if He had wanted too," and
- "Can Jesus be trusted to do good in the crises of life? Is He good, all the time?"

Would you not agree, dear reader, the resurrection of Lazarus took the sting out of each of them? Ah! With resurrection in Martha's and Mary's eyes, they were not even thinking about them. This is true because resurrection settles all doubts even as it shows God's greater purpose in our lives.

The resurrected Lord is able to minister to the needs of God's children everywhere, people of every ethnicity, including the far flung islands of the seas!

This also means the gate to eternal life has been swung wide open for all people worldwide who repent and believe the gospel, acknowledging Jesus as the Son of God.

THINK ABOUT IT: "No matter how deep our darkness, He is deeper still."—Corrie ten Boom

---

Yes, "What we suffer now is nothing compared to the glory he will reveal to us later" (Romans 8:18 VOICE).

Raising Lazarus from the dead was also prophetic because it suggested the pending arrival of the New Covenant. The same Jesus who was standing at Lazarus' tomb, would soon die and come out of His own sepulcher. The resurrected Lord would then be able to minister to the needs of God's children everywhere. Yes, those of every ethnicity would hear the gospel.

THINK ABOUT IT: The Lord's outstretched arms on His cross are themselves a great symbol—Jesus' open arms show His heart has room for all people. "The middle wall of partition" is torn down (Ephesians 2:14).

One arm was extended in love for all sons of Abraham and the other opened to embrace generously all Gentiles worldwide, drawing both into the unity and peace of His big heart (Ephesians 2:14).

Oh! the wondrous grace, even in death, of Jesus' outstretched arms.

The resurrection of Lazarus is also prophetic because it tells people about a special day ahead for all who have been born again:

We'll step out of our mortal clothes and slide into immortal bodies, replacing everything that is subject to death with eternal life. And, when we are all redressed with bodies that do not, cannot decay, when we put immortality over our mortal frames, then it will be as *Scripture* says:
Life everlasting has victoriously swallowed death.
Hey, Death! What happened to your big win?
Hey, Death! What happened to your sting?
Sin came into this world, and death's sting followed. Then sin took aim at the law and gained power over those who follow the law. Thank God, then, for our Lord Jesus, the Anointed, the liberating King, who brought us victory over the grave (1 Corinthians 15:53–57 The Voice; Isaiah 25:8; Hosea 13:14).

The Biblical record does not describe dinner that evening. One can easily picture, however, the delight in the family. Lazarus was back at his place at the table, healthy and normal, enjoying his sisters, and eating with a voracious appetite. In fact, I can imagine the teasing: "Lazarus, you're eating like you've starved for four days!"

Neither does the Apostle John record if Jesus and His disciples stayed for the meal. John's silence might suggest Jesus let this family of three have uninterrupted time together.

As for Mary, she no doubt needed time to assimilate everything that had happened, and especially her relationship with Jesus. To her credit, Mary did work through it all, as the remainder of the story will unveil.

The Results of the Miracle; Neighbors Turn to Jesus

11:45 Therefore, many of the Jews who had come to visit Mary, and had seen what Jesus did put their faith in him.

The result was "a turnaround for many of the Jews who were with Mary." They saw it and "believed" (John 11:45 MSG).

Yes, suffering can liberate us, including our friends and relatives, by birthing new and higher meaning in our lives.

THINK ABOUT IT: Naturalists believe in the existence of only material things. Hence, man is not a "living soul" because the soul is immaterial, and not real. It also means we "live" as long as our brains send the proper messages throughout our bodies. When that process fails (death), we cease to exist.

While several objections to this philosophy can be raised, the strongest is the highly attested historical fact of Jesus' resurrection. In fact, it is one of the best supported facts of ancient history.

Our faith says, because Jesus was raised from the dead, "the one who raised the Lord Jesus will raise us also with Jesus" (2 Corinthians 4:14).

The Resurrection Principle

Lazarus was raised from the dead bodily. But can anyone doubt several other wonderful *resurrections* stand out in this story. Mary experienced a "resurrection" all her own, and so did Martha. In fact, these sisters, along with their brother, were ushered into a totally different understanding of reality with all of the new meaning that went with it. It was a new world view for them, and they lived out their lives in the glow of how resurrection hope changed them [it changes us too]. Even the mourners in Bethany who believed experienced this form of the resurrection.

Joseph's world came to an end when his brothers sold him into slavery, but he experienced a *resurrection* in Potiphar's house. Joseph's life ended a second time when Potiphar threw him in jail. But after some years, he experienced another *resurrection*. The result was he walked out of jail and was exalted to second in command of Egypt, amenable only to Pharaoh himself. Joseph *died* to the hope of ever seeing his family again, including his father and his brothers, and especially his brother, Benjamin. But in the rich grace of God this long lost hope came to *resurrection* too.

We choose how we respond to what *crucifies* us. If we select the path of bitterness and cynicism, we will become negative toward life and frustrate the grace of God (Galatians 2:21). The road leading to the resurrection principle is Jesus' path up Golgotha to His cross. It is paved in the strength of Jesus' attitude: "Father, forgive them, for they do not know what they are doing" (Luke 23:24). This choice to forgive is at the heart of the resurrection principle.

THINK ABOUT IT: The resurrection principle leaps out at us: every ending has within it the seeds of a new beginning—every ending. Even death itself is an ending that results in a new beginning. This is true until we arrive at our heavenly home where there are no more endings (see Romans 8:28).

People who select this track and take up their cross daily to follow Jesus will discover grace working in their lives (Genesis 50:20; Luke 9:23). In fact, the message of the gospel is that the material the Lord makes crowns out of is crosses. Even if the months turn into years, and the years into decades, as was true with Joseph, the grace of God will ultimately bring us to a new beginning, and it will feel like a resurrection. The "crown" we will then wear will be made from the cross(es) we faithfully carried all those years until our "resurrection" came. Joseph's conclusion will then frame our new attitude:

> You intended to harm me, but God intended it for good to accomplish what is now being done, the saving of many lives. So then, don't be afraid. I will provide for you and your children" (Genesis 50:20–21; see also Romans 8:28).

11:46 But some of them went to the Pharisees and told them what Jesus had done. 47 Then the chief priests and the Pharisees called a meeting of the Sanhedrin. "What are we accomplishing?" they asked. "Here is this man performing many miraculous signs. 48 If we let him go on like this, everyone will believe in him, and then the Romans will come and take away both our place and our nation."

Love for Messiah, or Love for Position?

While the resurrection of Lazarus turned many Jews to Jesus, it also hardened others against Him. This stubbornness was most pronounced among the Jewish national leadership centered in the Sanhedrin (Isaiah 46:12–13; 48:1–11). Although the Sadducees did not believe in the resurrection, denying the miracle of Lazarus' resurrection was impossible for them to do; the evidence was just too strong.

If they could not deny Jesus' "many miraculous signs," they could reject their meaning. The result was they totally disregarded the wonderful blessing that resulted in new relationships between Jesus and Lazarus, his sisters, and their friends.

In their efforts to silence Jesus they chose to reject Him in nationalistic terms. Hence, they focused on Israel's tenuous relationship with their pagan Roman conquerors. To them, Jesus was a blasphemer who was a threat to national survival.

> The Jews who were with Mary...saw what Jesus did, and believed in him. But some went back to the Pharisees and told on Jesus. The high priests and Pharisees called a meeting of the Jewish ruling body. "What do we do now?" they asked. "This man keeps on doing things, creating God-signs. If we let him go on, pretty soon everyone will be believing in him and the Romans will come and remove what little power and privilege we still have" (John 11:45–48 MSG).

These leaders did not question the God-sized miracles happened; indeed they had been evident for all to see. They were most concerned about losing their "power and privilege" in the land.

Jesus Prophesied the Destruction of the Temple

Let it be noted again, what they rejected—the resurrection of Lazarus, and then the triumph of the Cross followed by Jesus' resurrection unto immortality, is what ultimately converted the Roman Empire. The path of the Pharisees—the righteousness they crafted, ended in the very thing they feared—the death of the nation and the destruction stone by stone of their beloved temple in the Roman invasion of 70–72 AD (Luke 21:6; John 8:24). Jesus foretold it in one of His most famous prophecies (Matthew 24:2; Luke 21:6).

The bond of the Jewish people to their temple was very strong; they actually fought wars to preserve their temple. It took courage for the Lord to even give the prophecy of its destruction. Doing so certainly came back to haunt Jesus because it was one of the accusations made against Him when He was on trial for His life (Mark 14:58).

No record exists that any priest, ruler, or prophet, including John the Baptist, foresaw the stone by stone demolition of the temple (Matthew 24:2; Mark 13:2; Luke 21:6). If Jesus had been wrong here, it would have driven a strong nail into His claim to be the Son of God. But Jesus' prophetic batting average is 100 percent!

The temple switch was completed at Pentecost, and the destruction of the temple followed about 40 years after the Lord's resurrection. Combined together they were powerful factors in opening the path on up for the gospel to go to the Gentiles worldwide, including the islands of the seas.

THINK ABOUT IT: Self-righteousness has always been on the wrong side of salvation history.

11:49 Then one of them, named Caiaphas, who was high priest that year, spoke up, "You know nothing at all! 50 You do not realize it is better for you that one man die for the people than the whole nation perish."
51 He did not say this on his own, but as high priest that year he prophesied Jesus would die for the Jewish nation,

52 and not only for that nation but also for the scattered children of God, to bring them together and make them one. 53 So from that day on they plotted to take his life.

A Corrupt Priest as a Prophet

Caiaphas was the high priest who led the temple system that sacrificed perhaps thousands of lambs during his administration. Caiaphas had already been cunningly scheming how they could appeal successfully to Pilate to order Jesus' crucifixion. A totally satanic "solution" had popped into his mind. "It's to our advantage that one man dies for the people," he told the Sanhedrin, "rather than the whole nation be destroyed" (MSG). In this way he could show his loyalty to Rome and at the same time get rid of Jesus. Caiaphas used exactly this reasoning when He led the mob at Jesus' trial in shouting, "Crucify him," and "We have no king but Caesar" (John 19:15).

Caiaphas announced in this meeting of the Sanhedrin, therefore, he was ready to use his ultimate weapon; his nuclear option. The high priest was convinced killing Jesus would stop him and his followers. Caiaphas did not realize how he, in his own freedom of choice, would be helping to fulfill John the Baptist's prophecy, announcing Jesus the Lamb of God who takes away the sin of the world (John 1:29; Genesis 22:8).

The Apostle John, however, offered an additional meaning. He said Caiaphas actually gave a prophecy that day, albeit unintentionally. Israel's Messiah, whom they had rejected, would become the sacrifice for "the Jewish nation" and the "scattered children of God."

Could the Holy Spirit use the lips of a corrupt high priest to give a momentous prophecy? This priest was enraged enough to conspire to kill his own Messiah. Of all people, could *Caiaphas* give a prophecy?

Yes.

During the exodus, the Holy Spirit used a donkey to speak the truth to Baalam (Numbers 22:21–34). Isaiah prophesied in the name of God that a pagan Persian king would rise up named Cyrus. He would reign in the role of the Lord's "shepherd," with orders from God to launch rebuilding the temple. Isaiah also said Cyrus would be the Lord's "anointed," and the Lord would take hold of his right hand in his conquests (Isaiah 44:28–45:1). Isaiah foretold all of this some two hundred years before the events actually occurred.

Caiaphas also kept trying to silence the Lord's followers after Jesus' resurrection and ascension. He presided at the trial of Peter and John after Pentecost. At the tribunal against Stephen, Caiaphas sentenced Stephen to death by stoning, making him the first Christian martyr (Acts 4:5; 6:6–7:60).

Before he faded from the scene, Caiaphas had the blood of God's Son on his hands, and had made Stephen the first Christian martyr. Caiaphas fought Jesus with everything in him as he tried to hold onto his position as high priest and his beliefs as a Sadducee. As a Sadducee, Caiaphas did not believe in the resurrection. Interestingly, it was the resurrection of Jesus that ultimately was his undoing.

In the end Caiaphas lost everything (Mark 8:36).

The name Caiaphas does not show up in history again until 1990. The Caiaphas ossuary is one of twelve bone boxes discovered in a burial cave in south Jerusalem in November 1990. The most ornate of the ossuaries is twice inscribed "Joseph, son of Caiaphas," and held the bones of a 60-year-old male. The limestone ossuary is now housed in the Israel Museum in Jerusalem. This ossuary fits the era of Jesus' ministry and death. Again, archeology gives witness to the historicity of the Bible.

Mickie Mantle Talked About What He Lost

In her biography of the pro baseball great Mickey Mantle, Jane Leavy recounts comments from Mantle's last press conference on July 11, 1995. Mantle had been an alcoholic.

It was a standing-room-only conference. His comic timing was still acute, but the robust physique, the Popeye muscles, and the untroubled face of American plenty were gone. His tracksuit hung on his desiccated frame...He looked like death.

"God gave me a great body and an ability to play baseball," he said. "God gave me everything, and I just... pffft!"

What would be remembered most was the anguished plea to children: "I'd like to say to the kids out there, if you're looking for a role model, this is a role model. Don't be like me."

A reporter asked Mantle if he had signed a donor card. "Everything I've got is worn out," he said. "Although I've heard people say they'd like to have my heart...it's never been used."[8]

At least Mickey Mantle had deep regrets. The Biblical record does not indicate Caiaphas ever looked back with sorrow for his very wicked choices he so freely carried out.

On the morning of the Passover at which Jesus was crucified, Caiaphas the High Priest carried out the Passover ritual dating back to Moses. He did it oblivious to having rejected the Messiah on His temple visits, and blind to the fact the Shekinah had been moving about in the streets of Jerusalem. In fact, it is reasonable to say Caiaphas had never personally experienced the presence of the Spirit of God. Then, when he did come into the Presence proceeding from Jesus, he misinterpreted the Spirit in Jesus as being an evil threat to Israel's national survival, including his own job.

In repeating the ancient Passover ritual, Caiaphas unintentionally had a major role in Jesus' last Passover and the birth of the New Testament (1 Corinthians 5:7; Genesis 22:8). In condemning Jesus to death, therefore, Caiaphas willingly took the lead in the drama of the cross.

Caiaphas so despised Jesus he wanted the Lord dead. But in carrying out his murderous plan, he also condemned to death God's Lamb. Caiaphas literally helped make it possible for Jesus to "take away the sin of the world" (John 1:29; 1 Corinthians 5:7; Genesis 22:8). As high priest he did not participate in Jesus' death for that purpose, but it certainly did have that result.

THINK ABOUT IT: Our awesome Lord is indeed able to make even the wrath of men praise Him, without ever violating their free will (Psalm 76:10).

Does God Love Me?

Can anyone doubt Jesus' great affection for Lazarus and his two sisters? This story is saturated in the love of God identified by the term, *agape*. It also continues to demonstrate why the message of the sovereign Lord is so very attractive to people in crisis. Jesus died on Calvary to do what is best for us, as only God can know the best. "Greater love hath no man than this, that a man lay down his life for his friends" (John 15:13 KJV).

Since Jesus' life was guided by God's love, it only makes sense the Lord gave the Great Command, "Love one another as I have loved you" (John 13:34). Acting in the best interests of others is the gospel's guiding ethic for all believers. The Lord's Great Command must always be the twin alongside His Great Commission. Then the worldwide advance of this "so great salvation" will be marked by humility, honoring the Lord who showed immeasurable love on His cross (Hebrews 2:3; Isaiah 54:2–3). Jesus continues to express this same love for all people today.

What More?

Author and speaker Brennan Manning's best friend growing up was named Ray Brennan. The two of them did everything together: bought a car together as teenagers, double-dated together, went to school together, and so forth. They even enlisted in the Army together, went to boot camp together, and fought on the frontlines together. One night while sitting in a foxhole, Brennan was reminiscing about the old days in Brooklyn while Ray listened and ate a chocolate bar.

Suddenly a live grenade fell into the foxhole. Ray looked at Brennan, smiled, dropped his chocolate bar, and threw himself on the live grenade. It exploded, killing Ray, but Brennan's life was spared.

When Brennan returned home, he went to visit Ray's mother in Brooklyn. They sat up late one night having tea when Brennan asked her, "Did Ray really love me?"

Mrs. Brennan got up off the couch, shook her finger in front of Brennan's face and then passionately said, "What more could he have done for you?"

Brennan said at that moment he experienced an epiphany. He imagined himself standing before the cross of Jesus wondering, *Does God really love me?* And imagined Jesus' mother Mary pointing to her Son, saying, "What more could he have done for you?" (see Isaiah 5:4).

The cross of Jesus is God's way of doing all He could do for us. And yet we often wonder, "*Does God really love me? Am I important to God? Does God care about me?*"[9]

This story also applies to Christian universalism—the view that people can be saved in the life to come. Consider. The Father has sent His Son into the world, at great price, in a supreme act of love, to provide the plan of salvation. This solution, when compared to all world religions, offers people their best opportunity to flourish in a fallen world, and promises eternal life in the eternity to come. Samuel Johnson (1709–1784) expressed this conclusion when he penned, "Christianity is the highest perfection of humanity."

If people refuse to embrace the heavenly Father's Son and reject his plan of salvation, what more can God do? The Father is left with no choice but to give people an eternity like they have insisted on living—separation from God. Hell will be hot because of the burning brimstone, but the eternal separation from God will be hell at its flaming worst (Matthew 25:41; Luke 17:29; Rev. 19:20; 20:10; 21:8).

Jesus' Last Retreat

11:54 Therefore Jesus no longer moved about publicly among the Jews. Instead he withdrew to a region near the desert, to a village called Ephraim, where he stayed with his disciples.

This was not an attempt by Jesus to run in fear. Instead, it marked His determination to control the timeline of His life. Jesus would not allow His death to come prematurely, thus failing to fulfill all righteousness. His hour, His moment, was for His death to occur at the time of the Passover sacrifice only days away. So to stay in control of *kairos* time, Jesus withdrew to Ephraim, a village "near the desert," and waited there with His disciples. This rest was built into the timeline from eternity, giving Jesus a few more precious days with His disciples. It would also be His last chance to have some time to relax before Calvary.

11:55 When it was almost time for the Jewish Passover, many went up from the country to Jerusalem for their

ceremonial cleansing before the Passover. 56 They kept looking for Jesus, and as they stood in the temple area they asked one another, "What do you think? Isn't he coming to the Feast at all?" 57 But the chief priests and Pharisees had given orders if anyone found out where Jesus was, he should report it so that they might arrest him.

The crowd's question, "Isn't He coming?" would soon be answered. Jesus fully intended to go back to Jerusalem, knowing exactly what was ahead. "The chief priests and the elders of the people" had already "assembled in the palace of Caiaphas, and schemed to arrest Jesus secretly and kill him" (Matthew 26:3–4). Part of their sly plan was not to arrest Him during the Passover festival "or there may be a riot among the people." But they did not understand Jesus was God's Lamb from eternity. Jesus would come to the feast all right. His mission there would be to surrender Himself voluntarily into the hands of His sworn enemies.

He would control the timing and then fall on the grenade—in our place.

"There is no greater way to love than to give your life for your friends." (John 15:13 VOICE).

THINK ABOUT IT: God-the-Holy Spirit is the divine Evangelist who shows people the love Jesus expressed on Golgotha's knoll (John 15:13). It is a serious mistake not to appreciate the activity of the Holy Spirit in the earth. Jesus served in our best interests at Calvary and has continued to do so ever since, day after day, and century after century.

Fueled by this great love of God, the gospel of Jesus Christ will continue to go to the ends of the earth.

ANOTHER LOOK AT MARY'S FAITH

12:1 Six days before the Passover, Jesus came to Bethany, where Lazarus lived, whom Jesus had raised from the dead. 2 Here a dinner was given in Jesus' honor. Martha served, while Lazarus was among those reclining at the table with him. 3 Then Mary took about a pint of pure nard, an expensive perfume; she poured it on Jesus' feet and wiped his feet with her hair. And the house was filled with the fragrance of the perfume.

Jesus went to Bethany again after His retreat at Ephraim. His timing was exact. His crucifixion was at hand. Then, exactly six days before the Passover, perfectly on His schedule, Jesus returned to Jerusalem (John 12:1).

Accepting the Sovereignty of Agape Love

Martha, "the server," is the woman of faith in the story of Lazarus' death and resurrection. Then, after the Lord's resurrection, at the banquet in Jesus' honor, Mary emerges again as the spiritual leader. This raises an important lesson. The Martha's of life who cook and wash the dishes can have just as much love for Jesus and just as much faith as do the Mary's who sit at Jesus' feet. In fact, they might grasp quicker the sovereign purposes of Jesus, who is the resurrection and the life.

Before Lazarus' resurrection, Martha received the revelation Jesus is the resurrection and the life, acknowledged Jesus as the Son of God, and expressed faith Jesus could raise her brother on the spot.

After Lazarus' resurrection, the tables turn and Mary received the revelation Jesus would be crucified, but he too would be raised from the dead. In fact, Mary actually anointed Jesus' body for His burial.

An important lesson should be learned here. Faith is a choice of the heart and is not determined solely by physical closeness to Jesus' feet. The reason Martha did not get the answer she wanted from Jesus in Luke's story was because she was preparing the meal as a duty, and not as a gift of worship. Luke said preparation of the meal had "distracted" her so that she did not appreciate fully the Guest who was in her home (Luke 10:38).

Mary's very real emotional pain had convinced her she wanted to live again; she did not want to live out her life in her condition. Her pain also helped her discover she truly did want Jesus as the bedrock of her life; a love deeper than her love even for her brother. When Martha told Mary Jesus was calling for her, a thread of hope sprang up inside her and she started climbing out of the pit of her pain. Then, at Lazarus' tomb she began to grasp and assimilate the big picture.

Mary's suffering had revealed what was inside her, making clear what she needed to work on in her relationship with her Lord. Said another way, she had to move from friendship love (*phileo*) with its set of obligating expectations, to the sovereignty of *agape* love that trusts God to act without conditions in our best interests. This requires believing He knows what is best for us, even when we do not understand His sovereign purposes. Embracing the *agape* love of God, in fact, is the foundation for accepting the sovereignty of God's goodness in our daily living (1 John 4:8, 16).

THINK ABOUT IT: Meaning and purpose for life are discovered in a relationship with Jesus that permits the Lord to be the Sovereign in our lives, not merely our family friend. Mary did figure this out and made the transition. Yes, this means Jesus' motives are to be trusted even when He does not answer our prayers the way we pray them, or even when He is silent.

A Study in Worth

The sisters and Lazarus surely talked about the gift they could give Jesus at the dinner that would show His worth to them. It is unthinkable Mary could have made a gift valued at a year's wage without her sister and Lazarus being in agreement. It was their act of worship too.

Mary was her old self as a worshiper that night. Jesus' retreat at Ephraim had given her adequate time to think it all through and climb to a whole new level of worship. She had progressively absorbed how her brother's death and resurrection had given such marvelous glory to God. She might have also begun to realize the miracle had blessed Jesus' disciples with new faith to believe Jesus was the Son of God.

Dealing with her guilt was part of the process. Remorse had probably hit Mary the hardest after Jesus left Bethany for the retreat. It is true she had woefully misjudged her Lord's motives. Quite possibly she shed some more tears as she realized her big mistake. In the process of her recovery, she no doubt began to comprehend how she had mistrusted Jesus and put blame on Him that did not belong to Him. She surely felt ashamed of herself, and a shamed conscience routinely results in guilt trips—often tough guilt trips.

The clouds in Mary's thinking continued to clear up and the *Son*light began to shine brighter and brighter in her soul. The conclusion Mary discovered actually transformed her into a prophetess.

Please picture Mary on her knees at the dinner. She became Jesus' servant, doing the work of a slave—but more than a slave. She washed Jesus' feet, not with water, but with very pricey, high drachma perfume. Then she wiped His feet with her hair. [The Apostle Paul later said he was the Lord's slave too (*doulos* = slave or servant, e.g., Romans 1:1)].

Mary's tears no doubt also mingled with the fragrance—tears of both regret and gratitude. It is reasonable to believe she poured out her heart amid her sobs.

What she did that evening was extravagantly worshipful. We are left to wonder what she said as she emptied the fragrance. Perhaps it was this:

"Thank you, Jesus, thank you. Thank you for what you did for my brother. And I'm so sorry; so sorry, please forgive me for mistrusting you; please, please forgive me!"

THINK ABOUT IT: The sweet aroma of the perfume "filled the whole house." Everywhere the gospel has gone this story of Mary's extravagant expression of Jesus' worth to her, her sister and her brother, continues to be told.

Is there not a spiritual sense, dear reader, in which every generation is able to scent the spiritual aroma of the fragrance, as you think of the inestimable worth of Jesus?

He is truly the "pearl of great price" who is worth the gift and so much more (Matthew 13:46).

The *agape* love in the heart of Jesus had already forgiven Mary before she asked. All was well between Jesus and her. Now she had to accept Jesus had forgiven her. Mary's love for the Lord was demonstrated in the family's gift of the perfume and wiping His feet with her hair. She had become the Lord's loyal servant for life.

Alabaster Jar

Gateway Music released a worship song in 2012 named "Alabaster Jar." A verse of the lyrics follows:

This alabaster jar is all I have of worth.
I break it at your feet, Lord,
It's less than you deserve.
You're far more beautiful, more precious than the oil.
The sum of my desires and the fullness of my joy.
Like you spilled your blood, I spill my heart
As an offering to my King.

Chorus:
Here I am, take me as an offering
Here I am, giving every heartbeat for your glory.
Take me.

THINK ABOUT IT: At its essence, *worship* is all about ascribing *worth*. How does your life manifest that Jesus is worth your becoming His servant, a slave of Jesus Christ?

12:4 But one of his disciples, Judas Iscariot, who was later to betray him, objected, 5 "Why wasn't this perfume sold and the money given to the poor? It was worth a year's wages." 6 He did not say this because he cared about the poor but because he was a thief; as keeper of the money bag, he used to help himself to what was put into it. 7 "Leave her alone," Jesus replied. "It was intended she should save this perfume for the day of my burial. 8 You will always have the poor among you, but you will not always have me."

Martha, Mary, and Lazarus were in agreement: they each knew Jesus was worth it to them. But disunity had raised its ugly head, and Judas was the lead culprit. Thief that he was, he would have been thrilled to get his hands on that jar of essence. Judas knew the value of the perfume but he did not know the value of his Messiah, the Son of God, who is worth infinitely more than a year's wage.

THINK ABOUT IT: Disunity was in the house and Judas had company. Judas was sure Jesus was not worth such a gift. But Judas was not alone in his sentiments. "When the disciples saw this, they were indignant. 'Why this waste?' they asked" (Matthew 26:8–9). Mark is more generic saying, "Some of those present" were indignant (Mark 14:3–5). In any case, the disciples had a shocked look on their faces as they followed Judas' lead.

We must never forget what a strong advocate and protector we have in Jesus Christ (Genesis 15:1; Psalm 3:3; Ephesians 6:6)

"Let her alone," Jesus said to Judas. "She's anticipating and honoring the day of my burial. You always have the poor with you. You don't always have me." (John 12:7–8 MSG).

It is a special strand of the gospel story that Jesus was anointed for His burial at this meal, about a week before His death.

THINK ABOUT IT: In formulating the great plan of redemption, the heavenly Father did not miss even the small details. Jesus' body was anointed for burial a week early by Mary in the home of Simon of Bethany, whose leprosy Jesus had cured. The Holy Spirit helped Mary comprehend Jesus was worth it, and she extravagantly carried out this detail.

Then, "On the first day of the week, very early in the morning, the women took the spices they had prepared and went to the tomb (Luke 24:1–8). Their goal was a customary after-burial anointing, but they did not get to do it because Jesus was already alive.

The Worth of a King

A notable example of the value of a king to his people comes from the historical record of the Allied invasion of Normandy on D-Day, June 6, 1944.

British Vice-Admiral Sir Bertram Ramsay had been the commander in charge of the evacuation at Dunkirk May 26–June 4, 1940, that brought home 338,226 British and allied soldiers when France fell to Hitler's armies. Ramsay organized snatching them out of the waters of the beaches on the English Channel.

When D-Day came in June 1944, Ramsey was in charge of the amphibious landing efforts of the British soldiers.

British Prime Minister Winston Churchill desperately wanted to join the expeditionary forces and watch the D-Day invasion from the bridge of a battleship in the English Channel. King George VI, a seasoned sailor who saw action in World War I in the Battle of Jutland, decided to stop Churchill's plan by proposing to join Churchill on the battleship. He knew Churchill would not agree for his king to be in danger, and Churchill did protest strongly King George's idea.

The two great leaders remained at civil loggerheads until they met with Ramsay. The admiral flatly refused to take the responsibility for the safety of either of these two luminaries. Ramsay cited the danger to first his King and then the king's Prime Minister. He also listed the risks of the planned operational duties, and the fact that both the King and Churchill would be needed at home in case the landings went badly and immediate decisions were required. This settled the matter and King George VI remained ashore on D-Day. Churchill did too.[10]

King Jesus did exactly the opposite. With royal courage He voluntarily surrendered His body to be crucified. On the cross He offered a king's ransom: His life for the life of His people

(Matthew 20:28; Hebrews 9:15). Himself sinless, He died in our place (John 1:29, 36).

Even in death, the crown of thorns that was meant to make a mockery of His royal claims actually exalted His kingly dignity.

As Jesus made His defense of Mary she perceived the full picture and it told her why Lazarus was taken from them. She heard Jesus say, "It was intended that she should save this perfume for the day of my burial." When Mary had been deep in the pit of grief, perhaps even depression, she could not anticipate, as her sister did, what the Lord intended to do for her dead brother. She needed her sister to serve as an evangelist to help her even go to Jesus (John 11:28).

Yes, Mary had figured out the answer to her "Why" question— *Why did my brother have to die?* It all made sense. Lazarus was the prototype, the example, of what was about to happen to Jesus. At this juncture in her understanding, Mary's act was prophetic; Jesus Himself validated it: "She has done this for my burial."

THINK ABOUT IT: Mary perceived Jesus would be next; His enemies would succeed in killing Him. But Jesus too would rise from the dead!

The Apostle John's record does not show Mary prophesied this with her words, but she certainly did with her deed. She had figured out a whole sphere of new meaning—resurrection meaning. A tomb would not be able to hold Jesus any more than it held her brother.

Mary, Martha, and Lazarus were just what Jesus needed to help prepare the Son of Man for the flaming ordeal of the next few days. It would all end in about a week with Jesus impaled on three nails on a Roman cross the woodcutter left full of sharp splinters.

To Judas, her gift was a waste; Jesus was not worth it. Distribution to the poor would have been the highest and best use of the fragrance's value—with Judas keeping a goodly percentage as his own "honorable fee" for his efforts!

"Our Own Ground Zero!"

After the wingtip of a hijacked plane sliced through the 78th floor of the Twin Towers in New York City on 9-11, a group of people huddled together in the Elevator Sky Lobby, waiting for help. Then they heard the voice. "I found the stairs – follow me!" It was Welles Crowther, a twenty-four-year-old equities trader, whose trademark was the red bandanna he had carried in his pocket since he was a boy.

With a woman on his back and a red bandanna in his hand, he led the group to a stairwell. He gave one woman a fire extinguisher, told the group to stay together and go on down the stairs. They made it out. But Welles didn't go with them. Instead, he went back upstairs to help others.

That's when another woman, badly injured, saw this man with a red bandanna over his nose and mouth, running across the lobby. He led them to an obscure staircase and then went back for others. Then the tower came down. They found Welles Crowther's body six months later. His red bandanna is on display in the museum.

Welles' father attended the 9-11 Memorial dedication. "I don't think for a moment," he said, "Welles was thinking about his own safety. He was thinking about the lives of all those people. Welles' last hour was his legacy."

A Ground Zero chaplain said, "When the ground is shaking all around you, find your cross at your Ground Zero."[11]

Welles Crowther was focused on others. So was Jesus when He headed to the cross (Luke 9:22; 11:25; 24:26; John 3:14–16; 8:28; 12:24; Acts 17:3). Otherwise, he would have never done it—of all things, not the cross (John 15:13). Jesus died on the cross so that we could escape (with 9-11 symbolism in mind), the fall of our own "Twin Towers."

Yes, when the world is shaking all around you, Ground Zero is always at the foot of Jesus' cross.

Martha, Lazarus, and Mary each believed Jesus was the Son of God; raising Lazarus was the final proof for them. This meant Jesus was their Messiah, and He was worth their very best. His value exceeded anything and everything they could give Him.

At its essence, *worship* is all about ascribing *worth*. In fact, the etymology of the word worship traces back to the Old English of the 1200s. Two words merged together over time, *weord* = worth + *scipe* = ship. By the 1500s, the word had become *worshipe*, and ultimately became *worship* as it is known in contemporary English. The basic meaning has remained the same through the centuries.

Mary had climbed from *phileo* to *agape*, doing it through the dark tunnel of deep grief. She was now acting in Jesus' best interests. Mary gave Him the most valuable possession in their home, doing it in full faith in advance of His own burial. In their hearts they knew the gift was not large enough, but it was their best, and Jesus knew it.

Mary's worship said worlds to Jesus about how they perceived His worth. It also told Him there were millions more like Lazarus out there worldwide, and many Marys' and Marthas' too who would honor the value to mankind of Jesus' crucifixion and resurrection. These people were waiting and hungry, yearning to hear the gospel and experience the forgiveness of God.

THINK ABOUT IT: Mary's gift was indeed extravagant, although certainly not equal to Jesus' worth.

God is also extravagant in His love for each of Jesus' disciples. The heavenly Father assures us we are worth it!

So many followers of Jesus let their value be defined by the curse of their sins. They never fully appreciate how the redeeming blood of Jesus redefines their worth.

Our worth to God, His great love for us, compelled Jesus to fall on the grenade in our place.

"Consider the kind of extravagant love the Father has lavished on us—He calls us children of God! It's true; we are His beloved children. And in the same way the world didn't recognize Him, it does not recognize us either.

My loved ones, we have been adopted into God's family; and we are officially His children now. The full picture of our destiny is not yet clear, but we know this much: when Jesus appears, we will be like Him because we will see Him just as He is. All those who focus their hopes on Him and His coming purify themselves just as He is pure" (1 John 3:1–3 Voice).

The writer of Hebrews expressed it:

"Do you see what this means—all these pioneers who blazed the way, all these veterans cheering us on? It means we'd better get on with it. "Strip down, start running—and never quit! No extra spiritual fat, no parasitic sins. Keep your eyes on Jesus, who both began and finished this race we're in. Study how he did it. Because he never lost sight of where he was headed—that exhilarating finish in and with God—he could put up with anything along the way: cross, shame, whatever. And now he's there, in the place of honor, right alongside God. When you find yourselves flagging in your faith, go over that story again, item by item, that long litany of hostility he plowed through. That will shoot adrenaline into your souls!" (Hebrews 12:1–3 MSG).

The Depth of Hate; the Height of Hope

12:9 Meanwhile a large crowd of Jews found out that Jesus was there and came, not only because of him but also to see Lazarus, whom he had raised from the dead. 10 So the chief priests made plans to kill Lazarus as well, 11 for on account of him many of the Jews were going over to Jesus and believing in him.

Not only did the chief priests and rulers in the Sanhedrin plot to kill Jesus; they also, unbelievably, consulted on a plan to kill Lazarus. They obviously could not deny his testimony; hence, the only way they knew to stop him was to kill him. They had not figured out yet even if they did kill him, Jesus could raise him up again. Lazarus was a star witness; a walking miracle—living evidence Israel's Messiah was in Bethany.

The undeniable facts of Lazarus' case spoke powerfully, and many ordinary Jews were watching and listening with open minds. Because the evidence was so convincing, they were also taking the big step of faith, "going over and believing in Jesus on account of [Lazarus]" (John 12:10 MSG).

Talk about Jesus turning Lazarus into a celebrity! People were actually coming from Jerusalem to see Jesus and to stare at "the formerly deceased Lazarus!" (John 12:9 Voice).

Jesus had successfully boxed these leaders into a corner. Their do-it-their-own-way-self-righteousness had no capability to celebrate an event as wonderful as the restoration of Lazarus. Instead, Lazarus' resurrection left them feeling threatened in their power base. They read their situation correctly because they *were* threatened. It had come down to a simple choice: celebrate Jesus or eliminate Him.

Celebrate Him as their Messiah was a choice they would not make; their self-righteousness would never allow it.

Their plot was never carried out against Lazarus, however. Jesus was clearly the person they were after. Stopping Lazarus would not have stopped Jesus. The ancient, 1800-year-old prophecy Abraham expressed to his son Isaac was about to come true: "My son, God will provide himself a lamb" (Genesis 22:8 KJV). These rulers and the people who followed them were blind to the fact they were freely choosing to fulfill Abraham and the prophets. The self-righteous plan they had developed was about to make happen the last thing they wanted—Jesus' revelation of Himself as "the Lamb of God who takes away the sin of the world" (John 1:29, 36; Isaiah 5; Genesis 22:8).

It is hard to imagine religious leaders with hearts this evil. But it reveals an important lesson of history: there is no corruption quite like the meanness of religion when it tries to eliminate its opposition.

These religious leaders were blind to the divine plan they were fulfilling, but they were not marionettes on a string God in heaven was manipulating. The sovereignty of God was fully able to bring them all together. But they were each sons of Adam, acting solely in their free will, doing what they believed protected their self-interests.

On this heartbreaking note Book Two ends—with a callous strategy to kill Mary's Baby and God's Son. At the same time the story is hope-filled that Jesus would rise from the dead.

Yes, the Good News of the gospel would go to the nations.

Now, to summarize this study of the death and resurrection of Lazarus.

Conclusions Chapter 11:1–12:11

1. *"We earnestly prayed, but Jesus did not answer our prayers."* Jesus is motivated by *agape* love. In His sovereignty, He always does what is best for us without preconditions, based on His perfect knowledge of what is right and best (Isaiah 48:17; 1

John 4:8, 16). In doing so, suffering helps us discover how to handle better some of the questions believers face.

This understanding also applies when we are in a situation of great need but our prayers are getting us nowhere because heaven has turned to brass and God is silent. Daniel's testimony reminds us that God hears our petition when we pray, although, in Daniel's case, it was twenty-one days later that the breakthrough came. The better choice by far is to walk in faith, trusting God, until our breakthrough comes, and keep walking in faith even if it never comes in our lifetime (Isaiah 8:17; Hebrews 11:13) .

2. *"God could have prevented this if He had wanted too."* Because Jesus had a higher purpose in mind, the greatest gift Jesus could give Lazarus was not to heal him, but to raise him from the dead as a revelation of God's resurrection power. This meant the story had a symbolic dimension for what was ahead—Jesus' own crucifixion and resurrection.

    Once God's love (*agape*) is understood, we can accept Jesus had a sovereign right to delay going to Bethany by two days, during which time Lazarus died. Jesus knew before He left Bethabara, in fact, how He would end the crisis Lazarus and his two sisters faced. The results Jesus had in mind would be so very good for each of them they would be *overjoyed* because they paid the price. This is the fruit of God's sovereign grace. The sovereignty of God was fully able to bring them all together in a new unity.

3. *"Can Jesus be trusted to do good in the storms of life? Is He really good, all the time?"* Throughout those painful days, Jesus displayed God's love, acting in Lazarus' best interests as only God knew what was best for him. The Lord showed this same Godly love to Martha and Mary too. Hence, the goodness of God overshadowed the entire crisis.

    It is the nature of the kind of love identified by the term, friendship (*phileo*), to expect Jesus to do what we ask, because this is what friends do. It is the nature of God's love (*agape*) for Jesus to do what is right and best for us, and it might not be what we asked. In this context we can see how friendship love can easily lend itself to placing restraints on Jesus' right to sovereignty in our lives.

In Lazarus' story, friendship love actually collided with the higher purposes of God. Mary walked down this painful road and it became for her a journey into the valley of grief that births hopelessness.

In His sovereignty, Jesus knew just the right time to invite Mary to come to Him—and with all her disappointed expectations she went. Yes, she went to Jesus!

God's grand solution began to make sense for Mary when Jesus called Lazarus out of his tomb. This new dimension of the love of God, "the great love wherewith He loved us," began to blossom the moment of Jesus' command that emptied Lazarus' tomb (Ephesians 2:4 KJV). From this point forward, Mary was on the road of recovery that unveiled the "manifold wisdom" of God's love (Ephesians 3:10 KJV).

Yes, resurrection was the great game changer.

Is there any doubt what Mary and Martha would say about Jesus' goodness after Jesus raised Lazarus from the dead and gave him back to his sisters?

Mary ultimately discovered a settled peace about God's pure goodness. She even came to understand God had placed an unseen umbrella of blessing over each of those stressful days. She had actually done all of her hurting, and crying, and mistrusting, while under that canopy of God's love. Like Daniel, who discovered God heard him on day one of his twenty-one days of intercession, Mary discovered the love of God was covering her too in the midst of each of her days of grief and depression.

THINK ABOUT IT: Mary finally understood! Like Mary, we usually do not comprehend God's sovereign purposes while we are in the storm. We normally begin to understand the mind of God in hindsight, as was the case with Daniel. Then we can see the whole picture better.

It is essential to understand in this context that God's love and human suffering are compatible in the same sense that a surgeon performs an operation. A physician cuts open the human body not out of any anger or malice, but in order to save life.

King David said it well: "The Lord is good. His love endures forever; his faithfulness continues through all generations" (Psalm 100:5; see also Psalm 34:8; 52:9; 119:68; John 10:11; 1 Peter 2:3).

4. *Friendship love (phileo)* will not only try to stop Jesus from doing what is best for us, it will also make the effort to stop Jesus from doing what is right and best for *Himself and His kingdom.* Clearly, Mary's expectations would have resulted in Jesus healing Lazarus. But that would have prevented the far greater testimony of Lazarus' death and resurrection, which brought such glory to God and forever wrote their names in salvation history.

Jesus' personal needs at this point in His ministry must be considered. When this is done, a follower of Jesus can witness the wonder of how the heavenly Father cheered His Son at Lazarus' tomb. Jesus was headed to the cross. The manifestation of the glory of God in Lazarus' resurrection was surely an important motivator to Jesus as He faced crucifixion. Did Jesus ever doubt His Father would raise Him from the dead? We answer He did not. Lazarus' resurrection, however, surely affirmed to Jesus what He already knew.

THINK ABOUT IT: How would Jesus have felt when He loudly called out, "Lazarus, come forth!" if nothing had happened?

What would it have done to His self-confidence facing His own crucifixion?

What would it have done to the disciples faith in Jesus?

5. *The joy of resurrection* is the wonder drug, the penicillin in this story. It continues today as the ultimate healer of the pain and suffering of crushed hearts with broken expectations. Filtering through all of it in their hearts, however, surely was painful for Martha and Mary, and took some time.

6. *The twin prophecies of Jesus.* The Lord foretold Lazarus' death and promised to resurrect Him. These prophecies served as additional proof to the disciples of Jesus' one hundred percent accuracy as a prophet. The result was a further anchoring of their faith in Jesus as the Son of God (John 10:14–16).

7. *The resurrection principle.* Resurrection follows crucifixion amid the hurts and disappointments of life for those who keep their trust in God and live with a forgiving attitude (Romans 8:28). As spring always follows winter and Mother Nature bursts into life again, so with God, every ending has within it the seeds of a new beginning. Every ending. This is true until we arrive at our heavenly home where there will be no more endings. We should never forget storms and rainbows always go together (Genesis 9:13; Revelation 4:3; 10:1). Sometimes much time may be required to find our rainbow of special meaning, but it is worth the wait.

8. *The question of trust.* A wisely developed "but if not" doctrine is essential for maintaining trust in God amid life's many challenges. This is true because circumstances will inevitably confront a follower of Jesus in which, at the time, he does

not understand God's sovereign purposes and cannot quickly find the rainbow in his cloud.

"There's more to come: We continue to shout our praise even when we're hemmed in with troubles, because we know how troubles can develop passionate patience in us, and how that patience in turn forges the tempered steel of virtue, keeping us alert for whatever God will do next. In alert expectancy such as this, we're never left feeling shortchanged. Quite the contrary—we can't round up enough containers to hold everything God generously pours into our lives through the Holy Spirit! Christ arrives right on time to make this happen" (Romans 3:3–8 MSG).

THINK ABOUT IT: The writer of Hebrews said there were heroes who "died in faith, not having received the promises" (Hebrews 11:13). They were able to go forward without "feeling shortchanged" precisely because the gospel produced this "passionate patience." They did see "it way off in the distance" and "waved their greeting" (Hebrews 11:13, MSG); Psalm 27:14; Isaiah 40:31, KJV; Romans 8:23–25). "I will wait for the Lord," Isaiah proclaimed, even when it feels like he "is hiding his face" (Isaiah 8:17).

Will you, dear reader, be willing to join rank with them? Will you continue to trust your Lord even if you never, in this life, discover fully the higher meaning in your situation; the rainbow in your cloud?

---

9. *The wisdom of obedience.* Many of Jesus' followers have made the decision in the valley of suffering to turn to God in repentance. Yes, suffering is indeed a great teacher and motivator. The Lord "wants you to listen to him! Plain listening is the thing, not staging a lavish religious production. Not doing what

God tells you is far worse than fooling around in the occult" (1 Samuel 15:22–23 MSG).

10. *Suffering and the sin-curse.* Suffering gives opportunity to face squarely the effects of the sin-curse. The rebellion against God in the hearts of all people is the source of all evil, sickness, disease and pain, including the brutality and corruption in nature. The ultimate result of the curse of sin is death itself, and explains why bad things happen to good people too.

   Lazarus' story shows Jesus is the solution to the curse of sin; He is the source of life. Hence, Jesus holds the power of resurrection, gives eternal life, and ultimately will restore the natural order (Romans 8:28).

11. *The afterlife.* Guided by the Holy Spirit in his writing, the Apostle John obviously chose not to try to unveil the specifics of Lazarus' afterlife; his four days in the grave. We should not get caught up with so-called near death experiences either. Instead, we must be content to major in what the Bible majors, and minor in what the Bible minors, and have the wisdom to know the difference. It is enough to "be confident," as the Apostle Paul expressed it, knowing "to be absent from the body" is "to be present with the Lord" (2 Corinthians 5:8).

12. *Restoration.* The resurrection of Lazarus must be most properly understood as a *restoration to mortal life.* Lazarus was not raised immortal and incorruptible as Jesus would be a few days down the road. Hence, Lazarus faced death a second time. Jesus' resurrection was infinitely greater. He was raised immortal and incorruptible, as the first fruits of the resurrection, never to die again (1 Corinthians 15:10). His resurrection was supremely superior, bringing immortality and life to light through the gospel (2 Timothy 1:10).

13. *The millions of smaller resurrections.* When the marvelous complexity of the human body is taken into account, including its trillions of cells, its blood vessels, and DNA, etc.,

the great miracle of the restoration of Lazarus can properly be understood as millions of smaller resurrections. King David 3,000 years ago did not know about DNA, but he did understand God made us "so wonderfully complex." And the great king added, "How well I know it" (Psalm 139:14 LB).

14. *Ultimate worth.* Suffering helps to discover true value—the importance of Jesus Christ in our lives. This leads us to agree with Mary, Martha, and Lazarus: Jesus is far more valuable than the very best gift we can give Him. *He* is the ultimate treasure and the pearl of great price" (Matthew 13:46). Jesus merits our love in this life and "throughout all ages, world without end. Amen" (Ephesians 3:21 KJV).

Jesus returned to Bethany six days before the Passover. After the dinner in Simon's home, the very next day, perfectly on His schedule, Jesus made the two mile journey to Jerusalem (John 12:11–12).

Book Three will start at just this point—John 12:12. It will begin with the story of Jesus' triumphant entry into Jerusalem, the event which launches the last week of the Lord's ministry. Packed full of the highest drama, it will chronicle history's greatest tragedy. Jesus' sworn critics were certain His death by crucifixion would be the end of their public enemy #1. At the same time His enemies were confident crucifixion would spread gut-wrenching gloom over His followers. In their minds, the crucifixion of Jesus meant the curtain had fallen on the final scene and the "Jesus problem" had come to an end.

But then…

Three days later the *logos*, the divine Word, the authoritative Word, put a surprise addendum on what they were so sure was the final act (Isaiah 25:8; 1 Corinthians 15:54–58).

ENDNOTES

CHAPTER 6

[1]Matt Woodley, Managing Editor, cited from PreachingToday. Com

[2] Ward Williams, "Walking on Water," cited from cited from PreachingToday.Com

[3] Lee Aclove, in the sermon, "Heaven," PreachingToday.Com

[4] George Muller, *Leadership*, Vol. 12, No. 4, cited from PreachingToday.Com

[5] Denison, Mark, **The Daily Walk**, (Fort Worth: Austin Brothers Publishing), 2013, p. 1.

[6] Dorothy L. Sayers, "Her Life and Soul," *Christianity Today*, Vol. 41, No. 11, cited from PreachingToday.Com

[7] Cited from PreachingToday.Com

[8] Soren Kierkegaard (1813-1855), Danish philosopher and theologian, cited from PreachingToday.Com

[9] David Holdaway, **The Life of Jesus**, (UK: Sovereign World, 1997), pp. 42-43, cited from PreachingToday.Com

Chapter 7

[1] Will Rogers (1879-1935), cited from PreachingToday.Com

[2] Flavius Josephus (37– ca. 100 AD), **Antiquities of the Jews**, Book 20, Chapter 9, 1.

[3] Dorothy L. Sayer, cited from PreachingToday.Com

[4] John Ross Cranleigh, *Leadership*, Vol. 12, No. 2, cited from PreachingToday.Com [105

[5] C. S. Lewis, cited from PreachingToday.Com

[6] Cited from PreachingToday.Com

Chapter 8

[1] Max Lucado, **Grace** (Nashville, TN: Thomas Nelson, 2012) pp. 53-54; cited from PreachingToday.Com

[2] Philip Yancey, **What Good is God?** (New York: Hachette Book Group, 2010), cited from PreachingToday.com

[3] Brian Lowery, Managing Editor, PreachingToday.Com

[4] Henry Bettenson, editor, **Documents of the Christian Church**, 2nd edition (New York: Oxford University Press, 1963), p. 210.

[5] Kanute Larson, **Holman New Testament Commentary: 1 and 2 Thessalonians, 1 and 2 Timothy, Titus, Philemon** (Nashville: Holman Bible Publishing, 2000) pp 22-23; cited from PreachingToday.Com

[6] David Slagle, cited from PreachingToday.Com

[7] Steve Brown, "Forgiven and Forgotten," Tape No. 139, cited from PreachingToday.Com

[8] Ravi Zacharias, "The Lostness of Humankind," Tape No. 118, cited from PreachingToday.Com

[9] Herbert Agar, *Leadership*, Vol. 17, No. 2, cited from PreachingToday.Com

[10] Johann Wolfgang von Goethe (1749-1832); cited from PreachingToday.Com

[11] Brian Nelson, "What Can 28,000 Rubber Duckies Lost at Sea Teach Us?" Mother Nature Network (3-1-11), adapted, PreachingToday.Com

[12] From the hymn, "All Hail the Power of Jesus' Name," composed by Edward Perronet (1726-1792); music by Oliver Holden (1765-1844).

[13] Eugene H. Peterson, **Five Smooth Stones for Pastoral Work** [Grand Rapids:William B. Eerdmans, 1992), p. 175; cited from PreachingToday.Com

[14] Phil Callaway, from Men of Integrity, April 16 entry [March/April 2006]; cited from PreachingToday.Com

Chapter 9

[1] William F. Albright, **The Archeology and the Religions of Israel**, Baltimore: John Hopkins Press), 1956, p. 176. Cited by Glen Harris, GospelOutreach.Net/Bible Nelson Glueck, **Rivers in the Desert: History of Negev**. Jewish Publication Society of America, Philadelphia, 1969, p. 176. Cited by Rabbi Glen Harris, www.GospelOutreach.Net/Bible

[2] Oliver Sacks, **An Anthropologist on Mars** (New York: Vintage Press, 1966), cited from PreachingToday.Com

[3] Abilene Reporter-News (5-18-00), cited from PreachingToday. Com

[4] Richard Moore, interview by Pat Coyle, cited from PreachingToday.com

Chapter 10

[1] Steve Gertz, *U. S. News and World Report* (12-10-01), pp. 24-32, cited from PreachingToday.Com

[2] Craig Brian Larson, editor, cited from PreachingToday.com

[3] James Dobson, **Life on the Edge**, (Carol Springs, IL; Tyndale Momentum, 2007) pp. 24-25, cited from PreachingToday.Com

[4] The history of the Maccabean Revolt of 168-164 BC that birthed the Feast of Hanakkuh is told in the apocryphal books Maccabees I and Maccabees II. A wealth of valid information about Hanukkah can also be obtained using your computer's search engine.

[5] John L. Allen, Jr., "The War on Christians," *The Spectator*, October 5, 2013.

[6] Justin Taylor, "Ravi Zacharias Speaks with the Founder of Hamas." Between Two Worlds Blog (12-3-12), cited from PreachingToday.Com

Chapter 11:1 - 12:11

[1] Chariots of Fire, (Warner Brothers, 1981), Colin Welland, writer and Hugh Hudson, director, Cited from PreachingToday. Com

[2] Lee Strobel, **The Case for Faith** (Grand Rapids: Zondervan, 2000), pp. 7-23, cited from PreachingToday.Com

[3] C. S. Lewis, **The Problem of Pain** (New York: MacMillan, 1962) p. 93.

[4] Scot McKnight, **The Jesus Creed** (Paraclete Press, 2004), pp. 55-66, cited from PreachingToday.Com

[5] Tim Keown, "A Man in the Game," ESPN Magazine (12-1-12).

[6] Gina Kolata, "Bits of Mystery DNA, Far from 'Junk,' Play Crucial Role," The New York Times (9-5-12), cited from PreachingToday.Com

[7] Professor James Tabor, is an archeologist in the Department of Religious Studies at the University of North Carolina at Charlotte. He reported on his archeological findings in 2004 in Jerusalem's Hinnom Valley at the International Symposium on Archeology and the Bible, and has written about the discovery in the James Tabor Blog. The site today is identified as the Tomb of the Shroud. Professor Tabor did not state the specific conclusion that the discovery defends John's record of Jewish burial practices, but it clearly does. Also see "God, Science and the Bible: First Century Burial Confirms Gospel Details" at UCG.org.

[8] Jane Leavy, **The Last Boy**, (New York: Harper Collins, 2010), p. 374, cited from PreachingToday.Com

[9] Cited and adapted from PreachingToday.Com

[10] Historical narrative summarized from the article on the Dunkirk Evacuation, Encyclopedia Britannica, and on Bertrand Ramsey in the Wikipedia Encyclopedia.

[11] Adapted from the series, "A Word With You" by Ron Hutchcraft, "Our Own Ground Zero," #7195, August 8, 2014.

FOR EXTRA READING

Claydon, David. **Connecting Across Cultures and Religious Boundaries.** (Melbourne: Acorn Press, 2000). An easy to read, practical book providing ideas on sharing the gospel with people of other religious backgrounds.

Strobel, Lee. "It's Offensive to Claim Jesus Is the Only Way to God." Chapter Five in **The Case for Faith**. Grand Rapids. Zondervan, pp. 145-168. Strobel also released a **Student Edition of The Case for Faith** in 2001. The Student Edition is an excellent beginning point for members of the body of Christ who are just starting their journey learning how to give an answer for the faith that lies within them (1 Peter 3:15).

Zacharias, Ravi. **Jesus Among Other Gods**. Waco. Word. 2000. This book examines Christianity and world religions by one of Christianity's brightest minds. A compelling critique of the claims of religious pluralism.